PREDATOR FACTOR:
HOW HUMANITY IS DECOUPLING FROM EVOLUTION

Steve Lesk, MD

Table of Contents

CHAPTER I THE CRUCIBLE 4

CHAPTER II THE DEFIANCE OF ENTROPY 55

CHAPTER III ENTROPY'S BIDDING 107

CHAPTER IV: IMPLICATIONS, CONTEMPLATIONS, OBSERVATIONS OF EVOLUTION'S FREE FALL: AN OBSERVATIONAL ANCHOR FOR THE CURRENT HUMAN CONDITION. THE CASUAL LENS. 134

CHAPTER V FUTURE VISION 224

CHAPTER I
THE CRUCIBLE

"Each new variety and ultimately each new species is produced and maintained by having some advantage over those with which it comes into competition; and the consequent extinction of the less favored forms almost inevitably follows."
Charles Darwin

"We stopped looking for monsters under our bed when we realized that they were inside us." Charles Darwin

"Evolution is written on the wings of butterflies." Charles Darwin

The crucible pits the intensity of daily survival with the mollifying effect of mutations. Those mutations that decrease survivability quickly vanish but those that improve longevity linger with a gradual honing of the genetic tree. Life is a grand experiment which serves to counter the hegemony of ubiquitous chaos and relies on DNA which exploits entropy's need for disorder, an impulse that actually favors mutations. Steven Lesk MD

Whether you believe in creationism or Darwinism, the following formula seems nearly inevitable: protoplasm + mutation x time = us. What does that mean? Living matter (protoplasm) progresses by random mistakes or mutations in the context of **extreme** survival pressure. That helical molecule called DNA that controls how cells are built and work,(and ultimately the blueprint of our bodies as phenotypes), screws up under the gruff influence of entropy which drools at the sight of disorder and chaos. Thankfully, for without those blessed mistakes, the changes that modify a cell's guidebook would not happen. (Imagine a world where the very first DNA molecule replicated, but never made those random mutational guffaws. The only life on earth would be that most primitive of cells, the precursor to us all.) And each one of those DNA slip ups is adjudicated by that greatest of all critics, natural selection. So, if a chimpanzee is suddenly born with fuzzy toes that curl a little more securely around branches, he has a distinct advantage over his brethren. The tree climbing function is given a boost and the next time that petrified chimpanzee is being chased by a ravenous leopard it will make use of those limb grasping digits in panicky escape by scrambling up the nearest tree a little quicker. When man trudged northward from warm to cold climates, his nostrils kindly enlarged (through mutations) to warm the chilly air he breathed. This clear boost in an unforgiving frigid clime won evolution's natural selection seal of approval, at least for those tribes that trudged northward. When an intense gradient is set up favoring one trait over another, good old natural selection steps in to rule on them (most much more subtle than curly toes) across mega bastions of time. The winners rock; those mutations that shank survival are doomed and quickly bear an ignominious death of extinction. And, of course, changing environments meant shifting evolutionary priorities. So eventually, given all the mutational odds, something like an US was bound to emerge.

Evolution is a sausage grinder, and an avid defender of organic matter, in direct opposition to entropy which aches for nothing more than to return living substance back to dirt and ash. In adoration of the organic, evolution eschews entropy's yen for the lifeless dust from whence we emerged, (we'll discuss entropy more in another chapter). In fact one could state, as I have, that **the purpose of life itself is to defy entropy**, but that is a debate for another time. Mother evolution fights like a scrappy street kid to promote living stuff, and worships oodles of time, honing its precepts to a superlative intensity, and if that intensity wanes, the whole vessel comes to a wimpy halt. The blasphemy of organicity in comparison with the eternity of the vast universe's time without such protoplasm, makes living matter precious to evolution. (One might easily question, as have I, why it is so hung up on promoting life? Rather than launching into a speculative harangue, let's just agree that it is, and it fights wickedly for it. Is this another of the 'basic properties' like gravity and entropy? You decide. Perhaps, since it is anti-entropic we should call it antropy. In the physicist Emil Schroedinger's book, "*What is Life?*" he grapples with the same conundrum. Evolution is entropy's greatest enemy and the luxury of time only matters to the living, and mostly to us sapiens. A walrus is not concerned about the clock, but we are which is why we label it, measure it and constantly gaze at our smart watches, since we are aware (unlike animals) that our time on earth is so limited. We also have gained, since the onset of language, the autonoetic sense of our existence forward and backward in time.)

From single celled organisms, to sponges and jelly fish, to bilaterally shaped beings with spinal cords (vertebrates), evolution is a grandiose trial and error rodeo of survival. Like a car manufacturer, different models are thrust onto the market to see what sells. Those that flop are sent to used car lots of extinction. (This explains why extinction, or the lack thereof, is the 'central paradox' of schizophrenia. A human mutation that causes hurdles at the exact moment the person is about to leave adolescence and reduces the chances of reproduction (or fecundity ratio) and survival must become extinct pronto, Darwin said. Well, schizophrenia is anything but extinct being one percent of the population worldwide. Any true theory of this malady must explain that fact. You may read more about this in my book, *Footprints of Schizophrenia: the Evolutionary Roots of Mental Illness*) (Prometheus)

That's the crucible. One then could predict that, as the crucible simmers its giant cauldron over eons of time and under the intense heat of natural selection in a jungle rife with predators, given the syncopated multiplicity of possible mutations that might arise and their outcome, an animal similar to a Homo sapiens would eventually make its heavenly anticipated entrance on the organic stage. Millions of mutations have been sent to second rate car lots, countless more have predictably remained to serve living matter, including us, well. These are evolution's blessed handmaidens. But the crucible demands the scrappy intensity that life and death drama sell, a theatrical production often lost by our primitive forebears.

And evolution has taken some wrong turns in its rugged journey… think dinosaurs, the dominant theme being size, not to imply that size doesn't matter. If an alligator is slithering up to bite you and you can flex one leg and crush it, you're protected. It stands to reason that when it comes to predation bigger is better: an elephant can defend itself against a fox, and a dinosaur could splat a raging elephant. Evolution tumbled down the rabbit hole of size, in a big, brassy way. The law of the crucible was to affirm those mutations that promoted survival and size most decidedly did.

But evolution went a little too far that time. The amount of food that dinosaurs gulped was truly massive, perhaps almost unsustainable, and yet the fatties, many of them herbivores, survived until, according to one theory, about 66 million years ago, a fiery asteroid smashed into the Yucatan peninsula, blackening the skies and burning up a lot of eats in hellish conflagrations. T Rex and his friends dropped like huge, charred flies. Either they suffocated, starved, or got scorched directly by the explosion. Here we see a course correction made nearly inevitable by circumstances that on the whole seemed perfectly reasonable. Evolution created an obese monster which folded under its own weight with a little nudge from its friend the asteroid. (In our nest of modernity, obesity is no longer a plus, so to speak, just another flagship to the mismatch of pre-historic lifestyle and our modern dietary gulps.)

So what did evolution do? Brutal necessity breeds change, and size, no longer the winning mantra, was replaced by something else. But what? What could possibly beat size in survival power? In its yen for a new steamy paradigm, evolution moved upward to the old cranium. While body plans were important, the behavioral repertoire was more decisive. Cunning became the new deity as mental intensity could outsmart a lumbering Bluto.

And this wasn't evolution's only course correction, since something else intervened more powerfully than a six mile wide asteroid. Language, with its far reaching cranial rewiring scorched the evolutionary earth with mastery and fit into evolution's new adoration of cunning masterfully. Language graced the mouths of us Homo sapiens about 50,000 years ago, and by ten thousand BC we'd wiped out all other species of Homo including the Denisovans, the Neanderthals and the Naledi. (There is some doubt about the Neanderthal's ability to form vowels given the shape of their cricoid bone, as well as their hearing acuity making likely that they just couldn't match our speaking talent.) Speech clearly made the grade as the most powerful mutational gift ever with its revolutionary implications about how we used ('complexified') our minds. But it was the intensity of crucible's heat, the life and death scramble that knocked on cavemen's door every morning that fed the mutational pruning that eventually led to us. Without that raging conflagration, the whole crap shoot shuts down like a giant fan whose plug just got yanked.

EVOLUTIONARY MENTALITY

Evolution exerts its promotional effects not just on the body but on the brain as it sees fit to do so. The bundle of nerves that control the organism also fell under natural selection's adjudicative spell. Our central nervous system's very beginnings inform the motion of that princely dance as we can assume that initially primitive organisms, including tiny single celled guys, just had simple reflex arcs, like knee jerks. These promoted survival by dragging the mini-organism pronto from the danger zone and urgently toward nutrients and pleasingly hospitable environs. Gradually, primitive beings like jelly fish, sponges, chordates, vertebrates, blossomed more complex central nervous system rodeos and repertoires, a complexity that was the opposite of entropy's grumpy desire. Options multiplied light years beyond forward or reverse, fight or flight. At some point a vague sense of intention popped up and the organism made some educated choices… like where to go and what the heck to do. Striated (or voluntary) muscles were tapped as the capacity of the organism to move by design increased and abstract decision making began to take root.

Freud used the word ego to denote the command center of the mind, particularly humans' minds. "Normally the control over the approaches to motility devolves upon it. (ego)" (Freud 1957, p.215) The primitive ego sucked up the functions of overlord of this intentionality. Captain ego juggled intention and choice… an informed choice that followed evolution's orders to survive and also multiply, go forth and prosper. Needing high grade info about the world at large, perceptual organs sharpened, (once again under the sway of natural selection) presenting clearer incoming data (sight, sound, touch, smell, taste) to the organism, and as they focused they improved survival directly. Information was the golden commodity to evolution, and the goal was an early warning system, blaring the alarm of predation and recognition of incoming torpedos or opportunities, the sooner the better. Like captain Kirk, the ego became the commander of this evolving ship, orchestrating crystal perception and intention. "…the self preservative instinct which must be assigned to the ego," Freud said. The ego's job was to protect and promote the organism, under the watchful eye of mother Ev. (Freud 1957, p.224) (Remember that Freud was a neurologist. His mental theories arose out of a deep understanding of the central nervous system.)

In the service of survival, memory started to donate its crucial two cents. A mental deal maker, it was added to improve the decision making odds, comparing the incoming data points to past happenstance, proffering solutions and recalling tragic missteps. Now decisions could be informed by what had happened before, a mega deal maker. If a gecko remembered that when it looked under a mossy rock it saw a snake, it could then avoid that shivery terror. Or, maybe it remembered where it had stumbled upon a luscious worm and so might saunter back for a second course. Elated, natural selection certainly gave the thumbs up to memory storage and retrieval. What an upgrade! All of these advances worked in mellifluous concert to improve the odds of survival as the mind differentiated into groovy individual parts with unique assignments, orchestrated by the ego, all of which pleased ol' man entropy not at all. The animal kingdom was surging gloriously in brainy abilities under the guidance of the newly enhanced central nervous system, and natural selection's harmonious nod of approval masticated over eons of time.

Eventually a vague quality called conscious awareness developed, a subject of infinite lugubrious debate. Avoiding the mystical, exactly what conscious awareness is is elusive, and dusty ponderous tomes have been scribbled about it, futilely inching toward a definition. Primitive man and animals could ultimately perceive something and have a sense of recognition and SELFNESS, I am, therefore I am. The protoplasmic entity could then ask if the approaching visual blob was a Godzilla or a rock, predator or brunch, as it learned to divine the difference… wordlessly. At what point conscious awareness barged onto the scene is unknown, but certainly prior to hominins (man and pre-man). Freud stated that just visualizing something was a very imperfect form of awareness of it since it eschews the linguistic part en mass. For millions of years humans had what one might describe as an experiential consciousness which was okay, or at least limped us forward. We saw stuff, smelled burning meat, touched animal pelts and each other, and those perceptions delivered to us the tools we needed to endure through the dense predatory onslaught of jungle terror. But at some point we became aware that we exist, not only in space but over chunks of time. For example, I'm aware that I've been typing and writing for the past hour and will be for the next. The term autonoetic is roughly applied to this.

Certain basic functions like breathing, peristalsis, and heart rate became automatic by using smooth muscle(as opposed to striated) long before we Homo sapiens emerged. This gradual goose step forward makes perfect sense since we wouldn't want to have to consciously tell our hearts when to beat, our lungs when to expand.

This primitive brain organization exists today. It existed in pre-verbal man for six million years before language. It is the stuff of animals, cavemen and young children, and users of shrooms and other psychedelics. And we revisit it nightly in REM sleep. We were physical, experiential Neanderthalish grunts through millions of years of evolutionary time, utilizing what mother nature gave us to scrape our way to survival. But what Freud dubbed the reality principle held little sway in the primitive thought module that entertained our pre-historic brains. This primitivity is on display in petroglyphs, those archaic rock carving depictions and the onset of linguistic thought complexity burns through in gradually accumulating sophisticated drawing, tool making, weaponry, clothing etc. Once language sizzled on the scene we wiped out all the other species of Homo, fanned out across the globe and now we own the world, some eight billion strong.

So, then what?

DOPAMINERGIC BRAINIAC

Like an evolutionary balloon, the brain swelled like a swollen wet sponge. For millions of years it was a wordless container, an experiential vessel filled with perceptions, feeling states, memories and intentions, like an octopus eyed computer sitting behind a closet humming away. The mind with its swashbuckling captain ego, worked silently on autopilot pulling as many clever strings as it could to promote the survival of the hapless grunt in an unforgiving jungle torture chamber. Sitting on a mossy rock Mr. Neanderthal pondered his next move wordlessly, his skull engorging the hefty energy and blood supply it demanded. Fluid streams of impulses, feeling states, memories, intentions and fears coursed through the brain as it adopted a plan of action. In that unpredictable jungle zoo of an environment, that daily schema, of course, had to be the safest, and most likely to succeed, to promote survival. Otherwise like his brethren, he'd be ground back through the sausage maker of evolution to hitch a ride to the dust bin of earthly inorganic matter, entropy once again victorious.

And, the human, that most physical of beings, like animals, ambled around on our own steam. No fridge, no Seven Eleven, we got up in the morning and would have to grouse around in search of delicacies for ourselves and our family. Let's say you're in the mood for wild boar, you ran, spear in hand to where you thought you might possibly find one. Anything we managed somehow to kill in the hunt we carried, often burning up more calories than the gourmet feast supplied. If a man needed a mate, he'd find her and chase her down. No matter what his impulses, he simply gratified them crudely, as best he could like any other animal, without the inconvenience of a superego. Children of nature, we were physical beings with an experiential noggin, but one that had unconscious fluid streams of "thought" that worked silently to promote our precarious welfare. (One might assert that most of the thinking we do now is still this same pre-verbal cogitation that humans engaged in for six or seven million pre-linguistic years while the wispy layer of conscious contemplation wanes thin.) Morality was not in our purview so much as survival, and would land later with language that groomed cooperation and ultimately civilizations that blocked our natural tendency to predation, and relied on its golden rule.

Ego, the orchestrating Oz or captain Kirk of the starship of the mind took control of intentionality. Catering to an endless wha wha baby demanding gratification, the ego did whatever it could to grab the demands of the individual within a most harrowing, unforgiving habitat, bearing safety foremost. Thus was the crucible, and with the help of the rest of the mind including conscious awareness and memory, it handheld the hapless cave person to thorny theaters of gratification. So, for example, a gnawing vein of hunger presented various possibilities while digging up memories of how it had been solved in the past. Revving into gear, the brain assisted us in bagging the sleekest and safest solution for this endless munchie. Sometimes the best laid plans vanished under a tiger's tooth or a cabal of hungry hyenas.

But evolution needed to deputize some influencing reward as it is only equipped to indemnify genetic events; it couldn't rule on moment by moment behaviors. The ego had been granted the mystical wand of intentionality, but these complex sapiens behaved with fluctuating purpose and made their own decisions. Educated by brutal experience, some behaviors were random and exploratory while others were pointedly goal directed, some more adaptive than others. Lady luck played a big role in the Jungle Book.

So evolution, anticipating Pavlov, approved a system in which good acts that followed the laws of natural selection were rewarded with a positive gummy of reinforcement. Good doggy, here's a little treat. Rotten, dangerous behaviors were denied reward, or at times even punished by searing pain. Evolution needed a sugary chemical that would function in the brain as its surrogate, a seductive reinforcer, and one that might even fashion the brain as a second evolutionary messenger, once removed so to speak. Painful stimuli had already been established to inform the organism of damage, as it was vital for protoplasm to figure out it had been chewed on. Conversely, it would also serve organic matter well to know it had carried out the mandates of Madam Evolution, and so a reward chemical was chosen by her called DOPAMINE!

Dopamine is a brain chemical, a neurotransmitter, and perhaps the most famous of them all. A cornerstone of mental illness etiology,(and some physical insults) this talented keystone rules the gelatinous gray matter kingdom. Talking technically, a neurotransmitter is a chemical released by one nerve cell to cross the gap between nerves (the synapse) and trigger the neighboring one, and it's welcomed into its specific receptor with great fanfare like a key lock. That receptor is the site of intense scrutiny by the chemical prescriptions tagged to fix schizophrenia and other mental bugs. It then gets reabsorbed into the first cell from whence it came requiring another lock and key receptor, this time called a transporter, to drag it back in.

Among other things it's released to encourage appetitive behaviors in a Pavlovian reward paradigm, and as such dopamine had a special place in evolution's heart. Reproductive behaviors were of course at the top of the list and are graced with a dopaminergic sugar high. As I said, evolution cackles with glee in the face of behaviors that promote living matter, and she is entropy's sworn enemy. Other survival adaptive endeavors like food gathering received dopamine's (and evolution's) consummate and immediate dopaminergic nod as did aggressive and protective stuff. Dopamine screams self-promotion as it is a drop of yummy secretion within the cranium. This 'deputized' reward system served Homo sapiens (and other animals) well. Evolution's handmaiden, it did its bidding and got evolution's highest nod, Le Prix d' Evolution. As in Pavlov's experiments, dopamine was the conditioned stimulus that made certain behaviors more likely. (see LeDoux, "The Deep History of Ourselves")

The simple art of cooking with fire shortened the bowel's digestion time and length leaving more rich blood supply for the brain, which uses about a quarter of the body's energy anyway, hogging the incoming reserves. In short, protoplasm's nervous systems went from simple reflex arcs to lumbering decision making computers, albeit silently, and evolution, reeling from the T-rex fiasco, had done itself proud this time. Although size still mattered and a large gorilla could rip a man to shreds (and often did), cunning's mystical prowess proved insurmountable and a sapiens with a bow and arrow might just fell the hairy ape from a distance. Moving from quadrupeds to bipeds, or walking on two limbs not four, allowed us to stand taller with an advantageous sightline, lugging tools and weapons in our hands across the grassy plains, and these boons to survival got dopamine's blessing. (Many of these changes in habits took millions of years. They were a result of climatic shifts, dietary changes, and sometimes just plain luck coupled, of course, with mutations.)

DOPAMINE'S PROMISE

So man was still not at the top of the food chain, (see Harari, "Sapiens") and the life of early man was a howling nightmare of fragility. Existence was not only not guaranteed, but disaster was nearly a heart pounding expectation. If a Neanderthal (one type of hominin, the general category of human-like animals, and another species of the genus Homo) for example, broke its hip, he was basically immobilized dead meat. Dragging himself to his cave if he could, he waited to die: no food, no water, no crutches, no Percocet. For the cave guy, scratching his way to survival demanded an aggressive, no holds barred sizzling furnace of intensity. He was used to terror and pain, and used to victory and all too aware of ignominious defeat. And in this regard dopamine served him well. Humans have more dopamine receptors than any other animal by brain weight. (see Vernier). It provided energy, aggressiveness and maybe even optimism, and suited the physical, experiential nature of our ancestors. (The ways in which our relationship to dopamine changes after language becomes a mega theme in our story. Stay tuned.)

Our primitive hominin had no use for morality, civilization's mortar. If he had an urge, the Neanderthal or sapiens gratified it, one and done. The need to procreate was highest on evolution's list of must do's, but in what manner primitive man did this we don't exactly know, while the assumption is that there was some capitulation of the unwilling, or more often brute force. (On the other hand, bunches of little family units no doubt served the purpose of protecting the pregnant mom and ultimately the small hominin kiddo until it could fend for itself.) The legacy of that gonzo, amoral pre-historic lifestyle lives on in us all. At some point in our infancy we draw a curtain across this terrorizing mental state and put it behind us. Freud called this the childhood amnesia happening around age 5 in which we forget the gruesome terror and brutality of that drama. Civilization is based on pushing it aside to create a quiescent civility. When we regress to a crazed psychotic state, those doors are opened up again and often reveal feelings that have been submerged since childhood; the door to the psychotic impulsive id. Is civilization based on a delusion of safety? Perhaps, or possibly just the need to maintain a sense of security that promulgates itself, in fragile pose, like a ballerina holding a pirouette too long. The maintenance of this civilized state of calm has much to do with the suppression of dopamine and this giddy molecule imparts pleasure and glee but has a closet full of other jobs. But civilization has devised a cadre of helpers to fizzle the hard wired aggressive prong within us all. Think religion, the ten commandments, jurisprudence, education, etc., all of which gang up on our inbred pulse to destroy and help suppress it. Substitute aggressive competitions like sports, jousting for the best mate or polished promotion gratify those ancient burns. So a polite society wrestles a fragile balance with the help of our suppressive efforts, released at night in the muscle paralyzed moment of dreams.

Eventually evolution shifted, and while size still mattered it shifted northward… brain size. (Things that once were external tend to move internally in the developmental schema of things.) The forces of adversity in the jungle environment overwhelmed: predators large and small, illnesses, injury, starvation, and extremes of weather all played a role in the unforgiving crucible of natural selection. Eons of time allowed these intense challenges to simmer. Eventually man's brain reached a critical mass and organization. "...the relative size of the entire cerebral cortex (including white matter) goes from 40% in mice to about 80% in humans." (Hofman) The brain of Homo erectus was about 900 cubic centimeters compared with the 1350 cubic centimeter Homo sapiens brain. (Leakey) "...the brain accounts for 2-3 percent of the total body weight but it consumes 25 percent of the bodies energy." (Harari) The mind, cunning, became the new evolutionary God. In concert with the body it proved its silent worth time and again, opening the sapiens door to blabbering speech. On a righteous path, evolution patted itself on the back, having finally redressed the dino fiasco.

But hold on... evolution had no idea what it was in for.

Chicxulub and Entropy

Sixty-five million years ago size reigned and the lumbering dinosaurs that ruled the earth did so under the aegis of mass. If anything promoted one's survival it was bulk; a tyrannosaurus rex could lift one foot and stomp a raging tiger into slime. These wandering hulks of protoplasm roamed the earth eating leaves from trees and other plant matter to nourish their zeppelin like form. Their brains were minuscule compared to the size of their bodies and functioned on a crude level while orchestrating the girth of their limbs and digestive systems with neuronal integrity. Evolution was satisfied with her choice and let the paradigm of size run amok. It made sense to Mother Evolution who sought, under the doctrines of survival of the fittest and natural selection, to promote organicity under any circumstance. And it worked, the earth enduring the footprints of mammoth beings who were in search of enough nutrition to maintain themselves. They roamed peacefully, these phantasms of size eating from the tops of trees, grazing at Mother Nature's offerings of fruits and vegetables although they were not all herbivores.

But then one day, while consuming their acres of plant offerings, they looked up and saw something different in the sky. Radiating an ethereal aura, it might have been a symbol of spiritual enlightenment, sent down from above to bless the living protoplasm that had gained a foothold against the wasteland of entropy's fondness for inorganic matter. Or it might have been some blessing of approval sent from somewhere in the hollows of the infinite universe. The dinosaurs watched calmly as this luminescence approached, intensifying in its brilliance.

Then a six mile wide asteroid slammed into the Yucatan peninsula, turning the world into a raging fireball of death and destruction. The skies blackened with thick smoke, trees evaporated, flesh incinerated and the dinosaurs crisped into carbon ash, sinking dutifully into Mother Earth's blackened womb, while Evolution watched its great achievement flit to dust. When all was said and done, It was time for a new paradigm, something subtler than girth, a principle that maximized complexity. Mother Evolution sat on the side of a creek bed and pondered, ultimately embracing an 'ah-ha' moment. Noticing the scurry of tiny mammals around her feet, she realized that it wasn't bulk that conquered, but something else… it was cunning. A piddling mouse could scurry around the craggy toes of a lumbering dinosaur avoiding attack, while going about its business of survival. Compared to its body size its brain outdid the dinosaur's, so, yes, indeed it was cunning that made the difference in Mother Evolution's equations of survival of the fittest and natural selection and she chose, declaring size, not body but brain size, as the new standard bearer.

But cunning did something greater than adding cleverness. In the game of organic matter, life itself defied the rule of entropy in its very existence. In fact one might conjecture that life itself is a bastion of entropy's opposite, or what I call antropy. In the debate about life's meaning, if any, theologians view it one way, physicists another, (see Schrodinger's *"What is Life?")* and the average human doesn't think much about it at all. For every profound principle there tends to be an opposite, gravity having centrifugal force, for example. The vast panorama of the universe is entropy's lifeless playground, with little opposing it. But, in certain sterling environments, with each detail golden and bright, entropy's adversary, antropy may take hold. And in those rare environments evolution, with the aid of light years of time, flourishes, brewing living matter which we may even define as entropy's nemesis. And as I have said, the purpose of life, then, is ***to defy*** entropy.

In its complexity of propagation, organic stuff, with super organization and energy and the blueprint of DNA, takes a rigorous stand against entropy, and with time's crucible allows Mother Evolution to do battle with entropy's desire and win bit by bit. In its quest for longevity and maintenance of the organic, evolution battles entropy sword by sword, making its inchworm of progress. Evolution borrows from its nemesis by using mutations, an offspring of disorder, to inseminate its progress, for, as I've said, without mutation, a product of entropy's talent for disorganization, there can be no evolutionary advance. Thus DNA's greatest talent is, like Robin Hood, to rob from entropy and give to evolution. So we can exhume two principles of living matter, the need for antropy whose banner is furled by evolution, and the caveat entropy who pilots its own ship, sucking us inevitably and rapidly back to the vast universe of inorganicity.

Thus the formula: *EVOLUTION PLUS TIME = ANTROPY.* Weaving its defiant dance around the boulder of entropy's desire in rare habitats like earth, (possibly the *only* habitat hospitable to life) evolution combines complexity and energy into beings, always just winning against the evil destroyer although in the short run, entropy inevitably claims it victims.

Freud made note of something he called the death instinct, something which we can now hog tie to entropy. And this evil foe delights in what we could designate evolution's greatest failure, the voluntary return to inorganic matter we call suicide. Clearly there is within us all a whisper toward a return to the inorganic primordial stuff from whence we came. In pre-linguistic times there was no suicide, no mental illness, when the only mantra permeating human's daily intensity was survival. But once language lifted us from this intensity and delivered a neutralization of most predators and an expectation of survival along with the group of mental illnesses that still accompany our recent transitional mindset, the seductive call to entropy's desire to have all organic matter dematerialize back to the inorganic weighs on some who suffer intensely under the horrors of insanity. Thus one can rightly say that suicide is a modern invention, spurred on by mental infirmity induced by our recent mental transformation and, lurking behind it all, the smell of entropy and the transition to language, a change we are still adapting to.

This force exists inside all of us and we take steps to avoid it. In future chapters we'll discuss the neurochemical correlates of this nemesis. But in its newly minted paradigm, evolution watched the fertilization of living matter in its yellow-brick-march forward, ultimately endorsing brain complexity as its sine quo non. And in this road to glory animals reached the ultimate synthesis of integration, the genus Homo. These hominins or human like animals, had it all, the motility, grasp, instinct for survival and of course, cunning, yet they were not at the top of the food chain. Over several million years its brain inflated from 900 cubic centimeters to around our current 1350. Neanderthals even went into the 1400 cc range and were brutally muscular, and primitively hearty. They might easily have dominated the earth, until something happened around 50,000 years ago, the most dynamic game changer of them all, even greater than a fiery asteroid… a little something called language.

"Our lives may be very different today from those of the first Homo sapiens, but our anatomy-including the size and shape of our brains-is practically identical. It may seem strange that natural selection, which has produced so

many impressive adaptations, would slack off this way. But natural selection is not some sort of conscious engineer, forever creating designs from scratch. It merely tinkers with genes and the bodies made by genes, sometimes generating new innovations and sometimes leaving well enough alone." (Smithsonian Intimate Guide to Human Origins, by Carl Zimmer, 2005, p. 145.)

"The perversions are neither bestial nor degenerate in the emotional sense of the word. They are a development of germs all of which are contained in the undifferentiated sexual disposition of the child…" (Sigmund Freud, in "The Cambridge Companion to Freud" edited by Jerome New, p. 179.)

It's clear that Freud viewed perversions as silt of the remnants of a premature type of sexuality that Homo sapiens simmer through during childhood and adolescence to arrive at the evolutionary resonance of ultimate union, genital intercourse. In short we all toggle through various stages of sexuality until ultimately arriving at the sine quo non which is most likely to please madam Evolution's zen for species propagation. Some may get snagged along the way by one phase of sexuality or another leading to a perversion or fetish which may run counter to the exalted mantra of reproduction. Freud singles out 'erogenous zones' including oral, anal and phallic to isolate organ patios that inveigle the young lad to participate in vital activities such as breast sucking, fecal excretion, and assertiveness. He paints a process of ongoing forward drive toward a specific evolutionarily approved goal.

But this process is also influenced by the prevailing wind of predatory necessity and intensity. To live to a ripe old age of 30, one must rapidly advance to sexual maturity in a climate of predatory insistence, and reproductive availability. And while our youngsters are biologically able to reproduce by age 12 or so, they are hardly in a position to arbitrate such a passion to fruition within the modern social framework. The complexity of our modern civilizational interactions necessitate further aging before consummation whereas the cave boy's pressurized lifespan and contextual predatory ardor necessitated a rapid climb to procreative readiness. So this all may encourage in some a tendency to gender boundary blurring by allowing the freer expression of perverse sexual inclinations that otherwise would not have had time to find any sort of action.

And this does not even address the mundane issue of morality which was imposed upon us Homo sapiens with the onset of something called civilization, a product of our fascination and mastery of language. Our caveman ancestors did not bother themselves with the inconvenience of morality, and were singularly ready to exercise any tendency toward gratification in light of the likelihood of predatory chomping. As civilization took hold, those nasty Oedipal/incestuous taboos weighed in forcefully creating extensive self denials and withholdings on a sexual level. All of this may be more of a breeding ground for sexual boundary dissolution than the uninhibited bohemian exigency of Neanderthal lifestyle. And with the recently prolonged lifespan of the average human, and the lack of predatory intensity, sexual ambiguities have more opportunities for expression.

Morality also is the product of civilization's need for order and safety, so that the animalistic instinct toward sacrificing other animals for our own need for nutrition is inhibited on multiple marketplaces. We no longer have the cave man's abandon to gratify their urges without consideration for the rights of our neighbors. This inhibitory milieu lends energy to the tendency to put off reaching sexual maturity and may also fertilize the potential for boundary confusion as the process of establishing the primacy of procreation in sexual endeavors is de-pressurized and drawn out in this modern era of longevity. Insemination is a goal post with some opposing team member interference. That interference is amplified by the lack of predation we now encounter as opposed to our caveman ancestors as well as the lengthier course of reproductive maturity. The intensity of cave man crucible predation hurried the process of sexual goal tending which disallowed the ambivalence that conceivably could lead to questioning the actual relevance of one's biological gender assignment. In short, Homo sapiens have been so successful at neutralizing the intensity of our evolutionary predatory wind that a process as crucial as gamete insemination is now in abeyance for an extended chunk of time which places its outcome in the category of indecision.

Countenancing the issues of declining birth rates, sexual boundary blurring, rising depression and anxiety among youth, and abandonment of expected social roles. we can grip the influence of predatory dissolve on our modern state of existence.

WE FIND OURSELVES IN A DECIDEDLY UNIQUE EVOLUTIONARY ERA, which, until flushed out, will continue to exert its effects on us invisibly like the wind. In my lifetime alone the life expectancy has jumped ahead by about 30 years. Homo sapiens were never designed to live much past the age of 30, so to encounter ourselves well beyond this goal post, on borrowed time so to speak, places us automatically in the terrain of the unknown. Entropy will conjure its degradation magic upon us from day one, and the skyrocketing to the longevity express opens pandora's box for all class of dissipative mischief.

The jet pack of evolution is the predatory intensity presented to our forebears for over 6 millions of years, and it is this hydraulic pressure that motivated us as prehistoric beings toward reproduction and survival. Absent this fuel indecision takes on a King Kongish swallow, and issues the elderly never even thought of dealing with surface ominously, leading youth towards existential crises of a cavernous nature. Once knee jerk reactions now become gaping indecisions. "What gender am I; should I have a family; should I work toward a profession; should I have offspring;" decisions evolution never meant to be grappled with, and which were taken for granted. You obey year parents, go to school, learn a profession, find a spouse have kids, two cars in the garage and a cute little painted house. By adopting evolution's mandates, civilization bent its structure toward facilitating them.

The geneticist T. Dobzhansky said, "Nothing in biology can make sense except in the light of Evolution." Like obstinate gophers, we bore our snouts through the ground of our own little existences and never bother to look up, backwards or forwards. Like Billie Eilish said, "I've been walking in a world gone blind," (Ocean Eyes). The changes endured by the youth of today in their milieu lifestyle are so momentous as to be dizzying, and the march of progress has zoomed so decisively over the past few hundred years, and even past 50,000 that not everyone could possibly be on board comfortably with this new panoply of mismatch endeavors. We Homo sapiens are truly disconnected from out pre-historic selves and as such face anxiety provoking decisions. The importance of gazing ahead and , mostly, backwards cannot be underestimated. We as humans are so cut off from our evolutionary roots, and the headwind that stretched the sails of her vessel, that we no longer have the luxury of direction. And this compasslessness fully explains the cataclysm of our current social apoplexy. The mismatch between our evolutionary past and our present includes how we use our minds and process dopamine, our dietary poisons, sedentary lifestyle indicators and much more. If we can't countenance these we are blinding ourselves to a key neon bellwether.

SUMMARY

Let's examine evolution's raucous impact on the landscape of current suffering.

1) Without the gut wrenching predatory nature of jungle swag, evolution's crucible fizzles to a simmer. That heat was the paring knife that cleaved mutations pronto into big bonuses or crippling drawbacks, and the latter quickly disappeared. Sans that searing heat knife, mutations can slink to a wishy washy ambivalence which allows them ongoing presence without enriching us or dragging us

heavily down. Without that hefty cleaver evolution nestles into free fall, leaving us advanced animals in massive indecision over issues never before considered ponderable. This gnarly indecision can foster anxiety, depression, and even suicide which we see on the rise in our youth. And suicide is evolution's greatest failure, (for a force that seeks nothing more than the promulgation of the species), and entropy's most joyous glee. In the not so recent past, there was no room for decision making when it came to gender, having a child, playing an adult role, you just did it. The luffing of evolution corresponds to the waffling of role adoption on a primordial level, a harrowing chasm for some.

2) The disconnect between our 7 million year old jungle lifestyle and our modern haunt elucidates a multitude of 'mismatch' illnesses including mental and physical. As we observe our sedentary and dietary excesses, we note the mushrooming of conditions like type two diabetes and heart disease as examples of this wrenching discrepancy since we no longer rely on our bodies for propulsion everywhere, and slobber gobs of fatty carbs directly into our aching arteries. And now that we are utilizing the miracle molecule dopamine differently since language, a mere 50,000 years old, we see internal brainy mismatch situations that we label mental illness due to the fact that not everyone is yet on board with this new way of processing the mind salve. Those least on board are dubbed mentally ill, or as I refer to them, 'evolution's dispossessed'.

3) We are experiencing a rapid jump in longevity, exponential in recent years. If for seven million years our bodies made it to about age 30, they are not used to the ongoing timelines that place our protoplasm into temporal extremis. Proteins start to break down under the influence of entropy (see "The Biology of Aging" by MacDonald) faster than our flaccid bodies can fix them. If the average lifespan in the 1800's was about 35 then it is only in the past one hundred fifty years or so that women expected to survive to or past menopause. Entropy's fondest desire is to return organic matter

to the inorganic and it begins its insidious drag at the moment of conception. In short, human tissue is not accustomed to age and we have more of that now than ever before, adding to the bustling bushels of chronic illnesses we are seeing currently.

All of this flotsam and jetsam adds up to the fallout of a new era, one that places evolution in a state of deflated ennui, and carries our bodies into a time frame that is entirely awkward in regard to entropy's desires, and evolution's promulgation. While cell phones may contribute to the bubbling anxiety of our youth, a bigger canvas is being painted by the moment we find ourselves and our bodies in. Juxtapose all of this mishegos with the uncertainty of civilization's ongoing progress due to climate change and potential nuclear conflagration, we find an unsettling questioning of every aspect of our lives in a rag tag dance of fear.

One must take a dynamic step backwards to observe that we are in a monumental evolutionary transition, one that will ultimately yield a different us, if we survive. If we have been around in one form or another for 7 millions of years, and other animals for billions, then the radical gut wrenching changes of the past 50,000 are so new as to be in their infancy, and they include monumental accretions. The insufferable mismatches in our lifestyle, longevity, how we use our brains since language including the new processing of dopamine and more are so spanking new that no one who gazes clear eyed at it could expect us to be anywhere near adjusted to these ardors. Yet it is hard to step back and fashion a telescopic assessment of where we are, even scientists just don't do it. But we must, if we truly want to understand who, what and where we currently are.

II: THE HEGEMONY OF LANGUAGE AND THE DOWNFALL OF MR. NEANDERTHAL

LANGUAGE'S TRANSFORMATIVE SPELL

Our brains were just waiting for it, and hominins had been around for some 7 million years, yet we were not at the top of the food chain and could be devoured en masse by packs of growling hyenas, ornery orangutans and feisty wildebeest. The genus Homo arose with an orchestrated leap forward integrating multiple advances into the body, especially the singular brain that distinguished us from all the other contenders. But the cranium could expand just so much for fear of getting stuck in the birth canal which would result in the death of both mother and unborn child. So the brain tissue had to be folded and crammed into the solid brain case. This folding created a variety of internal connections that ultimately gave the wise ones, the Homo sapiens the advantage. While we existed alongside several other species of the genus Homo, the gruff Neanderthals, Naledi, Denisovans and others, we were supremely adept at symbol formation, and this talent is the soul of language. After all, what is language but sounds symbolizing objects and feeling states, letters representing sounds that form the symbolic essence of words. In addition to this propensity for symbolization our voice box was more capable of sound creation than the Neanderthals' for example who probably could only form seven or eight, and their ears less acute sound dissectors.

Yet while our bodies had evolved into a sleek jungle carriage, our brains were stuck, having crammed and folded as much tissue into the box of our craniums as possible. Brain tissue swelled as much as possible, especially gray matter, over millions of years, serving Mother Evolution's bidding well. Yet there we were stuck in the brain case of our desires sporting a supremely evolved body with its prehensile thumbs and erect posture. We learned to use fire and cook thereby shortening the intestines allowing more blood for the head itself. But the brain needed to catch up. It needed something external as it had surmounted the pinnacle of biological gestation; it drooled for some gimmick as it were, a process to leverage its innate talents, some magic potion.

By 10,000 BC we had wiped out all other species of Homo. Most anthropologists agree that language was the force that altered the course of planetary existence. While hominins have been around for some 7 million years language has been adopted a mere 50,000 years ago, and language revolutionized how we use our minds. It helped foster art, culture and ultimately civilizations, tool making and weaponry advanced to protect us from the jungle marauders around us, and our rock doodling pointed to a solidifying mental complexity.

Around 50,000 years ago, and anthropologists are divided about this number, language made its meteoric appearance. This was just what our brains were yearning for, ready for some earthly paradigm to take it from a clattering jalopy to a sleek racing machine, and language did just that. I agree with those like Chomsky who feel that speaking exploded with a bang, while others assert that it was a slow march. The bang theory speaks to the depth of impact that language garnered, with a profundity that no other talent could elicit. Even evolution was surprised by the depth of transformation elicited by language's power, all positive from her point of view. One day humans began to speak and by 10,000 BC we'd wiped out every other species of Homo, and fanned out across the globe, and ultimately ruled the earth. As indicators of profound mental complexity, we start to see burials of the dead, the use of currency, more sophisticated cave art, and better weapons and tool making. The gifts of language were bestowed upon sapiens more than any other species of Homo and the results were impressive. Neanderthal's could only dream of benefitting from speech as much as we did, this talent quickly forging a brave new world. Gradually, over time civilizations began to take hold like wildflowers in an open field. The evolutionary benefits were enormous in terms of longevity, protection, and nourishment. With more advanced tools and weapons the town leaders could protect the residents from all sorts of predators. Walls could be erected against the fury of intruders both animal and human with solid gates. Agriculture began to flourish enabling a steady food supply with commerce fueling the aggregation and distribution of crops. (Although some have noted that reliance on agriculture was a double edged sword when drought and other phenomena of weather ruined the crops exposing the populace to starvation.) Talents like clothes making, shoemaking, weaponry and eventually metallurgy could be nourished with a more defined monetary reward module. These external talents quickly became evolutionary gradients when, for example, those with sturdy shoes were less likely to suffer cuts and foot infections which gave them a distinct survival advantage. Institutions began to form, supporting humanity against the chaos of the jungle's entropic embrace.

We erected structures, physical and symbolic to counter the lure of entropy's desire for chaos and disorganization. The treasured art of cooperation started to flourish as humans gained a sense of longevity and leisure, allowing creative minds to endure. Science, art, religion, education, jurisprudence and civil order all contributed to the modern human's need to counter the chaos of entropic forces that pulled us back to the jungle and still do.

Thus the flourishing of mankind hinged on language, and its cornucopia of gifts were limitless. The one predator that defied domination was one's fellow man who continued to wage wars and destructiveness throughout history, perhaps solidifying our need for organized army's and systems of government in protective nuance. This encouraged specialized functions and roles for individuals to wrap around their identity. We moved from natural selection and survival of the fittest to survival of the most reproductive, or sexual selection, and now we are moving even beyond that.

And it necessitated the adoption of what one might call a social strategy, a face to present to the world that informed one's relationship in regards to others. This kind of social strategizing was not even possible until sapiens delineated a higher level of consciousness. The type of thinking typical of a cave-person was not conducive to sophisticated social encounter and when patients regress to this pre-verbal mindset that I label 1.0 as opposed to the 2.0 mindset of modern adults. they too lose the talent for complex social interaction. Thus language in its ultimate accretion, 2.0 type of thinking, allowed us to cooperate in conjunction with civilization's advance. And evolution could do nothing but endorse an organization of human interactions that protected the sapiens from most predators including animal aggressors, weather insecurities, starvation, lack of housing, etc. Humankind was certainly better off within a civil structure, enriching survivals' possibilities including the gestative soil of free time with an expectation of survival.

The mind underwent this complexification once language took hold. Without this process the complexity of a social strategy, a mask with which to address one's peers, could not take place, and we see in schizophrenic regression that the ability to encounter the universe of others dissolves. And with it, that most needed element, cooperation wanes, and those lacking it are seen to retreat into their own version of reality. Thus the language of the schizophrenic is more eccentric and autistic in its content, more idiosyncratic than universal. In its desperation for advancement, the mind found a way down a developmental highway, following the universal rules of maturation as defined by developmental psychology: differentiation and individuation of parts with integration and hierarchical structuring within a functional organization. Symbol formation, the soul of language, was a brain fertilizing dynamo with its ever multiplying retinue of descriptives. (See Werner and Kaplan's *Symbol Formation, 1963.*) And the sapiens' brain was ever talented at this symbol forming task.

In short we left the brain of the caveman (1.0) and forged a mindset that was radically more complex. This mindset 2.0 paid off in a massive cornucopia of riches including the onset of civilizations with its institutions and cooperative orderliness. And this progression is the same one we embrace in our march through adolescence, with the benefit of education, discipline, conscious thought, and reading to arrive at the 2.0 adult rules of logic. After all, children's rules of thinking are not our adult precepts, but are reminiscent of the thinking demonstrated in dreams, ayahuasca users and cavemen. We transition from the idiosyncratic illogicality of kids to the universal communication of adults which involves multiple components including the ability to gate out the primitive beast of jungle mentality into a container called the unconscious. We learn to wall this off during childhood and adolescence utilizing considerable mental effort. Imagine oneself standing waist deep in a pool holding a balloon under water with both hands.

This is analogous to the effort required to submerge our primitive brain chaos into the unconscious. It is always threatening to pop up into consciousness and like a whiny child, demands our constant effort. This must-do is evolutionarily brand new and most of us are less than perfect at it. Balloon holding requires considerable energy and skill lest it emerge toward the surface in an exuberance of release. In short, the handy balloon holding is an antropic chore that partially eludes most of us and we find ourselves in a perpetual state of attempting. And if the balloon pops up to the water's surface the release of energy therein is a boon to entropy which is why once someone regresses to the mindset of schizophrenia it is a life long affliction.

The onset of language 50,000 years ago created a gargantuan psychic metamorphosis that reverberates still through the echo chamber of our modern society. We are all struggling with these recent changes imperfectly in their newness and it is exactly this situation that places some individuals in the crosshairs of mental dysfunction. In short they are a victim of the time in which we live and nothing else, not imperfect mothering, faulty life choices or profligacy. They are merely evolution's dispossessed. One other factor lurks behind this precarious assignment, entropy. Since we exert so much energy shoving the horrors of primitivity and childlike thinking under the water into the balloon of the unconscious, the energetic release of this balloon sides with entropy's lust for lower tension and non-complexity. As Freud pointed out, the mind seeks a climate of low energy, which fits in exactly with entropy's desires. In sleep the mind and body seek restoration from the day's intensity working its way toward the greatest state of entropy possible for a normal organic being.

To do so it gives up muscularity in the paralysis of sleep and allows the mind to regress in an environment of sensory deprivation without noise, light or skin impingement back to the more primitive thought process 1.0 of our forebears. The dorsolateral prefrontal cortex, the executive center of the brain, feels sensorily deprived and elicits the hallucinatory phenomenon of dreams to avoid atrophy. By processing the day's events in a more acceptable outcome, dreams allow the mind to sink into deeper and deeper layers of sleep which can be characterized as an entropic restorative habitat. When schizophrenics regress to the same primitive mental function during waking hours, the dorsolateral prefrontal cortex again feels deprived of sensation and solicits hallucinations. But in their quest to crush the ego these hallucinations often take a pejorative intensity.

They thus give direct expression to entropy in three ways: blunt ego attack by denigration, second by vitiating conscious thought with intense distraction ("kill yourself, you're a fool, your a homeless criminal") using phrases that are unignorable, and third by giving voice directly to entropy's yearning for the individual to return to inorganic matter by voicing its fondest desire, committing suicide. Thus in regressing back to the primitive thought pattern of our jungle stricken forebears entropy is handed a decided victory, and the energy that was invested in balloon submergence is now released, gratifying entropy's wish for the anergic trough.

External stress can accentuate the odds of becoming mentally ill. In the next chapter we'll explore entropy in detail.

ALONG CAME THE SPIDER: THE SIXTH SENSE

"We must reject the idea that the faculty of articulate language resides in a fixed, circumscribed point." Pierre Paul Broca, 1861

It was not planned. Certainly evolution did not foresee this turn of events. The brain of a Homo sapiens reached a critical mass and configuration, like the critical mass of plutonium that leads to nuclear fission, the onset of language led to an explosion far greater than the thunder of an atom bomb, the big bang, if you believe in language's abrupt arrival (Chomsky). And of course the atom bomb is one perfect example of what we were capable of once our language birthed contemplation. With the help of good old captain Kirk, the ego, the brain organized around this new principle… words.

Initially words were labels and they may have been object labels or syncretic, combination labels of actions and things. For example, a word may have developed for the action of throwing a rock at a moose, like moosculating. Starting a fire with a stick may have been mashed into one word, or the joy of eating a trout. However, words gradually assume specificity, modifying labels into more refined categories… it's not just a rock, it's a big rock; not just a flower, it's a bright red flower. That's not just a hippopotamus over there, it's an angry one about to charge… run like hell! All of these divisions and subdivisions, descriptives and qualifiers encouraged subtle mental differentiations that were previously impossible without… of course, speech.

Suddenly a dividing line was drawn between what was delivered to consciousness and what was held back by our friend the ego. Prior to words the consciousness of man was experiential. The dull Neanderthal took note of sensory inputs from our eyes, ears, skin, nose and internal feeling states. (The pathway to consciousness remains the sensory channels. When we think we talk to ourselves in the form of internal speech.) Our ego was primitive and had difficulty differentiating self from others, inner from outer. Just as children may believe that clairvoyant momma knows what is on their minds, primitive man was just as under-developed. Freud, in denoting his classic view of the mind, did not take pre-verbal man into account as definitively as perhaps he should have. Freud's 'meta-psychology' included the famous unconscious, preconscious and conscious areas. Sans language, those cubby holes are nonexistent. He did say however, "How does a thing become preconscious? And the answer would be: 'By coming into connection with the verbal images that correspond to it." (Freud 1957, p.213) In short, a flapping fish barrel of words began to coalesce in the sapiens' mind, a small vocabulary. Obviously not all could be in conscious awareness at the same damn time. But words allowed the ego to construct the mental apparatus that led to adult thinking. The ego became the word processor supreme, the street cop, waving some forward, stifling others. The ego gained the important task of fish finding, but not only this, along with it came reality testing, syntax and hierarchical organization of incoming stimuli. Captain Kirk earned a huge promotion. The demarcation between one's self and others was hardened, baked to a golden crisp. The traffic cop orchestrated the dance, the flow, the pattern of shoulds and shouldn'ts in the mental theater.

Initially, a small layer of preconscious labels accrued. Language's hypnotic influence masticated and intensified the mental actors. As vocabulary expanded, so did the preconscious (that part of the unconscious just next to what is conscious or aware.) Like guests on the Tonight Show waiting patiently in the green room, etherial thought blobs approached their word labels in the preconscious just before they took the platform of awareness. (We will discuss more about how this platform space clears under the influence of dopamine suppression, and is swarmed with angry ants like a sugar cube when dopamine is suddenly unsuppressed: think schizophrenic breakdown, an Ayahuasca cocktail, and even in sleep.) Modifiers, descriptives, and feeling states were all 'wordified'. The mind moved from diffuse to categorical specificity, a process unavailable to the pre-verbal, primitive (mental) organization. (Remember that term.) Words organized into sentences that obeyed the rules of syntax (grammatical mandates). (The importance of syntax in organizing our minds should not be underestimated. Some, like Chomsky, believe that it is an innate trait of a sapiens.) A master fisherman, the ego's task was to reach into the fish barrel of verbiage and pull out just the perfect terms to decorate those blobby fluid thought precursors. (Pre-verbally, Fido thinks this way, as did man, pondering silently, wordlessly, but actively nonetheless. Their smaller animal brains work to promote their interests as did the brain of Joe Neanderthal. And of course, our brains still do think this way for the most part, I would assert. Only a slim fraction of thoughts are promoted to the level of conscious awareness, more when we're actively thinking.) Syntax, with its subject, object, verb, adjective, etc., was one system that advanced brain development. Before reaching consciousness our ego commander dusted sentences off, reality testing them, and hanging them out to dry on the eave of awareness. Eventually this whole process reached a state of automaticity.

Thus, a fancy tripartite organization imposed itself on the mind. Words were scooped from the preconscious, organized into sentences, and inspected with a magnifying glass by the ego's reality testing function, then silently delivered through the auditory channels. (We consider the forebrain, most likely the pre-frontal cortex, our gelatinous mind's seat of consciousness.) The act of delivering concepts to it has many implications, like a crazy Amazon driver who does a dance as he drops your toaster oven on the front porch. For one, a chemical called BDNF (Brain Derived Neurotrophic Factor) is secreted and this stuff's MiracleGro for the mind. It promotes dendritic arborization, the little branches fanning out like tree roots. Without that the forebrain (analogous to any muscle) has a potential for atrophy, especially if it doesn't get enough incoming entertainment.

And, BDNF is euphorigenic. A gaping mouth hungry for info, the forebrain needs this input much as a muscle needs exercise to prevent it from withering. When deprived, in a desperate effort to avoid deterioration, it starts creating its own cinematic input. The stuff of dreams at night, during daylight hours they are hallucinations. (Mental illness interrupts the smooth flow of nutritious activity to the forebrain which needs that input. Restoring this incoming frequency is always the treatment goal and we do so by toning down or blocking dopamine, directly or indirectly.) As we grow up we re-experience this evolutionary brain intensification as the rules of talking go from diffuse, infantile idiosyncrasy, to specific, directed, informational and communal. (Werner 1984, p.289)) What the adult says the rest of us understand. With children, (and schizophrenics) on the other hand or psychedelic users, sometimes their responses are so unique to their own experiences that others just don't get it because they are still in the process of solidifying the congealing brain organization language bestows. In a great leap (over 50 thousand years or so) the ego took a 180 degree turn from the caveman's primitive organization, hurtling our cognitive development forward, in ways that were untouchable before we spoke. And it was the ego, the commander of this gelatinous gray matter, that got us out of Dodge.

So, our ego is at this point stuffing the forebrain with stimuli of a conceptual nature. It is now behaving like any other sensory organ (eyes, ears, etc.) only instead of a Bach concerto or a twilight panorama, it delivers the stimulus of organized concepts (not sounds, not sights) to our conscious awareness and it has become, so to speak, the sixth sensory organ. Language, at some critical juncture, moves from labeling and symbol creation, to thought when we realize we can talk inwardly to ourselves. And with this monumental progression, it has garnered several nifty advantages for the mind of humankind.

Now Freud's metapsychology with its conscious, preconscious and unconscious areas can be realized and defined in a word juggling context which, prior to language was a no go. With the ego we have a sense of identity, something that shreds to confetti if we drink Ayahuasca or take acid. Defining boundaries, our beefy egos drew a sharper demarcation between one's self and the rest of the world. Our cognitive abilities multiplied like horny rabbits. The ego had the function of a monolithic word processor. Scooping the best words out of the pre-conscious part of the mind, it hammers them together syntactically following the rules of grammar (which we all learn from Mrs. Petry in sixth grade) into gaily expressive sentences. Like inspector Cleuseaut it inspects those sentences using the rules of adult logic, presenting them to consciousness like a neatly bowed gift delivered by Federal Express. It was then consciousness' role to open that gift and contemplate it. Happy birthday.

Words hit the spotlight and danced. Not only did language serve the purpose of expression, but procured the mind's expansive enrichment. And, conveniently, when we wanted not to remember something, all we needed to do was dissect it from its sticky word label and leave it unattended, dangling alone in the pre-conscious. Or even further, as the unconscious was an even deeper burial, hiding it down the stairs and in the basement. Ideas, memories, or impulses could be banished there like a bastard child, rarely if ever to be seen, miles from the words that describe them. Civilization demanded that certain impulses never see the light of day. Impulses like: sleeping with mom; killing your neighbor; smearing feces all over were sent downstairs. Like unwanted relatives they rarely got an invitation to the reunion. Sometimes they got feisty and threatened to bust the door down. This, Freud noted, created mental symptoms as the mind struggled to keep gross uncle Fred from the appetizers and the other guests.

And words were the mind's ticket to a new dance with dopamine… suppression. The mind learned this clever feat of legerdemain from the motor system. We need to suppress dopamine, the ubiquitous neurotransmitter, to attain ballet smooth, coordinated movement. A magician's sleight of hand, the complex hurl of a knuckle baller all rely on this suppression. This brings dopamine into a delicate balance with another neurotransmitter, acetylcholine in the motor nerve tract called the nigro-striatal. But the mind lacked the tools to do this in the other dopamine tracts called mesolimbic and mesocortical, as if we lacked the limbs to carry out this conceit. Language gave them to us. We could now suppress dopamine in those tracts, clearing the mind space, gaiting out unwanted intrusions into our mental playground, supporting the mighty ego and assisting the complexification of our minds into adult rules.

We were now freed to enter the process of control that led to clear thinking nor did we need dopamine's reward function as dearly since we had our own mystical evaluator in the form of thought. Our minds were desperate recruits waiting for the tools to enact this precious symphony. Thus when dopamine DE-suppresses, either in a regressive way or under the influence of chemical stimulation or in; sleep, the mind space becomes flooded and disorganized. Hallucinogen users, meth addicts and schizophrenics will report this regularly… as do manics. How do we treat this? With chemical agents that brilliantly block dopamine's receiving dock, their receptors. But I'm getting ahead of myself.

A crude analogy might be as follows: a man stands on a rock at a stream casting a net into the gurgling waters. He is looking only for an engagingly unique kind of trout. He readies his net and when he spots the perfect fish scoops it out of the water, examines it, and, if suitable stores the flapping monster in his fish box. He does this until his box is brimming with the slimy swimmers. He organizes his fish box neatly until he has the right combination, then hauls it back home where his wife and kids are waiting arms crossed for their next feast. He hands it to his wife who looks skeptically over the menagerie and makes an assessment of their suitability for cooking. Depending on her judgement, they might have a delicious dinner, or a smelly garbage pail.

In this analogy, the man is the ego. He is there scooping out the flapping fish words from the preconscious stream. He, the ego, is choosing just the right ones. Then the ego organizes the words and delivers them, now formed into syntactical sentences and concepts, to his wife and kids (consciousness) who pass judgement on them.

And remember, without our new trait of dopamine suppression, the fish could only leap randomly up at the man perhaps accidentally falling into his fish box. This state of affairs might happen when the ego is really weak and unable to do much organizing, a state of de-suppressed dopamine. Suppressing dopamine strengthens the ego and gaits out unwanted mental intrusions. Or perhaps he had a few beers on the way to the stream, or, maybe took some acrid Ayahuasca, or licked a croaking Sonoron desert toad, resulting in DE-suppression of dopamine, and puff, dissolution of the ego. We see this state of mind in schizophrenics and manics as well, children and in what is known as REM sleep. It's a flooding tsunami of ungaited input the mind can't get a handle on. In fact, one could define the major mental illnesses as word diseases. What I would call linguistic deterioration is a hallmark of schizophrenia and mania (although there are differences: syntax is often maintained in mania). Why? Because our fisherman ego may become impaired and not be in control of the word choice, or the reality testing process as our chemical friend dopamine is not suppressed. These symphonic components must work together in clockwork incantation.

It was words and the utilization of them by the ego that got us out of our pre-historic Dodge in the first place. Without words we'd be glued to the primitive mental organization cave humans like Mr. Neanderthal had for millions of years before language. (Mr.

Neanderthal's voice box was not his only linguistic drawback. Apparently his auditory system was not capable of perceiving the grab bag of sounds that us Homo sapiens are able to.) This is another indication that mental illness is directly woven into languages' jurisdiction. (Yes, we actually are going to plunge into mental illness eventually. This is a lengthy, explicit preamble to that crescendo.) Again, in order for the mind to organize words and offer them a clear stage for inspection, WE MUST SUPPRESS DOPAMINE. You see certain trends emerging in all of this, trends that are indicative of the problems we note in mental illnesses, particularly dopamine non-suppression, treatable with… as I mentioned, dopamine blocking agents, putting the brakes on this ubiquitous chemical. But other medications hamstring dopamine too, albeit indirectly.

Not only that, but words created a second reality so to speak, a scaffolding around the structure of our feelings and perceptions. No longer was a state of hunger, let's say, the only thing connected to memories of starvation. Past solutions to hunger; locations of food; preferences, now the WORD hunger magnetized all of those dangling connections. A unique secondary plane of reality built up around the framework of words and their remembered stirrings. Something called laterality happened as the brain expanded on one side (the dominant, left side for most of us right handers) to accommodate language and all of its glittering accoutrements.

But wait, THERE'S MORE! This ego, newly minted and deputized, became our ticket out of the primitive organization. Sapiens went from the jungle to the disco and the primitive brain organization, that infantile mental state 1.0 by which pre-verbal caveman operated, was ultimately replaced by the post verbal, complex adult 2.0 operating system of modern humans. The captain Kirk of our brain ship Enterprise delivered us from the impulse driven, amoral, experiential-physical state of primitive souls to the civilized, law abiding, moral contemplative beings that we are today.

Religion was born as was government, institutions of higher learning, jurisprudence. All of this soared around our mind's new complexity, operating system 2.0. In the spirit of social cooperation we learned to live side by side. And another of Freud's concepts, (we never get TOO far from Freud when we think of the human mind, or Darwin when we contemplate evolution.) the superego, rewarded us for law abiding behavior. Embracing the golden rule, now we had a good feeling inside when we did the right thing, the basis upon which civilization rests. Wrongdoing felt bad.

The power upon which man once operated had been usurped by this new sixth sense, word processing, telescopic wonder. Where did captain Kirk get all his strength? From that primitive operating system itself that used to rule our minds. Kirk muscled up and took from the primitivity of our minds his supremacy in language's intricate ballet. Robbing Peter to pay Paul, anything that strengthened the ego took more from the old 1.0 and gave it to the new and improved 2.0. An impairment in the ego's power now reflects mental difficulty, a symptom of coming infirmity. When the ego is crippled, watch out. Schizophrenics may be described as suffering from ego weakness, (see article by Tausk) but this would have to be true for bipolars (manics) and unipolars (major depressives) as well, and lack of gating. Out of chaos comes order. And order is supplied by the ego with the help of dopamine suppression in the context of our spiffy new operating system. When order is lost the chaos of entropy which seeks disorganization and lower energy states, again reigns. (All of this goes along with dopamine de-suppression, as the fulcrum of organized thinking painfully reverses. A schizophrenic breakdown or an LSD trip use the same pathway. We see things like linguistic deterioration as syntax vanishes, flooding of the mind space as gating dissolves, and phenomena like blockage of thought or perhaps even 'word salad'. Their opposites were originally unified in a global dopamine suppressive growth pattern reproduced in all of us as we mature.)

And our egregious friend the ego grows from certain activities that accrue in the strabismal playing field of youth. We learn to suppress dopamine, number one and learn the art of contemplation. Those brain fertilizers like BDNF and VEGF accrue, enhancing the mind's own enrichment. Reinforced by parenting, schooling, discipline, rules, and socialization with its steady partner cooperation, ego grows. Dragging us out of our entropic primitivity, all of this propels us from primitive thinking to adult, modern conceptualizing. The child no longer says, "The moon is a big fat man that will eat you!" The rules of logic crystallize into adult conventions while the mind becomes the most anti-entropic, or antropic substance in the universe.

Developmental psychology tells us a lot about this. As a basic rule (see Heinz Werner) any process of development goes from diffuse, disorganized, and lacking in structure to specific, hierarchically organized, and with differentiation of parts. When the high school band leader blows the whistle the kids line up and start marching in unison. Children's minds, hallucinogen users' minds, primitive people's minds, schizophrenic's minds… all lack specificity. Vagueness that is indicative of early development reigns over childhood's incentives. There is also an idiosyncratic quality about their speech. Children respond in ways that are unique to their own experiences, as do schizophrenics in their brazenly autistic way. I once asked a schizophrenic man, "Why does the sun come up in the morning?" His reply was, "Tomorrow." I looked at him blankly. When I requested explanation, he said, "Didn't you ever see Annie? The sun'll come up, tomorrow…" and burst into song. Instead of addressing the question from a factual point of view, he simply referred to an idiosyncratic association he had to my question. Adult thinking is universal, and understandable by all who speaka da language. We will talk more about this in chapters to come, but it is a core symptom of schizophrenia… this regressive type of autistic thinking typical of children. At least, us evolutionists think so and most psychiatrists do as well.

ONE MORE THING! Freud taught us that there are two types of thinking, primary and secondary process. Akin to daydreaming, primary process is unstructured, a rollicking roller coaster ride. We stare at the lamp, our minds scatter in a million diamond shards of connection, glances of memory. Okay, but this is not the type of thinking that suppresses dopamine, hardens the ego, strengthens our adult conceptual rules or secretes BDNF or VEGF. Sorry. Our Neanderthal brethren indulged in it, only without words. Prior to language our participation in our own mind's clockwork ordinances was nil, none, nada. The ego is not exerting any structure or control over it. Psychedelics, for example, blast the ego from its moorings and put us in the state of evanescent daydreaming. Poof the ego vanishes. They do this by stimulation of a type of serotonin receptor called 5HT2a. (The 5HT part just stands for serotonin, five hydroxytryptamine.) Suck the ayahuasca cup and the ego shreds, all we can do is sit back, let our minds lead the way. There's no gating, no dopamine suppression, frankly, just the opposite.

Now the next type of thinking is called secondary process. This is the type of deliberate, effortful mulling that warps into problem solving, focuses on a chosen topic. You get the idea. Deliberateness. That requires the participation of the ego and… us. We all have these two mental modus operandi, Jeckyl and Hyde. The six million year old trail wandering, which for most of that time, went on without language but now employs words and visualization and rambles on autopilot. And, there is a new, ego driven jet stream which is less than 50,000 years old which goes on with muscular ego guidance; active participatory effort since it takes effort to think. Two modes, one ancient and one new. The ego evaporates leaving us in a state of passive, experiential consciousness when, as I keep saying, we take psychedelics, a hot topic in the psychiatric kitchen. We're dazzled by the mind's shift to a more primitive thought paradigm. When we actively think, using the muscular ego as a tool, we strengthen it; we can reach solutions to problems; explain and understand; we actively suppress dopamine, gate out unwanted intrusion, complexify the very rules of thinking itself, and puff up the brain with the indelible growth euphoriants BDNF/VEGF. A whole smorgasbord of positives which were likely unavailable to the Denisovans or Neanderthals. These ethereal brain chemicals cause the nerves to insufflate and branch out. Like a muscle, if you use the brain, it enlarges, if you don't, it degenerates, use it or lose it. Is it any wonder that schizophrenics are in danger of atrophy of brain cortex? No. Their mind structure is reverting back to pre-verbal times, little ego after they'd mastered the operating system 2.0. There is some dopamine suppression involved with coordinated movement referred to as body ego. (The forebrain needs conceptual input, just as a muscle needs to be exercised. The analogy between brain tissue and muscle is quite apt. Both are prone to dissolution without use and input. One could rightly say that thinking is muscular activity.) However, this loss of brain function is not inevitable since schizophrenics are still able to utilize secondary process thinking, albeit with difficulty.

Secondary process thinking requires dopamine suppression. In order to clear the brain space, or theater of cognition within the mind, dopamine must be suppressed. When schizophrenics break down dopamine painfully de-suppresses and their minds are flooded with a tsunami of un-prioritized stimuli. Their ability to think is vastly inhibited although not impossible. A dose of dopamine blocking agent can clear their minds, such as a thorazine tab of maybe 50 milligrams as it restores the gating function. Now the seat of contemplation is free to rumble, whereas before it was overwhelmed. The preferred input of conceptualization has been chaotically usurped by in-rushing stimuli which leaves the forebrain in starvation mode, akin to sleeping. The brain interprets this AS a state of sleep and begins to self-stimulate with dream like hallucinations. More on this later. (More analogies. The analogy between hallucinations and dreams is quite apt. Both are creations of the forebrain routed through the sensory pathways under conditions of sensory deprivation. When the primitive organization takes over in schizophrenia, the forebrain interprets this as a state of sleep and begins its daytime hallucinatory dreaming as a means of self-stimulating. (See the You Tube lecture by Oliver Sacks on hallucinations.) So we can claim, as I will, that the act of Freudian repression, or burying of unwanted mental contents, is akin to suppressing dopamine and this process strengthens the ego, and works towards a more complex mental structure, strengthening our tentative mental security.

*

This is just the very start of where we're going to go, for to grasp the influence of evolution and its changes on psychiatric infirmity, we have to understand what happened when the symphony of words arrived on the scene. Not just the radical modifications we inflicted on mother nature that were wrought by language but in our brains. Clearly the mind of a modern day accountant is not the same as the psyche of Mr. Neanderthal, that spear wielding, pelt wearing ogre (although he may have had many gentle qualities.) And, what we see in mental illnesses reverses some of those megalithic modifications.

So, let's review some of the mental changes that took place when Mr. Neanderthal went from the brutal daily drama of jungle survival to a Gen X'r with his earbuds in his ear, his computer in his briefcase, hopping into his electric car to take him to the office, stopping no doubt to grab a latte.

1) Symbol formation became our forte. Our minds sizzled at the options, taking to it like dope to an addict, our psyches buzzed with the enriching potential. Like Helen Keller in the movie *The Miracle Worker* we dropped everything and made the startling connection and it was electrifying. It pioneered our mind's transformation.

2) Our brain lateralized. The left side swelled to accommodate the enormity that symbol formation, meaning language with all its implications, was.

3) Words became the utter center for feeling states. Hunger's (for example) vast implications now had a label around which solutions, memories, dangers, and implications all coalesced. We erected a pile of ashes into a new configuration, an alternate universe. Taming, and in a sense rejecting our natural environment we created our own physical geo-dome in which to exist. Homo sapiens has put mother nature at arm's length with the help of words. Of course, for some six million years or so, we were in a perilous engagement with the predators she exposed us to, so it would be natural to mistrust her.

4) Evolution's deputy, dopamine, could now be demoted since we could engage in crystal decision making of our own, and clarity of contemplation, a clear brain space required dopamine's suppression. We needed to put that bad boy in its settled place once and for all. Conceptualizing took over, while cave-people crossed the line into meditative contemplation. A new model of brain-ism surfaced, on top of the old. Dopamine suppression gaits out the unwanted stuff, feeds the ego and its identity and self-awareness module, fertilizes the mind and complexifies, differentiates and structures the clockwork organization of our hungry psyches. Yes, all of that in its new operating system 2.0. What we see when dopamine un-suppresses in a return to OS 1.0, is a loss of the ability to make a point, or apointilism, with linguistic deterioration, and a tsunami of unwanted debris flooding the brain space, including hallucinations due to loss of the gating function. Perhaps our greatest accomplishment, the suppression of dopamine, set us apart from all other species of Homo. Evolution, knowing a good thing when it sees it, welcomed it with a smarmy, sloppy embrace. As for survival of the fittest, we gradually tamed our multitude of predators, morphed gradually into survival of the most reproductive and an

expectation of longevity settled in. We will see that, in mental illness, a painful wrenching of dopamine backward from suppression invariably takes place. Dopamine suppression, the fulcrum which allows us to focus and attain a clarity of expression with adult rules, sometimes goes into reverse. Unfinished in its newness, the evolutionary march plods on today.

5) Yet, it should not surprise you that the diseases we might relate to evolution are all dopamine driven; Parkinson's disease, schizophrenia, attention deficit disorder, Alzheimer's disease, stuttering, Tourette's and more. We can add to these those ubiquitous mood disorders major depression, bipolar mania, and toss in as well the common anxiety disturbances, obsessive compulsive, panic, generalized anxiety disorder, etc. Laying the seed of them all when it flows backwards from suppression, dopamine is the bad boy of psychic distress. It's the pin on which everything hinges and we shall see how dopamine de-suppression is lead dancer in the ballet. The suppressive process reverses course, and opens the door to an exquisitely painful reassertion of the dominance of dopamine that occurred for millions of years before language and, as we shall see, nearly every medication we use to reverse mental illness suppresses dopamine directly or indirectly.

6) Ego. In celebration of its scintillating orchestration efforts, it got the promotion of a lifetime. This word processing dynamo yanked the words out of the fish barrel and delivered them to madame forebrain. Voila, a whole new paradigm of mental modus operandi settled in. CONTEMPLATION! In a reward switch, not dopamine but BDNF/VEGF graced our shores as the Pavlovian conditioning stimulus. Thinking reinforces mind expansion, enriching your mind with dopamine suppression, and complexification of mental apparatuses. We now have the ability to construct hypotheses from preliminary data points. This paradigm of modus operand-us 2.0 is rattled by every mental disturbance known to man and every de-suppression of dopamine mucks it up.

Imagine a gen X'r at a zoo with his earbuds, i pad and laptop sitting on a bench and staring through a fence, not at a gorilla, but at Mr. Neanderthal.

The brute would sit on a rock and stare back at him, in wordless observation. The gen X'r would think to himself, 'who is this guy'? 'He is me, but what does he experience in his daily life? Does he think? No, he can't.' But beyond a lack of words there is a lack of brain organization within. The ego organized our brains around language and vice versa, conductor of the symphony grande, and in doing so got a huge promotion. When the ego weakens, (in concert with dopamine DE-suppression) the whole framework of our mental apparatus melts, distorted, limping, sputtering and the primitive organization gains strength again. The gen X'r thinks to himself, 'I wonder what it would look like if I took an old operating system from the 80's and put it in my new Mac book pro?' Some things would work on a primitive level and others not at all. That's a good analogy for when the schizophrenic's brain crumbles.

7) Evolution, as just stated, made a new course correction on par with the dino fiasco. Natural selection morphed to sexual selection, but now ultimately to what I label the selection by indecision. Survival of the fittest yielded to survival of the most reproductive as civilization with its new rules embodied a more humane courtship process. Embracing the memes, evolution took note of society's customs and mores that have a lot to do with choosing a mate. The horrors of nature's adversity that enslaved us for millions of years went bye bye so that survival was practically guaranteed. No longer would mutations that were clearly disadvantageous be discarded by mother nature as a drag on survival since those very forces that led to our destruction had been diluted by civilization's protective womb. And mutations that were clearly advantageous in our intense jungle boxing match now, even if advantageous, were less of an obvious blessing. So the diffusion of the cave man's intense milieu once civilization shrouded our

perimeter has made the adjudication of mutational assessments fuzzier, less dramatic and capable of ongoing survival without clear proof of being helpful.

And remember all of this took place in the last 50,000 years or so. If we represent the approximately six million years that hominins have been around by laying three yard sticks end to end to represent those years, the last 50,000 would be about nine tenths of one inch! And these changes didn't take place as soon as language appeared on the scene, it took thousands of years for all of this to gestate, and more to proceed from speech to internal thought. The crucible worked its slow magic, interacting with our changing brains to promote conceptualization and cognitive enrichment. The primitive brain organization that ruled man's mind did so for one hundred and seven of those one hundred and eight yardstick inches. The momentum of that time is certainly with the primitive organization 1.0, not the new and improved 2.0 Cadillac, but entropy favors simplicity and the disorganization of the old ways.

Length of time living one way isn't the only reason to pay attention to who we were. Evolution takes place in a context. We should pay heed to the conditions in which protoplasm and ultimately humans evolved because those are the conditions that humans adapted to via natural selection. Man evolved in warm climates. He ate whatever foods he could find nearby and also hunted. He was nothing if not a physical being. We evolved within Mother Nature's parameters, and those mutations that helped us survive within them got natural selection's seal of approval. If in the last 50,000 years different demands have been placed on us, then we are definitely not accustomed to them. We're still getting used to this radical acclimatization. While I'm not suggesting we live like cavemen, or follow a paleo diet necessarily, we need to pay homage to our lengthy primitive past. Our bodies, for instance have a need to move and were designed to do so. You don't take a tank, for example, that is envisioned for war, and use it to run errands downtown and go through the take-out window. A sedentary lifestyle is anathema to what humans were evolved to be.

We need to sweat more. Humans moved around in warm climates generally, which led us to lose our fur, and although there was some migration northward, activity in warm air makes one sweat. (Incidentally, the farther one goes from the equator the greater the suicide rate. We evolved near the equator. There may be a connection there. More on this when we discuss seasonal changes in mood.) Sweating may have been a much greater excretion paradigm than we're now used to. Go to a sauna or a steam room; there are studies that show that it reduces sudden death and cardiac mortality. Some toxins are stored in the fatty tissue of the skin, only to be eliminated as we sweat. Along with sweating we need to replace fluids with good old H2O. Drink from the stream. Dietarily, ancient humans no doubt ate occasional meats, but usually foraged around for edible plants and fruits. Not on a time schedule like modern office dude, cave guy ate anytime he found something edible.

Sitting eight hours a day may take more of a toll than we realize. We were not designed for that. On the other hand, evolution helps us adapt to these modern new demands. Those whose bodies are more tolerant of sitting have no doubt already been favored by natural selection.

If you built something to meet certain environmental demands, it flourished in those situations, but if, in the last inch of our three yardsticks we compromise those demands, our bodies or our minds will not be as prepared for them. Those uniquely recent demands become, in a way, the spanking new predators, and those novelties will gradually change evolution's priorities. Evolution crawls forward by the establishment of gradients, and those who conform most closely to the gradient's requirements survive, the others don't. It makes sense to pay heed to our past, even though the demands we place on our bodies (and minds) are now vastly different. We are still in the midst of that course correction that's happening all around us, but we don't see it; a silent revolution. We do notice it when things screw up with the process. Illnesses can be considered evolutionary misfires if they do not meet the criteria of Darwin's rules regarding genetic principles that usually would lead to extinction.

Which brings us to the point that this book will focus on. I've enunciated the vast changes that language brought to our minds. We have new demands in complexity, functioning, and expectation. The modern world is more of a Freudian one than a Darwinian one, I might say. By this I mean that language helped erect Freud's complex metapsychology. Modern man functions within that metapsychology, the ego, id, superego, the preconscious, conscious and unconscious forces that rule us, although sexual repression has no doubt lessened since Freud. As the mental changes listed above have all taken place in the past 50,000 years or so, the barge of evolution is making its creaky course correction, but it is still in the process of doing so and not all of us are yet on board. Perhaps one day 100% of us will fall into the mode of modern thinking and none of us will be repossessed by our primitive past. But for now we are not quite there, and our primitive past, favored by entropy, will haunt some of us more than others. Don't underestimate entropy's yearning for the simplicity, low energy, and obedience of our inorganic roots as a tornadic force in the return to our old operating system 1.0, a force that, like gravity, never rests.

The primitive organization I've been referring to, in some ways analogous to Freud's id or what some might call a paleo-cortex, is in all of us. For the vast majority of us, the ego drags us forward, leaving behind much of the primitive organization's influence and robbing its power. Most of us move from childlike thinking to adult thinking, from idiosyncratic speech to universally understood communication, from the physical, experiential to the conceptual, all of these due to the mystical blessings of language. The cage bars between the Gen'Xr and the grunt Neanderthal is the ego which becomes a syntactical word processor and ultimately a sensory organ designed to deliver to us a conceptual symphony through the time worn auditory pathway for our consciousness' delight. And contemplation (secondary process thinking) strengthens the ego as well as the forebrain as it suppresses dopamine, allowing us to construct new hypotheses from the ashes of data points. All of this is in the context of speech.

The ego strengthens and sets up a barrier to the forces of the primitive organization. With the dopamine suppression we can gate out those annoying intrusive unwanted stimuli. Freud said, 'where ego is, id isn't.' If the ego weakens, (as in hallucinogen ingestion, as in schizophrenic breakdown) this can open the door to a resurgence of the primitive organization along with a torrential dopamine flood. Let's begin to explore what all of this means.

So far we've touched on what happened to us over the past 50,000 years or so since language, not just in neutralizing the gruesome forces of adversity that surrounded us, but in our minds. What grew out of language was an entirely eccentric beast, one perhaps unintended by greedy evolution. Had evolution gone down another crooked highway? Like T. Rex, will language and its ramifications turn out to be another ponderous misfire? Was any of this meant to be? As we stand in the giant footprint from the Charles Adams cartoon, looking for signs of our brutal jagged past, we can only conclude that we are not who we were. It's best to define as accurately as possible what those changes were and to make note of evolution's screw ups, the few who are still either left behind or called back to a pre-historic state of mind that existed long ago for millions of years in a land we no longer inhabit. We're not in Kansas anymore, Toto. Evolution's baby may be cranky, disturbed, but overall far better off than it was before. Change creates glorious advances, and at times, collateral damage. As I touched on above, suicide, entropy's greatest victory as it drags us back to the inorganic, and evolution's most dramatic failure, may be one of those problems. Illnesses like schizophrenia, Parkinson's disease, juvenile diabetes, attention deficit disorder, Alzheimer's disease, Tourette's, stuttering, and others may be some of evolution's side effects, along with major depression and bipolar illness that are also off shoots of our Neanderthal past, the common thread entropy and dopamine de-suppression. We no longer live in the treacherous jungle beat of our forebears and these newly minted brain songs, and bodily readjustments fit some and shred off others like the serpent's oily skin. Perhaps in the future they will settle in comfortably as we distance ourselves from entropy's righteous call. We've placed our six million year old Neanderthal in Studio 54 and he may be disconnected from the synchronized beat and the flashing lights.

And then there are the problems that accrued from man's flash of new talents. Pollution, dietary disenfranchisement, sedentary lifestyle, the absence of green nature in our city landscapes, the sense of alienation that takes place among some… in those incidental ways we've outsmarted ourselves. We have landed men on the moon while millions here on earth were starving. Which is not to say that these problems were all created by progress, but that the process remains in flux and that we are still in the midst of it. But the jet fuel of evolution's ardor, predation, has drained and we are now in a position of decoupling from that time worn set of Darwinian dictums. Our behaviors, most of which were para-reproductive incidents like job seeking, owning a home with a room containing a crib, and eyeing a mate, have been shown to be waffling. One might argue that this is the result of newly minted conscious choice, but I assert that it is the remnant of evolution's pallor. The old broad is weak and teetering into malaise, enticing of resuscitation. Madame Ev's dictum to procreate is now on life support and we can see that reflected in the koi pond of society. Choices indicative of her infirmity are everywhere including not seeking a profession, or a home, or a spouse or a child, the keenest knee groin to Madame Ev's stately majesty.

And evolution is not only the standard bearer of baby making, but the proud flag waver of opposition to something I will focus on in the next chapter, the second law of thermodynamics or entropy.

CHAPTER II
THE DEFIANCE OF ENTROPY

"*The entropy concept.. in spite of its age…has kept an untarnished luster of novelty, an aura of unplumbed depth. It may well be that it holds further surprises in store for us.*" Peter Landsberg, in *Warmth Disperses and Time Passes*, by von Baeyer, p. 156.

In 1905 Ludwig Boltzmann traveled to Berkeley, California. His famous statement that entropy is disorder which tends to increase made him a popular lecturer, bombarded with questions from eager students who admired his genius. He compared entropy to his teenage daughter Madelynn's room in which disorder rapidly spun out of control. He enumerated multiple incidences of entropy's swell in the world around us and described the increase of entropy when driving a car.

He gave mechanical interpretations to the concepts of heat, energy and entropy. and was much admired for his work. A year later, while on a vacation with his family in Trieste, he patiently waited for them to leave the hotel room and go to the beach, so he could be alone. Quietly tying a rope to the crossbar of a window he pulled a small chair up to it. Placing a noose around his neck he deftly kicked the chair away and hung himself. Why we don't know. He was famous, successful appreciated. But ironically enough he was giving his old concept entropy one of its fondest desires, the voluntary return of a living organism to the inorganic world, although it's unlikely this concept had anything to do with his singular demise.

INTERNALIZATION OF THE DEATH INSTINCT

Evolution's fate is to be just one momentary step ahead of entropy, using its propensity for disorder to assist in the form of mutations, without which evolution could not progress. It has managed to maintain the edge in its hodgepodge Rube Goldberg machine of a bauplan, a helterskelter accretion of bodily organs gradually superseding one another. But entropy is inside of us all, like a can of white paint with a pump of blood red poured down the middle. We carry the death instinct with us and evolution, in its wily lust for organicity, has made use of it too. After all, animals, unlike plants, must turn into killing machines to hunt down and devour their dinner. They must have the ferocity to fend off predators, guard their territory, their families and the sole right to their mates. Mother nature cashed in on this death instinct or entropy in an attempt to preserve the conquest of one animal over another, something plants have no need for.

Cavemen did not dally in self-destruction as there was more than enough adversity in the jungle motif around them. But entropy and time are related concepts, with the entropic zest always declaring victory if one waits long enough. We are endowed with full antropy at birth which seems to gird until total bodily maturity then arch into a slow downturn that follows us to demise. Us moderns have neutralized much of the predation that plagued the Neanderthals and other pre-historic brutes. But the price we pay for this conquest seems to be a propensity for slow, simmering self-destructive habits like eating ultimately deadly food, or massive quantities that rebound into diabetes or in creating chemicals that kill pests but ultimately ourselves as well.

We've exchanged external killers for self-appointed slow cooking murderers like recreational drug use, deadly food ingestion, chemicals that kill, inactivity that defies our birth right of constant physical motion. And of course there is the regular rapidly acting form of self-demise that is engendered when the landlord entropy succeeds in the repossession of our minds. So the death instinct or entropy has taken up a different place within us as we conquered the petrifying attackers that routed our sapiens forebears. We have succeeded in replacing the growling tiger with a simmering fast food sandwich.

THE PURPOSE OF LIFE

This question has dominated our higher thought processes since we were even capable of them. Why are we here on earth enduring all this glory and tragedy, as if it was really necessary? The existentialist might tell you that life is a meaningless farce while the religious will proclaim it to be a tribute to God's wondrous inspiration. But viewed through the lens of entropy life can have one purpose only, to defy its cynical dictatorship.

THE PURPOSE OF LIFE IS TO DEFEAT ENTROPY. Fortunately antropy always manages to squeak out the win with the help of evolution over massive eons of time, but entropy manages to reclaim its victory in the short run within the singular individual. While the other planets, even the totality of the universe, consist of balls of dust, earth blooms with an enduring cesspool of teaming life. DNA, the chemical that utilized entropy's most vital characteristic, disorder, in the form of mutations, squeaks out the win. Given the DNA fulcrum which leverages a squeaky advantage using mutations, we are able to set the groundwork for evolution's symphonic fireworks which over billions of years eluded entropy's malignant evil and folded up a steady accretion of bodily advances until it came up with us, and we came up with language. Then SHAZAM, the rocket ship of our mentality thundered upwards with an entropic one up unseen in the history of gamesmanship. The antropy/entropy quiz show was buried deep inside our brains. And we've seen how the collateral damage that results from that eventuality proffers up what we label mental illness and some physical diagnoses as well like Parkinson's disease or Tourette's.

Our brains could not have taken advantage of language without the same entropy defeating ghost ship that endures in all organicity. We harbor the grid of entropy within our marrow, licking its chops to redeliver us to the inorganic dustbin of icy planets. It's just a matter of time before death fists its icy grip. Language could not have bestowed on us its advantage in any other way… the battle royal between entropy and antropy had to reside in its accretion, the death wish sizzling like an angry ant hill, a balance of forces as primeval as any forest. Antropy lines up with dopamine suppression, entropy its opposite.

Antropy embraces evolution, entropy dissolution and death, with evolution's focus the totality of protoplasm while entropy hones its deconstructive fire on the individual entity. Over the course of its development the child gradually replaces magical thinking with the reality principle, and enriches ego strength with the ability to gate out unwanted material storing potential energy and thus complexifying the mind developmentally. Freud's metapsychology bolsters this enrichment with the superego a residue of civilization's need to reward neighborly gestures, the unconscious imbedded in our mental crypt to lock away that which mankind cannot abide including his famous Oedipus complex. But we are not incapable of returning to the past legacy of disorganization, and as the primitive parts of the mind also mature and the pressure of gating out unwanted material increases with the energy of balloon submergence at a tipping point, the schizophrenic is sucked back by entropy's tornadicvacuum to our 6 million year old mental habitat with an explosive discharge of that potential energy.

Thus entropy gains not a victory of return to inorganicity but a victory of its old soulmates disorganization and energic release. All living things store potential energy. Sequoia trees do this by hoisting tons of wood into the air against gravity. This represents a major defeat for entropy and rewards some trees with thousands of years of life. Animal matter stores its potential energy in its biochemical processes, the ability to garnish energy in form of food and utilize it at a later time point, and the six pack of muscularity which accrues with effort. The mind stores its potential energy in its gating capacity, a power grid ensconced in the hydraulic repression of the undesirable. This too is hitched to dopamine suppressive antropy. So, entwined in the post linguistic mind is the ability to store potential energy, the direction of antropic mastery in the suppression of dopamine, the ego enrichment therein and the bundling of mental complexity inherent in its 2.0 reformulation and its adoption of the reality principle so well expected by Freud. This radical reformulation also embraces the Freudian metapsychology which Darwin's evolution devours like a starving lamb as it is so joyously survivable.

But within that upgrade lies the death instinct, the entropic strings that yank some minds back to the pre-historic mindset, or at least away from the gold standard of clock like machinery known as conscious thinking. So if the purpose of life is the stone cold defeat of entropy, we are like the proverbial steaming tea cup, set upon a beggar's table, cooling over time. Supercharged with the intensity of birth, we burst out of the womb like the sizzlingly hot mug, steaming with life and antropy, but it's at that point that the cooling begins. Even though we continue to mature outside of the womb's heavenly cavity, it's not long before we angle down towards entropy's grip.

The blaringsirens of deconstruction splatter themselves across our faces like the dust on the carvings of an ancient temple. Skin sags, connective tissue loosens, the spanking brisk sheen of newborn tightness begins to loaf. We are the teacup and as we cool the organs lose their joyous newness, the engine no longer rumbling in low pitched hum, diseases clearly accruing with age. Much of this accretion comes with the loss of organ differentiation and complexity. While maintaining their basic assignment, organs like liver, spleen and pancreas tend to fade in functional power over time, the temporal illness of deterioration seeping into the patency of our veins and the muscular resilience of arteries. Bones yaw in arthritic deterioration while billions of nerve cells peak and die thanks to entropy's glee. The hail storm victory over entropy begins to wane and surrender as the shadow of time deepens. Evolution's delight is to see us survive and to procreate at which point it wants nothing from us nor is it concerned with our fate. We leapt from the plane, chute popping open and glided to earth in time to procreate, so go where you will. Live, die, shine, fade, evolution has done its job as long as the gene pool struts on. Excavating the Hidden Artifact of a Mental Illness: Obsessive Compulsive Disorder Is it possible to view the fossilized structure and cryptic impact of something as convoluted as a mental disorder? Can we unearth the artifactual structure as plainly as the statues on Freud's desk? Let's look at obsessive compulsive disorder and see if we can dust off some of its more ancient underpinnings.

Our assumption is that obsessive compulsive disorder (OCD) is the bastard offspring of Tourette's syndrome. In the latter a surging dopaminergic blanket is punctured by bursts of acetylcholinergic effort in the form of involuntary tics or jerking movements. The muscular activity itself served to buffer dopamine's heft. Once language appeared on the scene some 50,000 years ago, these involuntary movements became semi-voluntary with the fortunate salve of obsessive ideas, albeit delusional, that coaxed the dopaminergic suppressive action forward. The sufferer not only had a repetitive dance but a faulty rationale such as, "I must keep checking the door locks ten times or I'll be robbed blind and living on the streets."

Thus it was the addition of language which saturated the cudgel of Tourette's into something quite different. This took place in the dawn of civilization, a bastard child of language's scintillating impact on the mind of a Homo sapiens which became more focused, less diffuse and intently more capable of socializing. A la developmental psychology's dictums, our minds differentiated, with individuation of parts, differentiation, integration and hierarchical structuring as explicated by Heinz Werner. Civilization gestated in its combat with the disorganized catcall of jungle living into an antropic carnival of structure, organization, cleanliness and repetitive order, all traits of the good OCD devotee. One could call it a foundation of civilization, a tentpole in the struggle to abandon the Neanderthal's swamp fest, an embrace of order decidedly antropic in nature.

We still rely on obsessive compulsives to forward the march of rebellion against the not so subtle embassy of entropy's gruesome desires. A wrinkle in this OCD portrait is that while compulsive activity, like any muscular effort, is dopamine suppressive, obsessions, which are delusional and thus closer to the more primitive mind frame 1.0 of a Neanderthal's core, is thus dopamine de-suppressive, therefore rustling in the opposite direction from compulsiveness. In its wheel greasing investment, a tornadic nexus is installed in which a de-suppressive force swirls intensely around a suppressive rage, thus solidifying its gelatinous stickiness.

This is one factor that makes OCD so frustratingly difficult to treat and maddeningly stubborn. The fix relies in using indirect dopamine suppressors like Prozac in mega-doses to dilute the dopaminergic blanket, obviating the urge to hogtie the beast of dopamine's influence. But we rely on these sufferers to guide civilization through the entropic jungle to a habitat of organization and order, and cleanliness which is next to godliness in its ancient beginnings.

"THE FUTURE BELONGS TO THOSE WHO CAN MANIPULATE ENTROPY; THOSE WHO UNDERSTAND BUT ENERGY WILL ONLY BE ACCOUNTANTS…"
Frederic Keffer (in von Baeyer, p 99).

The purpose of life is to counter the ectopic miasma that crystallizes everything in the greater galaxy to ice, burnishes the sprawling planets to dust and rock, or sizzling gas fire.

Life opposes entropy's desires but so does civilization. It was clear from the moment the concept of a society coalesced, that the terminal forces of disorder and chaos demanded a muscular statute of rigid grids, blueprints of symmetry, and construction of exactness within which to counter the haphazard squalor of nature. And obsessive compulsive disorder makes these mantras with their repetitive obedience to plan its worship. Orderliness, cleanliness, detail, repetition, germaphobia and routine all insufflated this new habitat. Things had to run smoothly and coordinate and for that we needed arrangers who could ferret out the details. Thus the OCDers were the perfect initiators of our newly minted togetherness. This disorder served a moment in time perfectly and was embedded into our sonic psyches thereafter.

Yet there is always danger of reversing this trend, giving in to entropy's desire for utter chaotic swarm. To engage in civilization, something entirely endorsed by mother evolution, we needed to manufacture what I call a social strategy, a face with which to confront the world of the other. And to accomplish this the mind underwent a wholesale complexification under the design of the adoption of 2.0 adult thinking, Freudian metapsychology, language's demand for a preconscious storage unit in which to dangle options before the ego's word processing whim.

The ability to gate out undesirable impulses and thought patterns, and the 1.0 primitive organization of thought, all required the suppression of dopamine. Tagging along with that was an intensification of ego and sense of identity and finiteness. Language also, with its captain conscious thought, fertilized the mind with chemicals like brain derived neurotrophic factor and vascular endothelial growth factor, and lateralized the left side of our brains, which swelled like a wet pumpkin. All of this change zipped by in the last 50,000 years and of course not all of us are yet on board. And when a schizophrenic reaches the point of immutable break down they revert to the thinking swim hole of 1.0 rules and lose the ego advantages and complexity gained by dopamine suppression as its opposite dances gaily in the corridors of our mental dustbin, pleasuring entropy's horny desires in a carnival of chaos.

"THUS NOT ONLY IS IT (entropy) A BASIS FOR UNDERSTANDING WHY ENGINES RUN AND CHEMICAL REACTIONS OCCUR, BUT IT IS ALSO A FOUNDATION FOR UNDERSTANDING THOSE MOST EXQUISITE CONSEQUENCES OF CHEMICAL REACTIONS,THE ACTS OF LITERARY, ARTISTIC, AND MUSICAL CREATIVITY THAT ENHANCE OUR CULTURE."

(Four Laws That Drive the Universe, by Peter Atkins, p. 49)

After all, defying entropy is an act of life itself, a protoplasmic orgasm that speculates on life's chances. The moon sizzles with entropy, as does mars and the rest of the planets. One cannot deny that entropy reigns the universe, turning any hint of life into its frigid and sullen opposite. And entropy acts out amid the vibrato of life, with the need for animals to kill and eat one another, the death instinct which can turn man against man and man against self.

When civilization became a vibrant opal, killing was institutionalized into the staid art of raising and processing animals in a mass production scenario far removed from a city dweller's daily grind. One no longer had to search wildly for a killable animal, expending yards of energy, before capturing and murdering it, gutting it and dragging it home for primitive roasting. The entropic instinct of murder was set aside into the chicken farms and cattle trails of mechanized mass production. But, like energy's first law, ENTROPY IS NEITHER CREATED OR DESTROYED (in the short run only, in general it tends to expand) and if it is not openly exercised in the cool haze of daily living it seeks a different home.

And this home was found in the slaughter of humans against one another, the adoption of slow cooking murders… deadly food, corrupting chemicals, cigarettes, seeping sloth and dietary incongruities that didn't match the purpose of our bodies, and machines that ultimately may have inadvertently destroyed our earthly wonderland by incinerating the oil remains of the dinosaurs who endured a mass extinction event of their own 65,000,000 years ago. All of these 'mistakes' gave vent to entropy's desires, returning more of us to inorganicity in a subtle, invisible drag. In the balance between evolution's desire and entropy's, evolution barely squeaks out the win and it's possible that on no other planet in the universe does it do so. In nabbing our mentality back to the regressed thought patterns of pre-linguistic cave person, entropy manages to give direct expression to its needs when it urges the schizophrenic to take their own life.

"Take all those pills, go on." "Walk in front of that train, you can do it." The schizophrenic may endure those echoing garbage phrases routinely, day after day, as well as the repetitive ego denigrations that feed entropy's desires, direct expression of its lust. "You're a homeless hoodlum" Bethany Yeiser's *(Mind Estranged)* voices told her; "You've killed thousands of people with your mind" Elyn Sak's *(The Center Cannot Hold)* voices proclaimed each time she went off her medications. The ego becomes the prime target of the primitive organization once it is reinstated as supreme poobah of the mentality, since the ego is the Napoleon who dragged us out of Dodge kicking and screaming in the first place, it represents a threat to the primitive organization's hegemony.

So our civilization, while managing to buffer us from the direct encounter with the animal killing machine, has subjected our souls the diluted influence of entropy's encroachment and while the poison is slower, it is steady and unrelenting. From the moment of conception it begins its archaic denigration of our body with cumulative internal mutations that may amount ultimately to cancers.

The connective tissue yaws and the internal organs squander their veracity. We literally melt into the inorganic ultimatum of entropy's drooling lust. Suicide is vastly increased in the mentally ill, as entropy's fist strong-arms the mind to its breast. The suicide statistics on major depression, bipolar disorder and schizophrenia not to mention other mental infirmities are disheartening, with bipolar being one of the highest. One could view this as a direct inflection of entropy's influence, an influence which has played a director's role in the formulation of said illnesses. The depressed person experiences a self-castration, inability to enjoy much of anything, maddening concentration slippage and bludgeoning motor retardation. Not to mention the fact that they adopt delusional self-condemnation which brings them closer to the primitive thinking of the schizophrenic.

When animals evolved from the plant strewn primordial ooze, they were endowed with the ability to roam the earth. Their organs were vastly more differentiated than plants with muscular, nervous and digestive systems to name a few. But entropy took advantage of these gifts and made us killing machines, capable of tracking, murdering and devouring our prey. Our aggressive and death instincts make entropy a built in facet of the animal modus operandi, bestowing the earth with the bones of our meals, although we are eagerly vegetarian as well, animals are the killing kind.

But civilization vastly diluted that proclivity, with its shiny golden rule setting up a superego to reward human kindness internally. But if entropy can be neither created nor destroyed where has it gone? Even our pets are largely nonviolent. In addition to the slow suicidal poisons we ingest, the foods, pesticides, and gases that also destroy the earth, there have been mass murders through the ages as deranged dictators testified to the 'necessity' to eliminate hordes of 'others'.

Crusades, genocides, coups and assassinations have dotted our historic landscape like spray paint on a blank canvas when entropy's lust broke through civilization's mellifluous mandates with the aid of the aggressive and death instincts. But in the main civilization has persisted given evolution's hearty endorsement of the ritualized societal placidity which eliminates the need to expend energy to obtain it. One could label the first fifteen years of our lives the antropic years. The symphonic influence of education, child rearing, impulse control and societal camraderie deposits our mentality in an entropic vacuum. But entropy neither likes or endorses that. What girds against it is the ability to recognize the other as a source of gratification, if not social, then sexual, and to finalize a stratagem that fixes one's relationship to others in a concrete locality. On a biochemical level this represents some fixity in the suppression of dopamine which may lock it in armor against its opposite.

But if this embrace of one's fellow citizen fails to happen, then the vulnerability to mental illness augments.

"*Qualitatively entropy is disorder which has a natural tendency to increase.*" Ludwig Boltzmann (p. 110, *Warmth Disperses and Time Passes*, by von Baeyer.)

While entropy sits in its feathered perch, masticating the universe, a tiny pocket of antropic fury blazes blue a while longer in the dying sun. Earth was chosen to deliver this counterintuitive message most likely due to the rarity of exactly the right combination of natural properties, including gravitational, the moon's influence, electromagnetic, temperature and other yet ill-defined plumes that simmered the perfect stew and we may well be the only pocket of lush green life in the universe, the rest rolling dust balls.

Despite the enormity of the universe, the specificity of incantations that are required to conjure the DNA molecule out of thin air, the only molecule that would hand evolution a win in its need for disorder in the form of mutations, might just match the universe's vast probability. Thus, entropy was defied, the sole purpose of life. Entropy and time are interrelated and we simmer back toward the inorganic in entropy's time wornembrace.

Man-made machines are also quite complex and therefore antropic but don't automatically deteriorate over time, rather with use. No matter how complicated, machines are still inorganic objects constructed by humans. We reproduce, an essential quality of evolution's natural selection and a faculty of organicity, but machines do not. We create machines, they don't make us and as such we can pull the plug on them, even the artificial intelligence that looms perilously in the foreground. They do not think, and thus do not follow the dopaminergic suppressive mandate. They are not capable of mental illness which requires inordinate complexity nor do they have superegos or morality.

Yet artificial intelligence might just be the one boon to mankind that can find the means of countering entropy's desires. It might be that artificial intelligence, created by humans, could solve the problem of mortality and perhaps the global warming crisis as well. The success of the sapiens brain gives testimony to its potential, and if we have truly created a second layer of intelligence, no matter how artificial, it might just be the nutrients of our possibilities. But to do so we first have to hogtie entropy's seductive destructiveness in the form of mass murders and suicides so AI is not folded into the machinery of inorganicity. The human brain is probably the most antropic substance in the universe and as such is capable of astounding feats of defiance of the entropic hegemony.

"*The immediate cause of Maxwell's dilemma was his vivid imagination.*" (p. 85, von Baeyer) Maxwell's Demon, a thought experiment, was utilized to illustrate the influence of entropy in the movement of atoms between two chambers.

One could say that this device was the catalyst that motivated scientists all over the world to consider entropy and began the concept's journey across an evolutionary mystique of development which ultimately landed in its ultimate iteration. The Demon was conceived of as a wiry, semi-naked homunculus who sat between two boxes of gases of different temperatures allowing certain molecules to pass through to the other box as a sort of gate keeper. This magical gatekeeper, who was described in anatomical detail by its creator, was the stimulus that fertilized entropy's gestation. Concepts, like anatomies, undergo a developmental process akin to childhood in which they gradually become more sophisticated, differentiated, integrated and hierarchically structured so that their essential moments come into crystalline focus. These 'gimmicks' may have momentous propitiating power. Language, then, was the gimmick that birthed human's antropic enlightenment. Analagous to DNA itself, once language blossomed, the sapiens mind exploded. But language could not have realized its transformative mystique without countenancing entropy. Redwoods grump entropy by rising dozens of stories into the sky, with 27 foot diameters. Any time a weight is hoisted against gravity it revs with potential energy since it could, at a later time, fall, releasing the stored heft. This potential energy is in direct opposition to entropy which seeks to level everything to the lowest energy and organization possible.

Thus trees exploit gravity to karate kick entropy and may live for thousands of years. But what could language, a non-physical gimmick do to counter the universes most Thor-like brute? In our journey away from primitive thought we needed a crypt to bury it. It wasn't enough to just transition to the reality principle, the old childish cabin of illogicality had to be walled out of site, vascularly demystified. At the same time we created a so called pre-conscious to allow the ego access to words easily plucked like hanging fruit from a tree. As such we created a dichotomous system, with one end steeped in contemplative discovery, the other a submerged area of cover up. So when we reinforce the system with the gold standard of mental muscularity, conscious thought, we are reinforcing the most antropic functional system in the universe, the post linguistic human mind which stores potential energy by forcefully submerging the unwanted contents into a storage bin. "

The largest giant sequoia is the General Sherman tree in Sequoia National Park. That tree measures 31 meters (101.5 feet) in circumference at its base, is 83 meters (272.4 feet) tall, and has a total estimated weight of 6,167 tons. A few other specimens are more than 105 meters (345 feet) high but have less bulk than the General Sherman tree."

(Encyclopedia Brittanica, electronic edition)

It is thousands of years old. No animal can top this magnificence or expect to remain in the state of organic existence as long. One could rightly argue that plants are more successful than animals, covering the earth with their presence. But the secret of their longevity lies not in their enormity but in their ability to defy entropy. A being that vaults tons of matter into the air against gravity is storing mastodons of potential energy which defies gravity. Potential energy is also stored in its pulp, the fibrous wood that, when dried, can be burned to release massive heat calories of zest, in the form of fire which can be transformed into work with a steam engine or other contraption. But depression, mania and anxiety disorders like obsessive compulsive disorder are entropic victories as well.

The trajectory of our childhood to adolescent storm is a courageous march toward the victory summit of 2.0 thinking led by language. The siege, marked by the suppression of dopamine in the meso-limibic/cortical tracts, joins forces with the adoption of a social strategy, and the unification with the R troop, the reality principle. Once combined in a certain synthesis of gear-like characters in a B grade rom-com, the kid arrives at a 2.0 fixity that, beyond age 25 or so, is often unshakeable. They can now line dance in a hootenanny of antropic victory, for the cunning E, entropy, has been laid low.

Entropy has been dealt a body blow, the source of all organicity's rapture, as the sequoia basks in the Malibu sun. A flagstaff is plunged into the ground, the banner of antropy unfurled and the gold standard of psychic address, conscious thought, declares the win. Yet in the evolutionary moment, the momentum of which is from a 7 million year heritage of unruled thinking, some remain subject to recall. Entropy exacts its revenge upon a few who fall under its insipid spell and the flagstaff of antropy gets raped by a defection. In a regressive landslide, the schizophrenic mind slinks all the way back to our Neanderthal moment when reality took second place to urge. The primitive organization undoes the trajectory of victory and reclaims the capital in a hyena howl of revenge. When we use medications to treat mental infirmity WE ARE MEDICATING AGAINST ENTROPY. But the mind is not so easily blown off and sets up barriers to its unhinging. The depressive slinks back from the icon of secondary process thinking into a morass of primary process swamp, a boil of masochistic revery and a hibernated immobility with the underlying imprint of castration.

The manic steps back too from the tuning fork of 2.0 contemplation to a Maserati swirl of disorganized pensiveness, sprinkledwith a grandiose euphoria and a hypo polarized brain stem, in defiance of self-castration by hyper sexual swirl. Both approach the primitive 1.0 thickness in their propensity for delusions of a nature congruent with their predominating mood, self-deprecatory in the melancholy, inflating in the manic. Yet both escape the morass of pogrom by the primitive organization of our past defining the schizophrenic motif, a not so subtle victory. We see something akin to this defensiveness in the physical realm. For example, atrial fibrillation, a condition known to millions renders the heart less effective but yet not so blunted as to cease bodily perfusion. Petit mal seizures trigger a brain defection without the global neuronal discharge of the gran mal tornado.

So one could view the diagnostic categories of major depression and bipolar mania as the brain's attempt to avoid entropic catastrophe in the form of a return to 1.0 primitivity with its release of gating energy and effusive disorganization. The mind protects itself as any other organ, and while it might have abandoned the gold standard of secondary process thinking, it's loathe to be sucked down the chaotic boulevard of primitive organizational swarm. I've mentioned that *ENTROPY BORROWS FROM FREUD AND BIOLOGY*. Freud's pleasure principle dictates that the mind flows in the direction of least excitation and anxiety. Thus the regressive implosion of a schizophrenic breakdown, with its release of gating energy, and the decomplexification of thinking, serves entropy, biology and the Freudian pleasure mantra.

Once it occurs it is no wonder that it's a fixed lifetime curse that doesn't tip toe off into the crystal haze of remission. Yet during adolescence we elaborate an antropic bubble within which the modern mind inhabits. This is a monumental combo-thrust of linguistic competence, school learning, instinctual discipline, submersion into conscious thinking and the reality principle, no mean feat that can go easily awry. For most, maybe 80% of post adolescent souls, this jumbles into a permanent fixity of dopamine suppression, but for the unfortunate others there is a propensity for desuppressive slippage. Certainly the social crucible of acceptable interaction leading to a feeling that others can be a source of gratification not to be so easily abandoned, provides a glue to a dopamine suppressive lock. But once attained, within this suppressive dopamine bubble Freud makes use of entropy.

So, for example, a neurotic symptom in its nativity raises the excitation and thus the dopamine desuppressive coinage of its modern adult habitat leveling extreme discomfort for its sufferers. Freud rightly attributed these discomforts to a burgeoning bull's kick to break out of the gating balloon which is submerged like a submarine into the unconscious. His job, he discovered was to pull that impulse out of the unconscious haze, present it like a pornographic billboard to the patient's ego so as to give the commandant more troops with which to gate the impulse out.

Thus, *anything that strengthens gating is mentally healthy*. This of course explains why traumatic experiences, particularly Oedipal ones, are so mentally jarring, the memories having an intensity of a Houdini to break free from the iron chains of gating. By presenting the fugitive impulse to the ego adding to its strength, the symptom subsides, dopamine suppression is intensified, and *entropy is gratified* along with the pleasure principle. Thus, those who have undergone some psychoanalytic treatment tend to have a lower sense of excitation and greater entropy than some others who shuffle anxiously along coping with a burden of insistent urges wha wha-ing for gratification, no matter how forbidden. So in this case Freud borrows from entropy in its ultimate field goal, *within the bubble of the modern mentality*. In the cases of sleep, schizophrenic regression, and psychedelic use the mind actively is drawn to placid entropic gratification even though there may be mental safeguards against it. In the case of sleep, we paralyze our musculature before entering the land of nod to prevent any nigro-striatal dopaminergic suppression. The mind teeters into primitive organizational control, leaving the dorsolateral prefrontal cortex bereft of its habitual input. Its knee jerk response is self-generated hallucinatory theater, self-manufactured sit com like in muscular comparison to avoid atrophy under the influence of the primitive regime that grabbed hold of the brain.

We see the same equation playing out in the syndrome known as Charles Bonnet in which mentally healthy seniors, as they lose hearing and sight, may start to manufacture their own theatrical creations in the form of voices or visions which are often more benign than the pejorative staccato of schizophrenic productions that may give stage to entropy's own desires directly. Psychedelic use and addiction behavior as a whole mirrors a pied pipers draw back to entropic nirvana.

It's as if once we free ourselves of entropic cling by entering the 2.0 gold mental standard, we seek to reunite with entropy's desires incessantly. Meditation also heads in this direction in its controlled reconnection with the nirvana of selfness, while eschewing intrusive thoughts. The ultimate threat to the brain is the regression to primitive thinking with its entropic victory. Gating is blasted to smithereens once the schizophrenic breaks down and the crescendo of its energy blasted into fueling the psychosis. To prevent this mental catastrophe, those with less secure dopamine suppressive intensity may adopt a strategy of becoming the psychosis, embodying it so to speak behaviorally. One might conjecture then that major depression, anxiety disorders and bipolar mania are 'behavioral' psychoses and indeed often verge into frank delusionality. In acting as if they have no sex drive, enjoyments, or motivations, essentially self cas-trated, the depressive embodies a psychotic posture as a defense against the tsunami of takeover by the primitive organization. The manic's allergic counter stance to depression, a tornadic swirl of hyperactivity, dissolution of impulse control and compulsive sexuality (in 'proof' that they have not been self castrated) also embodies a psychotic stature, and thus avoids primitive organizational rout by becoming the psychosis physically rather than mentally. Obsessive compulsives also, in their repetitive behavioral insistence and intrusive ideation bordering on hallucinosis could easily don the label of psychosis in their overall presentation.

The compulsive repetition, derived from the involuntary precursor Tourette's, is an attempt to suppress dopamine motorically, looping in the nigro-striatal dopamine tract known to be the wizard of dextrous movement. So in its attempt to fasten a dopaminergic suppressive flutter, it embodies a psychotic stance which is the very opposite of its intention, but is also enabled by a delusional premise that greases its absurdity. This perplexing concateny of events leaves the individual in a state of epistatic insufficiency which then resorts to a direct attack on entropy's majesty in the form of cleanliness, order, repetition and attention (or obsession) to detail. *One might say that any behavior that does not conform to Mama Evolution's mandate of survivalism and procreation might be labeled psychotic in its essence.*

Thus, major depression, mania, OCD and the anxieties en masse represent entropic deviations from our jungle mandate. To my knowledge we do not see animals engaging in such misdirected behavior. At the same time the desuppression of dopamine can become for some a masochistic enjoyment, not consciously chosen but indulged in by those who have not found the company of others to be a source of gratification, rather pain.

The complexities of modern interaction may be an effort for some who are less negotiable with society and then lapse into total misfire once theprimitive organization fastens its iron grip. But the desuppression of dopamine falls into three major tributaries, schizophrenia, depression/anxiety, and bipolar or manic depression. The second two work their way back toward schizophrenia without actually clinching the deal by adopting a'behavioral' psychosis. In this regard delusions are inevitably means of dragging the desuppression one sanctimonious step further toward the primitive organization's kingdom, as if avoiding the swarm was not enough, the sufferer had to move one step closer to entropic apocalypse. Thus one can explain delusions entirely by their ability to further the illness farther down the road of dopa/desuppressive trudge which explains why they have nothing whatsoever to do with their content, merely their ability to "move the dopaminergic needle".

Depressive patients who ram the torpedo of their illness one step farther by adopting a radical mood-congruent delusion of guilt have merely chosen it based on its efficacy in dopamine desuppressiveness, and that alone. This also explains why they are so hard to dislodge, rational thought so irrelevant to their purpose. Manics too don the cape of delusion easily in an attempt to march deeper into the desuppressive fixity which they have inhabited in behavioral excitation. They may, for example, insist that they are inevitable lottery winners who will soon have millions to spend and begin throwing around large sums prior to the lottery's inevitable loss. So the ability to inhabit a psychosis just as one wears a glitchy sequined overcoat finds a wacky solace in pushing the process toward a delusional baseboard. This dangerous game moves them closer to entropy's cultish grip and may ultimately translate the behavioral adoption of psychosis into the mental sphere with takeover of 1.0 engulfment. Let's not forget that the iconic illness obsessive compulsive disorder, (OCD) embraces delusional thinking in the form of obsessions to grease the wheels of compulsion, the latter art-fully designed to spank the hammer of dopaminergic suppression home. Thus we entertain a near perfect balance of compulsive suppressive activity enjoined by an obsessive delusional desuppressive wind.

This balancing act is shifted slightly in compulsion's favor and the individual engages in repetitive action such as checking the lights, or locking and unlocking the door ad infinitum. In its compulsive victory OCD became one of civilization's foundations in the struggle to suppress vs desuppress dopamine and in the adoption of then frankly antropic habits including cleanliness, orderliness, repetition and insistence on detail, a slap in entropy's face, and a boon to the construction of the anti-jungle metropolis of modern inhabitation. We needed guidance in moving from the jungle to the disco, guidance given by the wizard of OCD. Meditation, especially certain types, attempt to isolate the nirvana seeker from the last 50,000 years of human history by encouraging a focus on bodily sensations alone, sans verbal intrusion. This focus brings one closer to the entropic reality of cavemen who were nothing if not experiential/physical beings totally in touch with their somatic senses.

But of course, like tossing off a heavy coat, the abandonment of all language brings one closer to the land of entropic Oz. This feeling of 'nirvana' is nothing more than the experience which we spend the first 15 ramshackle adolescent years of life absconding from as we learn to speak, think, mull and reason. Meditation seeks to reclaim that state and as such is a nether land between waking and sleep. This can be compared to the state of hypnosis, one of Freud's earliest techniques ultimately abandoned, in which the subject waddles into a conscious state of suspended animation with the encouragement of the entrusted other, not sleeping yet less in control of their mental compass. His goal was to resolve the resistances to his inquiries, and it worked well initially until he found that some stalwarts were simply 'unhypnotizeable' and that he could achieve the same constabulary of effect by slow accumulation of the free associations of the patient when lying in a comfortable couch in the office vestibule of his home, which was filled with ancient artifacts and mellifluous colors. In short, since we eviscerated entropy with our hyper acute sponge-like absorption of language we have sought nothing more than to return to it. We are able to approximate this resonance nightly in sleep, a restorative moment, in which we heal the day's wounds, and decelerate our bodily functions like heart rate, respiration and the peripatetic wrenching of the gut, among other things. We restore the mind too, in theatrical rerun of the day's events, corrected to reduce excitation.

This theatrical menagerie, created within the primitive organization's 1.0 disorder, rewrites the prior day's history in a more acceptable stew, disguises it then sends it to the dorsolateral prefrontal cortex for examination. As fully elaborated by Sigmund Freud in his book *THE INTERPRETATION OF DREAMS* the final product is sanitized and dripped dry by the ego for acceptable entrance into the court of conscious awareness with an overall resultant decrease in mental excitation.

The caveman's dreams did not require such costuming as civilization, with its forbidden impulses had yet to avail itself. Sleep then is our homage to entropy, the closest we can get to entropic beast's lair sans suicide and disturbances of sleep are baked in the wool for illnesses like major depression and manic depressive swirl. It's as if the struggling mentality is not allowing one to engage in entropy as it has taken a step closer to it as a tithe and fears immolation a la schizophrenic collapse. Restoration of sleep is a crucial element in the treatment of mental illness and can signal the beginning of a return to health. So then we see the dictum that all mental health involves suppression of dopamine and all mental illness involves its desuppression.

Suppression, like a cabal of costumed merry makers, gathers with it the benefits of ego intensity, reality principle adoption, brain expansion through secretion of chemicals like brain derived neurotrophic factor, and the adoption of the modern mentality 2.0 and a healthy gating out of 1.0 thinking and other societal undesirables. Not a bad payoff for the adolescent marathon to attain language, conscious thought, deductive reasoning, without which great problems arise. Autistics who are at times unable to adopt language, often are functioning at a marginal level requiring near constant care. And now we can indubitably say two things: that *all mental illness can be considered psychosis,* and that *all mental illness involves the desuppression of dopamine.* I'll attempt to justify those positions. We can define healthy behavior, the sine quo non of mental soundness, coinciding with evolution's desires.

Mama E wants us to follow the roadmap of natural selection with its mantra of survival of the fittest. Those actions that promote our wellbeing, ongoing success and reproducibility are baptized and those that don't find themselves down the toothless road to extinction. So in our modern post-linguistic reincarnation, learning an occupation that will provide an income and security which can foster love interest snagging and eventual procreation are evolutionarily gleeful as they work toward the goals of survival and projection of the gene pool.

Animals start as cubs but eventually learn to be killing, (learning to pursue, kill and eat other animals) fornicating machines that serve Mama E's bequest to prolong the species into distant eons. Like entropy, evolution is much obsessed with time, but eons of time which it has used to its species' advantage, just as entropy has cornered the market on the reclamation of the short lived individual. We too are animals and our destiny as we trudge through adolescent grief is to find other humans as a source of gratification but to also become competitive, fornicating machines. While civilization has beneficently graced us with leisure time, since we no longer must expend mega calories to obtain a caloric intake of nutrition, and that down time also can be utilized in honing physical and cognitive skills such as bowling, knitting, and stamp collecting which also meet the flagship of evolutionary blessing. Our arrow toward becoming the animalistic competing and procreating machines we are, serves up la Mama E's desires, and with language dealing the clincher to old man entropy. Mental illness then is any behavior that does not specifically coincide with natural selection, Darwin's heavenly contribution to our understanding, the crucible with its simmering stew.

The dopaminergic tsunami of schizophrenia, detours the individual into regressive thinking that abandons the reality principle of Freud. A menagerie of voices, visual exclamations and delusions deliver the schizophrenic into some thing routinely lower functioning and often non procreative in our modern complexity. So we are now in a position to redefine psychosis as *anything that does not coincide with evolution's desires* thus placing *all mental illness in the category of psychosis,* a term formerly reserved for what could be singled out as 'craziness'. The assumption is that our Neanderthal and other forebears did not suffer the weighty albatross of mental illness which would in essence lead to their demise in the hair raising crucible of jungle evisceration.

When the morbidly depressed individual is lying in bed unable to move, devastated by anhedonia and a paltry self esteem, exorcised from the evolutionary mantra, they are acting just as psychotically as the schizophrenic who runs down the street waving their arms like a chicken. Yet the melancholy individual is different in that they have not been overrun by the primitive organization and its ungated menagerie of symptoms marked by primitive 1.0 thanking. And depressives differ from schizophrenics in another way, both depression and bipolar illness are cyclical, meaning they come and go in waves of intensity dispersed with hopefully months or years of normal existence. Between attacks the uni and bipolar genuflect to evolution's dogma just fine. We can define the psychosis of these diagnostic victims as a behavioral one, rather than a psychosis of thought and mentation. They are desuppressing dopamine but on the way to the haunted villa of primitive organizational thought they hold back and *adopt a behavioral psychosis* in lieu of total 1.0 takeover. So depression and mania serve the purpose of sidestepping primitive organization rout by tossing it a bone as it were and inhaling a stance of psychosis internally rather than mentally with the payoff of remaining intact between episodes even if they act in a non-evolutionary manner when ill.

The dopamine suppression is evident by the fact that we used medications that bludgeon dopamine indirectly at first. The antidepressants, by stimulating the auto receptor, the little thermostat at the end of nerve terminals that detect and regulated neurotransmitter concentration, bellows out a signal of cease and desist once the flood of serotonin or norepinephrine spikes in response to a dose of prozac. And this cease and desist order dampens the dopaminergic swell. When these medications fail, we then add antipsychotics, the most direct dopamine blockers available in an effort to curb dopa-the-mean directly.

So the couriers of major and bipolar depression are half steps toward dopamine desuppression and are treated with indirect dopamine subduers, just like the response to a minor insurrection can be handled by the national guard, as a full-scale coup attempt requires the army to subdue. Since the depressive has not been swarmed by primitive organizational takeover there is no obliteration of the gating system, or shift of mind central away from the dorsolateral prefrontal cortex to what might be called a paleo cortex or primitive organization, which then causes atrophy and the need to elicit hallucinations. Nor is there obliteration of gating releasing energy that pours into psy-chosis for the schizophrenic. The depressive and manic are saved by their bodily inhalation of psychosis. Furthermore, in support of this argument, one could rightly say that the diagnoses of major depression, bipolar, and obsessive compulsive disorder are all based in delusional thinking. The depressive seems to be haunted by a delusion of personal guilt and responsibility for some imagined wrongdoing and or sense of castration.

Manics are caffeinated by a sense of invulnerability if not outright wizard like prowess, even if unconscious to them. They may tell you they are the next Spielberg or the new Norman Mailer. The icy unreality of these conditions is always perpetrated by an underlying delusion that stokes the engine of their maladies. But you're detecting a contradiction, and rightly so. If the psychosis is behavioral now you are saying it is anchored in the mentation of delusion, so which is it? Well the answer is that it is both, but in the nonschizophrenic infirmities the delusional part, steeped in the unreality principle, is often unconscious or only partly so. The depressive may not tell you that they have destroyed the world or that they are guilty of great crimes and have been castrated for them, they just ACT that way.

The manic doesn't (usually) say that they have godlike power over the universe, but they do act along those delusional tenets. A victim of ungodly panic attacks won't say that a dangerous predator is about to pounce, but they act that way in a crescendo of autonomic spritz. Obsessive compulsive disorder may garner the 'prototype of mental infirmity' award. Language brought us to the reality principle with the sparkling new 2.0 adult modern thinking module it installed in the brain of the post linguistic sapiens. But what I have called the unreality principle remains bubbling inside of us, the throwback to Neanderthal 1.0 mindset that captures us at night, during psychedelic use, as children, and when schizophrenics devolve. As the reality principle took hold with dopamine suppression and advanced reasoning, a battle between the reality and the unreality principle fomented. OCD displays this battle in gory detail as the compulsive actions work toward the dopamine suppressive stance while the obsessional delusion that fuels it works to desuppress the mean-Mr.-dopa. At a cataclysmic moment in our history the reality principle and the unreality principle must have been in balance within the populace. As emblematic of this struggle, the physicality of compulsion fused with a delusional compound to enable it and the two were nearly equal in strength, the compulsive blood slightly more viscous than the delusional, the latter drawing its coal from unreality principle.

So in desperate need to further the suppressive stance, the brain enlisted the antropic ice picks of orderliness, cleanliness, structure, and repetition. These qualities went into the formation of civilization itself, allergic to jungle chaos, as we architecturally brought forth cities and towns laid out on grids, buildings honed to precision, criss crossing byways and a reliance on routines, the latter cloth bound to time. Ultimately this dragged us from the jungle to the disco. Thus, OCD is a foundational illness also built on delusional thinking and as such is not cyclical, being too close to the schizophrenic genre, it never just goes away. We medicate it with high dose anti-depressants and, when they fail, antipsychotics to bolster the levy against dopaminergic engorgement. Thus we are in very real sense medicating away entropy. Obsessive compulsive disorder then can be awarded the label of prototype upon which other non-schizophrenic illnesses rest.

They display an endless infusion of two palpable cross purposes: the reality and the unreality principle, the latter which, as in OCD, serves to grease the wheel of the dysfunction entirely, but often unconsciously. At this junction I will make some bold statements about mental illness as a whole. *ALL MENTAL ILLNESS CAN BE CONSIDERED A PSYCHOSIS* both in behavior and unconscious delusionality especially in light of evolution's mandated script with the possible exceptions of attention deficit disorder and afflictions of post traumatic stress.

ALL MENTAL ILLNESS EXCEPT SCHIZOPHRENIA ARE ATTEMPTS TO AVOID IT. In short they throw the primitive organization a bone by inhaling psychosis behaviorally, and not mentally, although the latter happens easily at times since they are closer to that calamity than the average. Obsessive compulsive disorder is probably the closest to schizophrenia with its motor attempt to dismantle an oppressive dopaminergic load. The dopamine suppressive motor compulsion is infused with a desuppressive delusional obsessive flagship that lubricates those dopamine suppressive actions. We often see OCD with schizophrenia as it is so neighborly and because the balance between the desuppressive delusion and the dopamine suppressive hammer is so thin.

ALL MENTAL ILLNESS IS ANTI-EVOLUTIONARY since the behavior of the sufferer is not in line with Mama E's survival of the fittest karma. *ALL MENTAL ILLNESS IS DOPAMINE DESUPPRESSIVE.* We use chemicals that the wise man Homo sapiens devised to counter the return to pre-linguistic archaism, indirectly at first with the uni and bipolar but ultimately adding direct dopamine blockers, the antipsychotics, when indirect antidepressants fail. *ALL MENTAL ILLNESS IS ENTROPIC.* This can hardly be disputed. Obsessive compulsive disorder, as previously mentioned, may have set the stage for every disorder to follow, another clue to its primordial character. As human kind moved from primary 1.0 thinking to modern 2.0 machinations, Homo sapiens struggled to suppress the grand poobah dopamine. So we see the modern pall bearer of suppression melded with the disordered conceptualization of Neanderthal past.

This balance between suppression/desuppression was just barely won in the affirmative, explaining its repetitive nature. Each boring repetitive act barely moves the suppressive needle forward, so the individual searches for a direct sledge hammer to its position and finds it in directly antropic activities like cleanliness. orderliness, repetition, everything our jungle past was not, a brick and mortar balustrade to the this new thing springing up called civilization. The totem pole butterflied into obsessive compulsive order, a howl away from chaos, utilizing obsessive compulsive glue.

So civilization trumped the Freudian doctrine the pleasure principle by moving the brain needle from disorganization to its opposite. The cover of my first book, *Footprints of Schizophrenia: the Evolutionary Roots of mental Illness* (Lesk, 2023) symbolizes this nicely as a string that progresses from a disorganized tangle to a precisely interwoven maze. (see front cover). As the brain sauntered from chaos to disco. the mind hurtled from primitivity to orderliness. in tandem with the need for the suppression of dopamine, and perhaps, as I have said in the past, DOPAMINE SUPPRESSION IS THE GREATEST ACHIEVEMENT OF A HOMO SAPIENS from whence all else flowed, although not without its collateral damage. This damage is not just mental but the physical canards of Parkinsonism, Huntington's disease, Tourettes, stuttering, restless legs and more that all suffer from guilt by association to dopamine. Alzheimer's disease is also implicated in the heist as it involves a seeping away of dopamine's partner in crime, acetylcholine. Autism, on the other hand, may be largely a disease of failure to attain language, especially in those most afflicted.

Body dysmorphic disorder is an OCD related condition in which the sufferer believes falsely that they have a hideous body part that everyone stares at and they avoid going out, repeatedly checking the mirror for the supposed defect. Here we see frank delusionality. If there is any abnormality at all, it is of a minor, inconsequential nature. We see the obsessive compulsion replaced by a repeated checking in the mirror at the elephantine horror, the obsession, delusional and dopamine desuppressive, the belief in any sort of defect at all. The same mantra of swirling a physical suppressive action with a delusional rationale moves the boat forward. This has become the standard modus operandi of mental ills.

The body dysmorphic patient has an unconscious delusion of castration, not unlike the depressive who has convinced themselves that they are being punished for some imagined transgression. The difference, in major depression or manic insanity is that there is no attempt at dopamine suppression, just an effort to embody the psychosis physically instead of mentally, to avoid a late schizophrenic takeover by the primitive organization. The depressive actually makes use of the delusion to move the needle further down the road while avoiding the blitzkrieg of mental implosion.

Their delusinality is generally UNCONSCIOUS. The body dysmorphic patient is aware of some distortion in their thinking but not of their belief in self-castration as if they were walking around with a bloody stump to be ogled in horror. So, with obsessive compulsive disorder the prototype, the dye was cast, ancient and hollow by OCD for the other brain disorders to follow: a delusion must hold the hand of any mental discord, accompanied either by a monotonous attempt at dopamine wrangling or an avoidance of the schizophrenic mega-regression by embracing a psychotic posture. Exclusions to this rule may include attention deficit disorder which then signals an acetylcholine excess, or autism, which highlights a failure to capture language's beneficence. Dopamine's sister neurotransmitter and partner in crime, acetylcholine couches the mirror image of the collateral damage levied upon us by our modified detente with mama-dopa.

Alzheimer's disease reflects in part an acetylcholinergic drought, treated with potions that enhance this complex chemical. Acetylcholinergic perturbations may also color conditions as diverse as restless legs, bruxism, and the wayward side effects of many medications that, as noted, suppress our boy dopa, acetylcholine rising in glee as the strongman gets lassoed. The molecular see saw of dopa and acetylcholine means one goes up as the other sinks, an inverse sisterhood which then incriminates one if the other is dragged in for questioning, a guilt by association. Of course entropy lurks behind all of this, licking its chops for an opportunity to dismantle the golden standard of antropic mentality, conscious thought. It even gains a tickle in the mental retreat from secondary process Sherlockian reasoning to the unstructured, windswept tornado of primary process day dreaming. It is well known that the common mental blows of mania and melancholia make it nearly impossible to just think. Why? The entropic glee thus induced is well noted, as its dripping jaws salivate over the welcome gift. And while the mood distortions are an attempt to scoot around a primitive organizational takeover, the move is a step closer to entropy's venus fly trap, and as such render them infinitely more susceptible to it's fondest desire. Suicide rates among the depressed, hackneyed manic and the jittery anxious are much greater than average, bipolar disorder a standout.

And why not, when the most dreaded burn, depression, inevitably oozes in once the manic superman implodes. And the failure of this initial stratagem is in essence a double insult. The collapse of one compensatory zeitgeist into the jaws of the detested other, expands the sting, and too many bipolar captives decide to end it all, the most suicidal month being May. This no doubt relates to the upswing in daylight hours which jars them from comfortable depressive womb into the mishegos of ramshackle decompensation.

And let us not forsake the well worn paradigm of gating which one might proffer as the underlying engine of mental repose as ALL MENTAL ILLNESS INTERFERES WITH GATING, MENTAL HEALTH STRENGTHENS IT. The ubiquitous sore of poor concentration is an indication of a gating rupture, in need of global tinkering. Depressives arguably suffer the most when they find themselves unable to cement a blissful mentality of sedate reasoning. Instead they are at the mercy of windswept thoughts that teeter in an unruly mob through their brains like tap dancing thugs. Manic patients notice not only the gaping wound in their gating bulwark but rev the jet propelled ideation space-bound by hypo-polarizing the brain stem, correctable with hyper polarizing anti seizure-potents. In tandem with this illumination is the fact that dopamine suppression is the salve to the gating kryptonite, its standard bearer conscious thought. Meditation too is an attempt to strengthen gating by barricading incoming thoughts to the nirvana-seeking practitioner, returning one to the physical/experiential zeitgeist of señor Neanderthal, the wordless clunk. One thus takes a step closer to entropy as in sleep, and indeed many of us find our meditative endeavors morphing into cat naps.

As civilization coalesced, it became screamingly clear that certain naughty impulses and outdated modes of thinking 1.0 were in need of curtaining if one was to idle in modern adult mentality and decorum. Thus the gating muscularity was beefed up to Hulk dimensions and the psyche seasoned into a bicameral dynamism. On one end the modern 2.0 mentality rested with its freedom from king Oedipus and its complexified modus operandi of Sherlockian deduction, the rarified air of mental theater cleared by gating out unwanted intruders. On the other end resides the submergence of a gang of thug-like unde-sirables held captive by an iron clad gating moat swirling within the unreality principle of 1.0 rules. When the moat dries up the thugs burst out rampaging the whole peaceful village. The modern mind bows to this dynamic polarity as opposed to Neanderthal's unicameral dirge. And so we have a high def scan of modernity's psyche, a taut dividing line between the gated and the ungated, yielding a protected spotlit stage of sedate contemplation. This dynamism of modernity is cinched by language's exuberance in dopamine suppression in the meso/limbic and cortical tracts, previously unreachable by the physicality of our jungle guy. And the suppression delivers us to the reality principle reasoning 2.0, thick gating, ego intensification, and the expansion of neuronal tissue with chemicals like brain derived neurotrophic factor, not a bad bargain for the adolescent in his quest to dominate the linguistic world of thinking as opposed to just experiencing. Meditative techniques like vipassana yearn to discard the last 50,000 years of evolution to deliver our butts back into physical experiential actuary. The regression to a schizophrenic entombment not only returns the sufferer to 1.0 type of thinking with its unreal adjudication of delusions, it leaves the former brain command center the dorsolateral prefrontal cortex bereft, leading to hallucinatory phenomena in a context of sensory deprivation, but opens the door to atrophy which is a fairly routine out bank of the schizophrenic commune.

Schizophrenia, then could only conjure its phantasm in light of being THE OPPOSITE OF LANGUAGE'S GIFTS. This suggests that our Neanderthal buddies held no evidence of the schizophrenic embodiment, lacking as it were in its opposite. When the schizophrenic suffers its absorptive regression to a 6 or 7 million year old mind that hominins catered to, they are abandoning the last 50,000 years of evolution, but clearly the momentum is with the caveman's brain. If we take three yardsticks laid end to end in a metaphorfor the six million sun circles of hominin life, language engages barely the last inch of those measurers. We are still in the nascent umbilical cord of that profundity, a decisively unholy mentality for some, while another 80% are fully aboard. This evolutionary moment will probably work itself out in the next five to ten or twenty thousand years, and my prediction is that mental illness as we now know it won't exist then. But it does now and until that time it makes sense to see it for the evolutionary dispossession that it is. When the schizophrenic breakdown there is loss of the dynamism of modern polarity between 2.0 reality embrace and the suppressive, gated unconscious grab bag of discarded litter from our past including 1.0 rules of thinking, and societal taboos, those Freudian no no's that terrorize us. This taut string-like dynamism is utterly lost in the schizophrenic mind, to the delight of a Moriarity named entropy. The schizophrenic lacks enjoyment, the result of an impoverished ego, the source of active demise and has siphoned into the mugwump of mental flaccidity similar undoubtedly to a Neanderthal, but worse since the cave dweller never reaped the gusto or language in the first place. We see in the end stage schizophrenic a sort of devolution into Bleuler's four A: ambivalence, anhedonia, alogia and flattened affect. In fact one might suggest that a deepening of affect results from the intensification of dopamine suppression induced by conscious thought. The residual type of schizophrenic enjoys little and may harbor quiet delusions as the intensity of positive, exaggerated symptomatology has averaged out to a muddled entropic ego-less bargain, lacking the dynamic guitar string of modernity.

So we can attribute to conscious thought, the bastard step child of language, many tasty delights including 2.0 thinking, Freud's reality principle, ego enhancement, brain swelling as in a muscular paradigm, the blunt suppression of dopamine and the beneficence of gating without which modern dynamism evaporates. But we can even outfit another craggy benefit, the stuff of trees, in which a massive weight of wood is launched skyward against gravity. Might I suggest that *conscious thought is a means of storing potential energy*, just as much as the sequoia tree's might that leverages into centuries of longevity. It snags this legerdemain by storing more and more material into the gating balloon which takes energy. You remember the bright rosy gating balloon that we all vow to submerge under the water table of conscious awareness? As we think, more and more contents are stuffed inside, and greater gating musculature accrues along its well defined border. So, in a very real sense, the linguistic inheritance supersedes communication and even deductive reasoning by allowing the brain to be a potential energy storage monster that, as much as a redwood hefts lumber poundage skyward, our brain stores greater and greater bric a brac in the inflating balloon requiring of us insufflated bundles of heft to shove underneath the water. Thus the success of a Homo sapiens relies on the fact that *OUR BRAINS STORE POTENTIAL ENERGY AGAINST ENTROPY* which places them in the realm of antropic survivor. I have asserted that *THE HUMAN BRAIN IS THE MOST ANTROPIC SUBSTANCE IN THE UNIVERSE.* Much like a muscle it bulks when flexed and withers when neglected. This said, we can conclude the inverse that language *is not* merely a symbol formatting exercise in labeling with its indexes, icons and symbols themselves.

Language *is not* just a labeling dictionary, although initially it functions as such. The child learns to identify things by name and points to them, "Bunny!". Since we're in the negatives language *is not* just a communication device, although it certainly has performed admirably in this stunning paradigm, opening the pandora's box of human discourse and information exchange, no doubt invaluable grease in the unfolding of civilization itself including cooperative efforts and the ballet of sapiens endeavors as variegated as science, government, jurisprudence, education and so forth. Language *is not* just means of expanding our brains while suppressing dopamine, although the left side of our brains does swell in response to linguistic complexities, and the central nervous system's bloating salves of brain derived neurotrophic factor and others enhance neuronal tissue bludgeoning atrophy. Furthermore, it *is not* just a device to engage in conscious thought, the reality principle and 2.0 reasoning, lifting us from the chaotic morass of jungle-ness into the light of modernity and splattered success globally. Not just those earth quaking tricks. But *IT IS A POTENTIAL ENERGY*

STORAGE DEVICE DESIGNED TO DEFEAT ENTROPY which gives it its greatest incantation and defeat of the inevitable collapse into inorganicity, which entropy drools for in anticipation. This explains its true star quality achievement which to this day inflates our longevity punching forth the antropic win. When assessing any mental phenomena we need to excavate its various dimensions to scarf onto the life buoy of explanation. In this book I've drawn on a gruesome cadre of Halloween ghouls, as offbeat as physics, neurobiology, Freudian psychology, Darwinian evolution, language theory, and more. Our brains are patched together by a garden of whacky and eccentric wildflowers, so disparate as to make their gut dissection nearly impossible. Yet with conscious thought, the battering ram of reality principled contemplation, that iron block which moved the Homo sapiens up the ladder of stardom, now to own the earth, we can uncover the shifting sands of obscurity and drag home a prize artifact. Sleep offers us a windswept paradigm with which to compare other mental states, and Freud viewed brain disease as a waking somnolence. Accessed as an attempt to approach entrop-ic nirvana as closely as possible, we see muscle paralysis a key feature, flaccid sensory input with dim light, buffered sound and gentle tactile advance the rule.

The caveman used it to restore the body to survival mode from the day's gross insults, cuts and bruises healing, aching bones melding into redress. In this insensate vacuum, the dorsolateral prefrontal lobe is deprived and, fearing atrophy, elicits dream input, and those passion plays are bent to the task of reconstitution. They replay the day's events in less anxious form, slave to Freud's pleasure principle, to contribute their tithe toward ogre entropy and reducing intracranial excitation left over from the day's bloopers. Dreams then stand as a banner paradigm for the hallucinations seen in schizophrenics and others, a product of the displacement of the mind's centrality by the primitive organizational coup to something one might refer to as a paleo-cortex. Leaving the governmental capital so used to receiving a tax of conscious thought input, the primitive organization hollows a bereft state of disinclination and the prior seat of government issues forth an elicitation of input in the form of hallucinations, auditory (most commonly) or visual or tactile or even the funkily created olfactory input. We see this in the Charles Bonnet syndrome in which the mentally healthy elderly, waning in sight and hearing, start to hallucinate in a manner strangely disturbing, enough to warrant antipsychotic potions, despite the fact that the geezers bear no psychotic diagnosis. So on three counts, sleep, Bonnet syndrome, and schizophrenia we see a coalition of processes: sensory or thought input deprivation elicits a summoning of hallucinatory phenomena, just as a muscle denervated by severing starts to twitch. Muscular activity we have surmised from the iconic example of Tourette's syndrome is used to suppress dopamine in the nigro-striatal tract. But the nigro-striatal and the meso-limbic/ meso-cortical tracts are fraternal twins and when dopamine suppression occurs in one, it is also experienced in the others.

Sleep, as a dopamine desuppressive phenomenon, paralyses the muscles in order to prevent the backward slide from being interrupted. In obedience with this paradigm, catatonics, who are often steeped in a semi-paralysis, are no doubt attempting to theater the same plot, avoid all dopamine suppression via immobility so as to usher forth the desuppressive onslaut. Depressives also find themselves waxed into what is referred to a psychomotor retardation which may very well be an attempt to avoid all suppressive inclinations so as to further their shot at primitive organizational leapfrog which is also served by delusional thinking. Yet their melancholic trajectory is ultimately crafted to AVOID a full blown reactivation of the primitive coalescence by veering off into a sideline tributary. Psychedelics which deliver the stoner back to primitive organizational zeitgeist on a silver platter, stimulate a receptor called serotonin 2a. My theory is that stimulation of this receptor encrypts a massive dopaminergic desuppression while carrying the psychonaut back into prehistoric mentality. In support of this wild-eyed conjecture is the fact that all of the newer antipsychotic medications also BLOCK serotonin 2a receptors adding a layer of security against the whims of psychosis, in addition to their dopamine blocking barricade. In fact they block the 2a receptor of serotonin more than they block the erstwhile D2 receptor of mean Mr. dopamine. The acquisition of language is a dopamine suppressive venture as much as the pursuit of coordinated movement from childhood whimsy to adolescent mastery. One can make a convincing debate that the brain is as much a muscle as the biceps or the trapezius, enlarging when flexed, decaying to atrophy when ignored. It's quite feasible that the onset of schizophrenia in the late teens, early twenties has to do with the fact that once language is mastered there is a dilution of dopamine suppression allowing the primitive organization to make its furtive move.

This primitive seat of mental government also requires a period of maturation before its army is fully trained for assault, but once it gets a foothold it is as vicious as any terrorist cabal. Efforts to forestall the coup may include flights into psychotic depression, attacks of rabid mania, obsessive compulsive disorder all of which leave the pre-schizophrenic with a trail of tattered diagnoses before the schizophrenia becomes full blown. When this happens there is collapse of the iron-clad gating system, leading to a release of potential energy that pours into the psychosis like molten lava, explaining why schizophrenia is a lifetime diagnosis whereas major depression and bipolar disease are cyclical, coming and going with periods of normalcy in-between. Entropy hasn't had the chance to reassert itself in the thug like form of gating evisceration which takes place in the schizophrenic debacle. The affective disorders have evaded recapture by Neanderthal's mind frame, (which was their purpose) and entropy has been denied its heavenly reacquisition thereby allowing a return to normalcy once the mood raider leaves, possibly on its own in six months or so, or with the assistance of our devilishly sly re-orchestrating chemotherapies. And these medications are designed to reestablish the evolutionary gains of the past 50,000 years or so, and thus are ENTROPIC SABOTEURS. So we find ourselves in an evolutionary moment that gives credence to our six or seven million years history of Neanderthal mentality whose momentum is certainly swarming compared to the piddling 50,000 drops in the bucket since language induced its transformational conjuring trick. And in this moment we are still in the phase of adjustment in which some regress wholesale back to the prehistoric mentality, others, utilizing brainy natural defense mechanisms avoiding the full monty by veering off trajectory into affective or anxiety disorders. But it is not just the evolutionary momentum of 7 million cave person years of pre-linguistic silence, it is the sucking force of entropy's lust that seeks to undo all complexity, and energetic organization, returning it to the lowest level of disorganized anergy that facilitates this evolutionary moment's hardships.

The broken harbors of mental division are not just million year old habits, they are habits seduced by the entropic pedophile of universal chaos. This entropic homogeneity equates within us to approximately Freud's death instinct. Plants have no egregious animus and have not been known to attack and kill each other. Their energy devolves from the sun, their nutrients sucked up by capillary action from the womb of mother earth's soul and soil. They expend no energy seeking nutrients, they simply soak up life from the sun. Animals, on the other hand, have inherited momma Evolution's mandate for survival which includes tracking, killing and eating other animals in a desperate quest for preformed protein. Mr. Cave dweller was just as capable of slaughtering and roasting a pig over the spit as getting eaten by a grouchy gorilla. His marching instructions disavowed morality, the mantra of survival their worship, and evolution heartily endorsed the wholesale splattering of animal guts against the rock cliff of natural selection. This tenet gave blunt voice to entropy's fondest desires, the return of all organic matter to inorgancity, the complex energy dynamisms of life force splurged to dust and sand. So while evolution borrowed its benefit from entropy's need for disorder in the form of DNA mutations, entropy staked its claim in the brutality of animal chomping. While plants have no such pastime and the animal kingdom thrives upon its bones, plant life has a much greater longevity on average than diverse kingdom of animal homicidality. A part of each animal is the need to kill, and this is the death instinct fashioned from entropy's bones. But once civilization hobbled together its creaky tent post there needed to be an intuitive quiescence. Golden rule, religion, morality all served as rich soil for civilization's claim to secu-rity and satisfaction, and evolution, switching gears, gleefully bought in big.

Entropy suffered a defeat as we farmed out our killing instinct to slaughter houses and chicken farms. Instead of tracking, murdering and devouring animals we went to the grocery store and dropped a plastic wrapped package of chicken breasts into our wagon. Civilization has largely solved the problem of ENERGY EXPENDITURE TO GARNER CALORIES, one of its greatest accomplishments, and another reason Momma Evol. scarfed it up. But, just as the first law of thermodynamics states that energy can neither be created nor destroyed, I propose that ENTROPY CAN NEITHER BE CREATED NOR DESTROYED also. So when it suffers a rout in one alley of murderous return of organic to the inorganic, it seeks expression elsewhere. Freud mentioned that civilization was founded on impulse control, and as such harbored numerous 'discontents'. The dance from jungle to disco exploded the gating function of our minds as more and more societal outcasts, and impulse nonstarters had to be shoved into the red ballon of repression and held underwater, a balloon that included primitive organizational rules, and the death instinct. The latter stages an all out media blitz comeback as entropy gains greater control of our minds, gleefully fomenting self destructive voluntary return to the inorganic in the form of suicide once diagnoses of major depression bipolar disorder and schizophrenia are pigeon holed. the death instinct encompasses aggression as well as self aggression, anything that bubbled up toward the return to inorganic stuff. And in schizophrenia it finds a direct voice through the hallucinations that order the individual to off themselves as unworthy. But in its burned out yearning to find expression, it has wriggled around the societal vacuum of individual atrocity to make its reappearance on stage in the form of genocides, mass murders, and world wars that snuffed out millions of lives, totally unnecessarily. So entropy, in effervescent wisdom, finds a path to expression when blocked by sedate societal restraint. Substitute gratifications in the disguise of sports displays, competition at work for the big promotion or to grab the coolest babe, the hottest car or the highest leveraged house is ubiquitous. Yet these do not gratify the sleeping giant of our death instinct, whose overlord, entropy, never rests, won't fly to Miami for a tan or hob nob through the streets of mardi gras. Could it be that other planets, or even most, began as ours and that the entropic Moriarity managed to dust bust them all to gas and rock? Possibly, but most planets are now considered climactically uninhabitable, but perhaps at one time they were.

The bluish haze of mother earth is a welcome sight from space, unequaled in its teaming forests and blue whaled oceans. Could language have been the pandora to our success as well as the engine of our demise? Let's hope we are not now facing another mass extinction event, of which there have been many, not the least of which was the Chicxulub asteroid the size of Manhattan that plowed into the Yucatan peninsula plunging the earth into entropic carnage 65 million years ago. So much for the dinos whose mass was far greater than their brain in weight and size, but who managed to flourish by sheer bulk alone, any predator facing massive hydraulic foot force if they dared to attack T rex. Could it be there were many earths, now vacuumed into the dustbin of planetary uninhabitability by our nemesis entropy and that we remain the last holdout of a freakish entropic demise? Perhaps worth considering as we plunge headlong into a climactic challenge unheard of in our ancient scrolls.

Hopefully it will be one that unifies the human race into a single effort of the wiley sapiens known to surmount challenges in his brainy way, thanks to language. One might ask if entropy is always involved in the etiology of mental sickness. The answer, obliquely blurted is that yes it is, but in some cases more obviously blunt than others. We can look at the phenomenon of paranoia, a particularly ubiquitous worm. Paranoia can exist within the context of a full blown, flag waving schizophrenia and often is, but also make its unwanted appearance on the stage of torments less overtly dominated by the primitive organization of our forebears. It can make a standout all on its own, neglecting the cape of 1.0 regressive thought patterning. The erstwhile DSM 5 has a diagnosis of paranoia unfettered by the carnival of high gear schizophrenic posture.

These are people who navigate the world relatively normally but maintain a delusional aspect in their thinking that meets all definition of delusion, as a fixed, false belief. Folie a deux is a rare condition in which a couple maintains a screamingly illogical contention, unshakable by rational argument. The blood vein of paranoia can be as subtle as believing that one's coworkers are gossiping negatively about them or as intertwined as the conviction that the government has sent robots to spy on the person, bugging his phone while beaming pornographic images onto his mind via implanted microchip. The latter usually implies full blown primitive organizational rout whereas the former may be a dominant theme of the most otherwise rational. How are we to piece together a construct of this ubiquitous scourge? Body dysmorphic disorder is considered a form of obsessive compulsive disorder and dons the cloak of obsessive compulsiveness. The sufferer is convinced of some physical defect or bodily grotesqueness such as hideously bad breath or other offensive odor, thereby inducing an avoidance of others so as not to encounter their painful scorn. This obsessive delusion follows the blueprint of obsessive compulsive disorder in that it greases the wheel of a compulsive act such as checking the mirror constantly to inspect the elephantine horror or counter the state of their odiferousness. So we see a delusional obsession greasing the wheel of a compulsive act, the accepted modus operandi of garden variety OCD. But the paranoid scab held within it is the conviction that others are countenancing this hideous sore; commenting furtively about it. So a disorder as quirky as body dysmorphic can harbor the ubiquitous insignia of the paranoid, a suspicion of condemnation, delusionally hatched. We treat body dysmorphia with high dose serotonin reuptake inhibitors like prozac which, when lamely helpful are added screaming bore antipsychotic potions.

Freud in his inimitable thinking prowess, gave us an unusual answer which seems to leap out as we scan the jagged landscape for clarity. Daniel Paul Schreber was a German judge in the late 1800's and around 1900 was slammed into an asylum with a scorchingly blatant psychosis. In his brainy way Schreber decided to write a detailed memoir of what he was experiencing, in bloody specificity of both internal and external perception. This superlative window, *MEMOIRS OF MY NERVOUS ILLNESS*, into a thousand horse power psychosis offered an erudite painting of his intra-psychic bulwark. Among other things he was convinced that his doctor Flechsig was trying to murder him, that God was out to scuttle his ability to reason and that in defense of his mental hyperacidity he was in need of turning into a woman.

He felt he had a beggar's choice between losing his faculties completely or becoming physically female. In response to these options he asked, who wouldn't chose the latter? Schreber referred to his 'voluptuousness' and felt that God was intimidated by the sheer attractiveness of his newborn feminism. This bizarre memoir caught the eye of a famous neurologist who, despite never having met Schreber, felt capable of doing an analysis of its whacky contents. Ultimately Sigmund Freud ushered forth a framework within which to spotlight the singular mishegos of paranoia, roughly exposing what he viewed as its inimitable roots. Schreber's problem was one of physical attraction toward the parent of the same sex and this gruelingly dystonic homosexual libido required deep plunge into the nowhere land of the unconscious. Yet the power of this flaming impulse burned intense in Schreber's mind which resorted to a regression to 1.0 primitive organizational thinking in essence to achieve the only possible gratification available which was a delusional one. By the time Schreber left the asylum he was much less psychotic but totally convinced that he'd been magically metamorphosed into a woman, so much so that he invited a scientific examination of his body, an offer that apparently no one felt inclined to accept. This 'father complex' was so unacceptable that the individual who suffers from it projects or attributes it to the other person. "It is not that I love him (the father substitute like his doctor Flechsig) but that he loves me." Yet once more this is not an acceptable proposition to the repressed father longing which turns it into its direct opposite hate, then searches delusionally for telltale signs of ire in the father substitute.

So we may hear from our patients that so and so is "F…ing" with me, meaning that they are in some way screwing around with them antagonistically. This blueprint grows tentacles flowering into "He is trying to kill me" or "plotting my demise" or that "God is trying to take away my reason." This complex formulation assumes many disguises and is seen in stimulant abusers who have leveraged a whopping dopaminergic surge into a paranoid psychosis in which the imagined persecutors are buzzing them by satellite, howling at them through the heating vents and beaming pornographic images into their computer. They can suffer frank hallucinations and it is not that unusual to hear from them that a chip has been implanted into their brains which is causing the voices to skitter in their ears like radio static. Thus paranoia can be leveraged by a dopamine surge (either chemically induced by the meth or in response to regression to the primitive organization) into frank hallucinatory complexity with a basis in Freud's humble formula. A 'father complex' is projected onto the love object then turned into its opposite, hate. And one might say that the ubiquitousness of paranoia is due to the frequency of such gallingly indecent impulses toward the parent of the same sex, impulses subject to the same gating balustrade as any other squalid indecency in the sufferer's mind, but that under the right circumstances including a regression to 1.0 thinking it can suffer an exponential mushrooming into full blown icy conviction. But, one might ask, what role does entropy play in this ill conceived cartoon of paranoia? Well we know that delusional thinking drags the victim further down the path of dopamine desuppression.

Delusions are utilized to barter a major depression, for example, further along the road to primitive organizational wackiness without actual takeover by this behemoth. In fact it secrets it away down a nip and tumble tributary that defends against an entropy orgy called schizophrenia. Once the primitive organization has taken over, paranoia can do nothing more to entropize it. The ubiquity of paranoia then is chalked up to the almost inevitable attraction of a child for the parent of both the opposite and the same sex, especially when attraction for the opposite sex parent is incarcerated by the chains of repression and terrorized over by a castration threat thus making it safer to be enveloped in a 'father complex', or 'mother complex" for women a la Freud.

In spite of this the usual scenario remains attraction for the parent of the other sex with urges to kill and replace the same sex parent. These are gradually buffed over by an identification with the same sex parent and a search for a replacement for the opposing gender parent in the external world leading to an echo of gratification by the outside society at large. The homosexual, according to Freud identifies with the opposite sex figure instead of the same sex role model. What then leads to transsexualism is difficult to say, exactly why one individual adopts a homosexual lifestyle, the other insists on bodily transformation. Much more research is needed about this ballooning phenomenon. But we can say that all mental illness has a bipartite escarpment, the conscious behavior and feeling of it and the unconscious, underlying dirge-like anchor of its root structure. The depressive labors under the delusion that they are guilty of some egregious act and will soon be facing a well deserved punishment. As such, or perhaps in a quirky effort to avoid this punishment which equates to a castrative bludgeon, they have unmanned themselves psychically. Now incapable of enjoyment they redress the universe of the living with the bloody stump of their self infliction on their sleeve. Manics dance with the unconscious delusion of a messianic invulnerability, and in avoidance of the depressive un-balling engage in an esprit de corps of sexual debauchery. When it all collapses into the mud swamp of dreaded depression, manics can become quite despondent and indeed have a high suicide rate. Anxiety disorder patients labor under the unconscious inflection that a predator is about to attack, and plunge saturninely into the autonomic fight or flight contusion of the Neanderthal encountering a starving cheetah.

The prototype of these earthly canards is the affliction known as obsessive compulsive disorder, a core foundation disorder. Here a compulsive, repetitive act is spurned on by the delusional obsession. This set the prototypical swarm for the rest of the mental scams that burst forth from it as a miscarriage, and an avoidance of the ultimate primitive organizational swarm, schizophrenia. The obsessional delusion is often conscious, but not always, straddling the craggy border between Tourette's, an involuntary tic blotto, and the major mental illnesses that navigate their existence in the dark. Obsessive compulsive disorder has shifted wholesale to a semi-voluntary dance, fumbling in the atmosphere of dopamine suppressive ardor. But the major mental contusions may creep over to delusion which, as I said drag the scene of dopamine de-suppression a tad farther, but not in the direction of primitive organizational takeover. As the gating system yaws under the weight of major depression, for example, a conscious delusion congruent with its tuberous thrust will make a salivated appearance, like an unwanted guest bearing its face at the door of a surprise party. And this creaky rupture of the gating paraphernalia not infrequently accompanies the major psychic maladies. This will end our discussion of entropy's role in the mental illnesses and its vast influence over the universe of our mentality. But like a puppet master it lurks in the background, an intoxicating aroma pervading every aspect of our being, both mental and physical.

The classic example of the steaming cup of coffee laid on the table and returned to 40 minutes later is the icon of energic dissipation. Entropy woos disorganization over its polar opposite and language's spell on our mental evolve gut wrenched it by weaving us into complex mental atrocities, differentiated, individuated, reintegrated and hierarchically structured a la developmental psychology's guide book, thus making the post-linguistic human mind the most antropic substance in the universe. Face slapped and narcissistically peaked, entropy grabs greedily at whatever shards of our psyche it can, dragging some back to the primitive organizational 1.0 disorganized hovel of our momentous six-million-year-old history which certainly has the momentum over a mere 50,000 years of linguistic mastery.

And those who aren't lassoed all the way back take a momentary bargain of semi dissolution by adopting a depressive or manic or anxiety ridden behavioral psychosis underwritten by an unconscious delusion as prodromes by our icon of maladies we call obsessive compulsive disorder. So, at least two forces march against the adoption of our modern disco mentality, the length of time we've spent unschooled in it and entropy's desire for mind fucking chaos. In the usual brainy sapiens manner we've learned to fight these calamities with manufactured chemical congeners, a brilliant barrier to evolution's sucking return. And we know that our caveman ancestors, the Neanderthals, Denisovans, Naledi and the like live minuscule banks of time, some thirty years or so on average we presume. In that case, our bodies have evolved to live perhaps one half to one third of our current lifespan expectation. So while me may view our jettisoned longevity as a victory, it places us on a jittery plank with which to walk on in our later years. And entropy takes advantage of this bit of fortune by breaking down our proteins faster than we can repair them, leading toward inevitable mechanical and organ failure, dribbling bits of accumulated break down. So, as our minds have outwitted the grand wizard of disorganization on diamond facets of existence, time alone provides walk ways for its inevitable victory over us all. One images then the framework of DNA's anti-entropic Rube Goldberg machine as the body itself clatters and jangles its way into the unexpected agedness our reality testing minds have conjured up.

"How fleeting are the wishes and efforts of man! How short his time! And consequently how poor will his products be, compared with those accumulated by nature during whole geological periods. Can we wonder, then, that nature's productions… should bear the stamp of far higher workmanship?"
(Charles Darwin, On the Origin of Species, Chapter 111)

Time, that griffin of most eager disciplines, has eluded us all, animals and plants alike, in hoarding itself away from the endurance race that all living beings suffer during our brief existences. While we may view our lives as endless, and certainly the past 150 years or so has garnered a swollen expectation of survival unrivaled in history, in reality our paltry earthly residence is but a mosquitos bite in the echo of evolutionary time. The concept of time itself is no doubt so misunderstood that humanity can no more grasp it than it can a greased pig on a sweaty Sunday afternoon. Evolution has used time to its advantage, but not our individual lifespans but the ongoing nature of organic tissue which, over eons of time, is able to morph into ever greater anti-entropic, or antropic particles. Evolution cares little about us as unique beings, only about us as a species with ongoing thrust into the cavity of time's vault. It has been able to defeat entropy, not in the short run, as the latter's power is to rapidly devolve us all, but in the long game in which time itself is the major player, tipping the scales in evolution's favor with the help of DNA. Time then seems only to emerge significant in the ongoing battle between entropy and evolution which has end gamed the latter with Homo sapiens now roaming the earth at 8 billion or so strong.

But it would not surprise you that we, as the bearers of evolution's triumph, spend our lives in earnest worship of entropy's seductive gifts. Animals in particular bear the oceanic pattern of entropy's high and low tides. And in this corn maze of battle evolution has once again slyly utilized entropy's spirit to motivate instinctual demands. So, for example, when the waking animal is hungry entropy suffers until the being gratifies its need to ingest at which point in time entropy increases, the excitation quelling with each bite. One could rightly say that animals in particular, as opposed to flora, spend their lives in pursuit of entropic satisfaction, and three situations exist which gratify this calling most directly... sleep, orgasm, and death. Let's examine each coin side individually.

In sleep we seek to lower excitation and do so by paralyzing our muscles so we can return to the animalistic mentality that existed for 6 or seven million years prior to language. We indulge in this regressive, primitive mental organization which swells entropy's pride and undoes the day's more vexing, anxiety provoking events with the aid of hallucinatory dreams. As we know, since Freud, we camouflage these mental productions to paper over the primitivity that dyes their rancid acts, like a movie where all the costumes have been switched and the habits of speech reversed so as to be painted onto the wrong characters. Even though we are paralyzed and can't act on these caveman habits they are so egregious insults to what we have called the civilized superego that we prefer not to encounter them bluntly. We spend our lives submerging these impulses more or less successfully, the legend of the death instinct, an ash of entropy's bargain with evolution when animals first roamed the land. And, of course, as I have mentioned previously, certain drugs can usher in regressive thinking including psychedelics. In fact one might assert that the basic allure of addiction is its ability to, in various ways, return us to states of greater entropy than sobriety could ever offer.

And in orgasm, too, we achieve a sensation of entropic calm, the post coital gift that evolution has allowed entropy to indulge in since it serves ol' madam E most handsomely. If the greatest yearning of evolution is our ongoing reproductive ardor, than what better way to insure its sustainability than to exploit ol' man entropy's very yearnings. And so we reach a state of post coital entropic nirvana which dons the cloak of deconstructed anergy. Not only is sexuality the most pleasurable sensation known to humans, it rewards itself by wallowing in entropy's playground for a period of time. What a brilliant coup to evolution's sly endeavor that one ups entropy again, as does DNA, in utilizing entropy's fondness for lower states of existential energy to promote its most raging demand, procreation, a demand which we are now seeing humans, unlike any other species, abandon in record numbers as if entropy itself no longer held allure for them, a catastrophe that could only happen if evolution itself no longer held sway!

And most finally, we return to entropy's playground upon demise, and resume that inorganic state so desperately longed for by its smarmy facilitator. Life then is an anti entropic swarm that rages against that destructive pressure until the moment of death at which time we succumb to its endless power which starts working on us all at the moment conception. If the purpose of life is to defy entropy, then the purpose of death is to give up that protest, and sink into entropy's luxuriating womb. And we must never forget that we've stolen from entropy's coffers for only a minute echo of time, but that our battle with it is won if our offspring live on furthering time's embrace so to speak. Again, time plays the pivotal role in this combat, and on planets where entropy has succeeded in vacuuming all organic matter from its surface, time is wholly insignificant. No one sets a clock on Pluto. Death then, may be viewed as a positive, for the mortal combat against disorganization can then be dropped, and we can sink into our graves no longer fighting.

In fact one may rightly view life itself as an aberration, something so absurd as to be unobserved in the universal eco system. The little green men, so highly touted in area 51 or Roswell, in New Mexico, have yet to make an appearance. Despite our best observatory efforts, no aliens have offered us their hand in salvation or attempted to scuttle our behinds with super lasers. And if life IS an aberration, something so rare as to exist only on this bluest of all planets, then death is the rule, not the exception, and we may return to it with some relief that our mortal combat with ol' man entropy may finally call it quits. In fact disorganized inorganic states are the rule not the exception, and we find ourselves sinking back into what nature or physics or something has had in store for us all along. So, when we observe humans forsaking evolution and eschewing the dance of child rearing, they are unwittingly embracing entropy, favoring its thorny chaos over madam Evolution's quirky protoplasmic bent.

Those who ultimately write off procreation will find the open arms of entropy awaiting them, with blessings. So in addition to the lack of predation ruffling the windless sails of evolution we find a second underlying motive or motif, the intoxicating vacuum of entropy's sucking chasm. For to abandon evolution is to embrace entropy, a megalithic force so pervasive in our midst that we might as well just banish the complexity of organic structure altogether. The organic exists to grab as much time as possible against the entropic chaos all around us, and Homo sapiens revel in the 8 billion of us that now exist. One might want to point out however that in terms of biomass plants far exceed animal tissue and most of that plant putty is cellulose.

So we now have two grandiloquent forces bitch slapping the expected roles of Homo sapiens existence, the waning of evolution due to predatory mist, and the sallow embrace of entropy's desires. When we choose to skip the bulwark of reproduction, we are choosing death and chaos over organization, structure, and the expected defiance of the second law of thermodynamics. We exist in a state of existential yearning for the mellifluous flutter of entropic amorphousness, and we are taking a step in that direction by not having a kid, sticking it to evolution in a major way while embracing the siren of entropy's call. The addict ropes in disorganized mentality with his ingested congeners that recreate the primitive mentality of our Neanderthal forebears passing on the linguistic inheritance that delivered reality testing to our door like an Amazon delivery gal. With our defiance of evolution's procreative mantra, the ambivalence in adopting the parental and societal role, the puzzle regarding gender identity, and the embrace of depressive indecision we are, make no mistake about it, faltering in our inherited mandate to club entropy in the cajones, a mandate ONLY observed on mother earth.

The planet must have eccentrically unique characteristics to have nurtured this rebellion against universal chaos, a specifically rare combo of habitat odors and hang outs. This unique menagerie of talents nurtured the one world that stuck to entropy big time. The revolution against evolution is not just a rejecting stance, it embraces the universe in which chaos and simplicity rules over the exquisite organization of candlelit nights and political imbroglios. The phenomenon of life is so rare and extraordinary that we take it for granted.

Don't.

CHAPTER III
ENTROPY'S BIDDING

"On the basis of speculations regarding the origin of life and of biological parallels, I drew the conclusion that, beside the instinct preserving the organic substance and binding it into ever larger units, there must exist another in antithesis to this, which would seek to dissolve these units and reinstate their antecedent inorganic state. That is to say, a death instinct…" Sigmund Freud, *Civilization and Its Discontents*, 1994, Dover Publications, p.48

In our shaky quest for survival, we have learned both to procreate and to accumulate the industrial strength needed to harvest calories by methods known as hunter-gathering. To do so expended energy, and this humongous expenditure often outweighed the intake of a measly bag of rotting strawberries or a fistful of walnuts. Even the garnering of a petrified, cornered animal by a cadre of spear wielding cave man peers, once captured, executed, cooked over fire and eaten barely equalized the caloric expenditure of so doing. (The acquisition of fire proved vital to speeding up digestion due to cooking, shortening the gut which allowed more blood to flow to the brain, thus blessing its enlargement which it did gradually over eons from some 900cc to our present 1350cc, although the Neanderthals had over 1400cc.)

This, of course, is a problem trees and other flora shrugged at with indifference since they harvest nutrients passively by capillary action from the dirt in which they choose to root and the gaily shaped solar panels that they drape sunward called leaves. As an advantage this was massive and trees have no need to orchestrate the symphony of civilization's rewards any more than they have the need to cremate their floral brethren. Yet mamma evolution, no patience for fools, endorsed the advantage of a system of food delivery that reduced the grating expenditure of energy and this was a major flashpoint of the onset of civilization's benefits, which, among others persuaded her to bless the blustering scheme. And, as if this weren't adequate, the neutralization of 90% of our natural born predators clinched the civilization deal (born of language) for our momma, and her blessing fertilized piddling villages that first dotted the landscape, coalescing ultimately into nation states that bore names and defended their honor. And so it was that in evolution's yearning to create a being that could actually roam the earth's patina of dust and effect more than a passive influence upon it, she notarized a covenant with old entropy in which these so called 'animals' would carry out his bidding while allowing them brief moments of survival. And this jungle debut wore its coat admirably until it became clear that a civilization was the way to go, and with it, the necessity to forgo any type of reckless human assassination.

The golden rule shown brightly as the pole star for society's egalitarian breed. But this credo withered incessantly in the Homo sapiens declaration of peace, as the mandate of Moriority entropy was not so easily dismissed. "Men clearly do not find it easy to do without satisfaction of this tendency that is in them: when deprived of satisfaction of it they are ill at ease." (Sigmund Freud, *Civilization and Its Discontents*, 1994, p.42)

And so as if to rise up in salvation of evolution's infatuation, something called a superego began to manifest in the minds of the Homo sapiens. This superego, when finely tuned, was an internal righteousness monitor, slyly implanted into the cranium of the unsuspecting samaritan. It would reward civility with its yummy goodness, and deal lightning bolt wrath to its opposite, or even the thought of it in an effort to avoid the often harrowing consternation of the arbitrary and potentially whimsical societal authority who was also wrapped in self interest. This operating system, installed in all of civilization's cobalt game players, was the solution to the jungle killing and fornicating machine that roamed its chaotic habitat prior to the onset of civilization's credence. It has served civilization well, although there are always those who err slightly in its installation.

And, even more searing, the superego death blow to entropy was an excruciating clobber which needed redress, according to our universal destroyer. His will, Lucifer's emblem, be thy done, and nearly every era found a way to carry out his assignments wholeheartedly in the form of genocides, mass murders, crusades and other swords of chaotic reenactment. Thus, humans end up in a situation of imperfect perfection in which the internal operating system installed with civilization's blessing goes directly against vicious entropy's desire, But the superego offers us another window into the problem of the most common mental malady of depression.

Now we can see that not only does the unconscious guilt rise up when the gating grid undergoes rupture, exerting its woeful influence on the sufferer in the form of a hibernation like attack, but it is met by the superego which, unable to decipher delusion from fact, comes down with its Goliath sledge hammer dealing its awesome power upon the sufferer whom, even more squashed, hyper-ruptures occasionally into frank conscious delusionality. So this emblem of civilization's shining comet can lend itself to god awful unnecessary suffering in the costume of a misguided depressive attack. Lacking a solid reality testing function, its blunderbuss shatters into the glass of mentality on a regular basis when delusion floats up to the surface of pre-consciousness tripping its wire of alarm. But in this act too, even the superego is carrying out ol' entropy's wishes, for in endorsing a delusion, it is siding with the 1.0 mentality that travels with the de-suppression of dopamine, the regressive thought cadre enunciated by the pre-verbal individual cave guy or children.

Words dominate the child but adults dominate words, and in this craggy crossover during adolescence we clutch onto the reality principle, waving adios to the jingle jangle unreality of childhood fantasy and the psychedelic user's hallucinations. So in glomming onto the unreality principle and dopaminergic desuppression, the superego is actually doing entropy's bidding, despite its mandate to bull pen the alacrity of antropic civility. And in its support of the depressive ilk that some 15% of the population will suffer, mostly women, the issue of suicidality also gratifies the morbid interests of entropy. We see elevated rates of self destruction in all the mental infirmities, and as such, entropy finds a way to enlist even civilization's flag ship, the superego, in its gruesome endeavors. But Freud gave us a deeper dive into the superego's nascent sprouting by fingering its genesis in what he called the Oedipus complex. Early civilizational Homo sapiens with some theoretical regularity experienced a revolt of the teenage males against the aging father figure, killing and castrating him so as to dally with the women for themselves. This gruesome anthem needed burial in the unconscious if civilization were to advance and thus it becomes the principle element of gated contents in the childhood mandate of thou shalt nots.

Males who, as kids, have a longing to kill ol' dad and take his place with mom, eventually learn a healthy respect for pop and look to find a substitute for mom's affections in the global community around them, if they are able to countenance their peers as a gratifying cadre of souls, not just a mortifying mafia of rejecting attackers. (Too often the latter is the unfortunate assessment by the pre-schizophrenic and makes bullying a serious insult.) In so conquering this Oedipal mythology, which coincides with the mastery of language and the adoption of the reality principle, the mini-human learns to bury those impulses deep into unconscious crypts, and therefor knows nothing of them.

Yet, in depression, as the gating hydraulic force begins to waffle, the full impact of patricidal (or matricidal in women) urges re-emerge like an enemy submarine complete with nuclear capabilities. And so we can now see that this fantasy is what surfaces bluntly in the depressive, floating warily up to the preconscious to manifest its hideousness, catching the eye of the superego which reins fire and lightning down upon it as if impulse equaled action.

Hence the ubiquity of depression. This effort by the child to plunge Oedipus into deep six is a major source of potential energy brain wise, dealing a blow to entropy. So when the repression creaks, entropy is somewhat gratified even by a depressive simmer. After all, a dismount from the gold standard of dopamine suppression, conscious thought, aids entropy and carries the individual back toward 1.0 conceptualization (and away from brain expansion, ego enhancement, and gating power). Mania, which entertains not just a fantasy of messianic invulnerability but a delusional glee of Oedipal victory, nauseated by the potential of succumbing to Oedipal indictment, curls off into whirlwinds of hypo-polarized, sleep deprived impulsivity some of which is designed to prove the lack of castratedness by dabbling in sexual impropriety and a mud raking fuselage of impulsive rigamarole.

All of this is designed to escape the superego's notice when gating fails and the Oedipal impropriety is countenance by the pre-conscious. A release of potential energy and a withdrawal from secondary process thinking in the hail of zooming mental intrusions, is thus an accompaniment of mania as well and entropy is partially gratified, although not as tickled as it is by the schizophrenic energy blowout. Anxiety disorders signal an alarm as the Oedipal fantasy floats ungainly close to the pre-conscious, in danger of touching superego's trip wire, and pours the contents of autonomic discharge out into the panicked sufferer in a manner whose underpinnings remain entirely clueless but supplements a squashing effect on the uprising in its utility.

This condition is probably the least infected with potential energy bits, so its presence gratifies entropy the least. But this model deepens the explanation of the frequency of anxiety disorder as an accompaniment to depressive mishegos which fully encounters the delusional Oedipal myth in the preconscious. So the anxiety comes not just from fear of imagined condemnation and punishment which is in the hazy form of something castrative but in the signaling of the impending cloudburst of eviscerated potential energy release, coinciding with a fantasy of predatorial vanquish. And so we see that the structural foundation of civilization in the form of Oedipal mastery (a strong-arming of this particular form of the death instinct) and submergence in the crypt of the unconscious dovetails with the onset of linguistic clarity and necessitates a boat load of umph to repress, stored as potential energy against the sympathy of old Mr. Entropy.

This potential energy investment, plunges the mind into complexity and dynamism, all coinciding with the childlike to adolescent mastery of language and the Oedipus complex, again asserting our principle that *words dominate the child, adults dominate words* as the march toward adulthood proceeds to utilize them for their usual omnipotence which hovers in the arena of universal communication. All of this is in the service of civilization's static calm, and reinforced like a thumb tack in the wall of time by the superego's emergence. Many things are happening at once in the child hood march to maturity with an energetic horsepower rev of the gating edifice fusilladed by language and the Oedipal assignment, a need to utilize words in their rightly appointed manner and dominate the cognitive mandate of reality principleness, transitioning from 1.0 primitivity to 2.0 adult rationality and in so doing also encountering the social bluster of life rafting onto one's peers for gratification and succor.

We can assume this process recapitulates the struggles of humankind as we stumbled forward over the past 50,000 years or so. The death instinct, so sedately uploaded by evolution's greed for the ripe fruit of animal motility, (an earth rover that could actually influence its surroundings unlike plants), with its special bluster Oedipus, tripped ahead until running bluntly against the symphonic adipose tissue of civilization's siren. Demanding burial, this death instinct born of entropy, joined forces with language to countenance a bedrock of reality principle in which to deep six its homicidal covenant. The killing-fornicating machine had to temper its delirium and genuflect to the golden rule with the help of something called repression, which stored potential energy against the vein of entropy, a double nut blow to its grandiosity. Not only was killing to be outlawed, but the mind was to blossom in flowery heft as it muscled its way to repressive ardor of all associations related to kill, with the gimmick of disentangling the words from their intended objects and plunging the balloon of repression heftily under the water's surface. Wallah. And so was born something gladly accommodating to the structure of a civilization with its more complex minded citizens, aggregating the potential of 2.0 thinking as opposed to the opposite 1.0. And of course, as we have enumerated, the participation of dopamine suppression leading to enhanced muscularity of gating, ego six-packing, brain expanding menagerie of complex human intracranial exigency mushroomed. Entropy sat in a corner and licked its wounds while the earth inhabited itself with all manner of customs, institutions uplifting civilization and infrastructures.

The latter were politely educated by the obsessive compulsive's patina of order, rigidity, and repetitiveness which lent its passionate charm to civilization's rant against the chaos of jungle inhabitance. So one can rightly say that, just as the purpose of life is to defy entropy, *THE PURPOSE OF CIVILIZATION IS ALSO TO DEFY ENTROPY.* It marches in counterpoint to the chaos of jungle jingle jangle, with its rigid infrastructures, time deadlines, institutions designed to uphold its honor, structures that lift even greater tonnage skyward against gravity in its skyscraper forest, repetition and grid-like organization, drawing much of its talent from the menu of obsessive compulsive disorder. The latter, of course is designed to suppress dopamine, which is a primary function of the embrace of language.

The suppression of dopamine is the core talent for which Homo sapiens can posit their fortune, and perhaps the *GREATEST ACHIEVEMENT OF A HOMO SAPIENS IS THE SUPPRESSION OF DOPAMINE.* As enumerated, the suppression of dopamine, born from the inhalation of language, fosters the gating function, beefs up the ego, expands the brain with fertilizing chemicals and shifts the nexus of mental control to a full set of 2.0 choppers.

No small potatoes. The entire process of civilization's whirlwind expanse focused around the dopaminergic hogtie, and carried with it a mincemeat of stunning achievements, all in opposition to the bricbrac existence of our cave person forebears who found their existence precarious in the extreme. Entropy, suffering multiple blows, and smarting from evolution's reneged promise to uphold its morbid insistence that animals return other animals to inorganic pulp, seeks roundabout means of self-expression and has found many. Freud said something like, he who cast the first word instead of the first stone at his enemy was the founder of civilization. This puts due emphasis on the bedrock structure of language in the process of impulse control due to gating. The stronger the gating the more robust the mental health and security of the individual, and of course this involves dopamine suppression, not just in the nigro-striatal but in the meso-limbic and miso-cortical tracts as well. One might also add to Freud's dictum that he who threw the first football instead of firing a mortar or threw the first baseball instead of a hand grenade were also civilization's fathers given the universal unbridled popularity of sports worldwide.

This substitute for homicidal muckraking like that seen in the coliseum of Rome, offers up a tepid but palpable tithe for entropy's death instinct, warping its victims to the sidelines in disgrace rather than evisceration. And it is not uncommon to see injuries take place in sports which occasionally cross the dividing line into entropic splendor. Furthermore, physical activity, with its dopamine suppressing pallor, serves the master of gating intensity as an added bonus to its instinctual mollification. In that sense it is serving civilization's glue with aplomb by offering up a substitute for hunting down, killing and eating its victims but also strengthens the gating powerball of those participants engaging in it, and one could say that most of the devotees of sports also try their hand at the ol' ball game so to speak themselves. But entropy and its offspring the death instinct is not satisfied with this masquerade of substitution. The hideous "war to end all wars," World War 1, was rapidly followed by the heinous and gruesome World War 2, Korean war, Vietnam war and many others including the incendiary conflicts we currently endure.

While entropy laughs we watch helplessly as thousands die at the hands of his mischief, which one would clearly add, relies on the delusional capitulation to the need to eliminate one's so called enemies. It can easily be asserted that there is no good reason for one person to kill another, yet it is flourishing and always has on a mass scale. And, because we are still in a nascent transition from jungle disorder to civilized 2.0 mentality, there is a chance that as we become more cerebral and less physical/experiential beings like our Neanderthal forebears we will conquer entropy's trope with even greater alacrity as the trend is toward dopamine suppression and gating intensity with ego strengthening, and a robust mental inflation. Yet we find ourselves in the devil's paradise of potential earthly inhospitality with global warming simmering ever rakishly, which threatens, if not to end the planet, to alter our habitat on a goose bumping fusillade of panic. We will need to learn to adapt.

The carbon dioxide levels in the atmosphere are steadily increasing placing all of us at risk of imminent immolation in a pallet of meteorological mishegos while we remain significantly unconversant with the grapple hook of any real rope pull of solution. Perhaps artificial intelligence, with its mechanical industry of wired contemplation, will proffer up a salve. We've bombarded our foods with toxic pesticides, antibiotics and hormones which no doubt contribute to the swollen incidence of cancers. We've adopted eating habits so alien to the caveman's bric a brac diet that we confirm diseases entirely self induced with hydraulically over fatted and sweetened goods that could only arise from the industrial revolution's food processing Rube Goldberg machinery. We numb our minds with flickering screens and endanger our souls with typhoonish bouts of sitting, as dangerous to one's health perhaps as smoking, another entropically gratifying habit that is only slowly fading despite the searchlight of evidence of its clear arrowhead toward demise. In short we do everything possible to kill ourselves and others without overtly labeling it as such, as if it's okay to adopt a passive stance toward the death instinct sans blatant illumination.

All of this going on while the institutionalized killing of food animals in slaughterhouses proceeds out of sight and mind when we saunter down toward the Piggly Wiggly in our gut busting El Dorado's and scarf a plastic wrapped chicken breast from the cooler. All the while entropy is smiling in its muted but decisive victories, awaiting the full fledged genocidal termination of zillions of our species. And these wars not only decimate human and animal flesh to ash but flatten vast pieces of infrastructure that will take decades to rebuild if they are rebuilt at all. And one of the guardians of civilization is infrastructure. Cities are laid out on a grid and sprout up like trees within this cautious border. With even greater tonnage than the sequoia we hoist massive concrete obelisks to the sky, countering gravity, storing potential energy and defying entropy's quiescence.

We adopted the obsessive's need for order and used it to fashion our constructs and communities, routinizing our lives within the flotsam and jetsam of anti-chaos. It's as if the structures themselves, with their iron clad invulnerability to nature's whims reinforce our secure footing against the entropic jungle swarm. Structures, roads, order, routines all lend credibility to our defiance of the icy ruler of the universe, a refusal on our part to vanish into dirt and dust. Time is only important on earth, and only to the Homo sapiens who place intense view on it with our clocks (which themselves are a model of obsessive compulsive detail and gear arrangement) watches, dials and digital readouts that bang us over the head incessantly with the passage of that priceless commodity. To no other being, animal, planet or universe does time enunciate its moaning passage, and we note that entropy utilizes it to carry out its insouciant message. (Evolution also embraces time with the help of DNA which stole a redress from entropy with the catalyst of mutations which evolution learned to use to its advantage. In so doing evolution outdid its despicable enemy and forged into time the sculpture of antropic rebellion.) We dress our lives around the rigidity and fixity of time and live by its dictums, getting up, fasting, sleeping, working and eating all to its beneficence.

We worry over time's passage and realize that ol' entropy needs time to carry out its prerogatives, to cool the gurgling cup of java and fizzle the tissue within which we cartage our bag of bones. Both the structure and routinization of society is a testimony to our defiance and when wars emerge like ducks from under the water, we see the chaotic loss of our lifelines. Once chaos and entropy begin to tear down the husk of civilization it is very hard to recreate it. Entropy has gotten its greedy toenails into our bullwarks so why should it let go? But prior to the warlike evisceration of our structural creations, what goes first is the moral compass that guides antropy forward.

Entropy grabs a foothold of satisfaction in endorsing immorality as a step closer to its A-bomb-like path. Thus men gain a modicum of satisfaction by disparaging others while indulging oneself and deviating in variable measure from the golden rule. This rule weakens under the pressure of incivility and the need to fashion a kill, if not in the sense of tissue and bone, but in the mode of incivility and downright careening across a wide boulevard of sapiens behaviors which may, but usually don't, cross the line of societal retribution. These 'little murders' gratify on some level the entropic death instinct needling away at us in our deference to the catwalk 'thou shalt not kill'. Yes, but thou shalt stick it to the other guy in any way that skirts illegality. These mini murders too give a slither of gratification to our entropic death instinctual souls which in that spotlight helps prevent more grievous monstrosity. We all pay a tithe to entropy's corral of misadventure. But of course entropy is not satisfied with that and in some twenty percent of the population it grabs hold of the machinery of conscious thought, bending its metallic bow into what we label mental illness. In these unfortunate souls entropy seeks to express itself in different ways, in the direct return to the inorganic that is suicide, which occurs with regularity in those who suffer psychic disease.

So civilization, in its rejection of entropy, finds itself attacked from without and within, which ponies up anything from mass murders to genocides to suicides, hovering blandly in the majority as the mini murders entwined in the social strategy of the average citizen. As we progress further down the road of passage from the onset of language's metamorphic onset, we will see, perhaps some 1000, 5000, or ten thousand years from now the escape from this entropic jello into a world without the need to victimize our fellow humanity. We will have pulled out of entropy's gravitational smell into the clear viscous morning of rationality. We await that moment.

So, I've stated that *THE PURPOSE OF LIFE IS TO DEFY ENTROPY.* This is a proclivity for which some trees have a startlingly effective organization which allows them to hoist acres of wood skyward against gravity, condense potential energy in their pulp which is released on burning, and avoid any necessity to hunt, kill and eat other organic brethren. Animals, however, in evolution's nifty bargain with entropy when it decided to dabble in earth roving reconnaissance beings, were saddled with the entropic assignment of becoming killing machines, thus gratifying entropy on a level flora have no lust for. So in that sense fauna can never be on the defying end of entropy as much as trees and hence cannot live as lengthy a span on planet earth. Language allowed us the blasphemy to defy entropy by complexifying our minds, storing potential energy as a tree by forcefully submerging ideation and impulse into an unconscious red balloon which swells over time. (This is one explanation for the onset of schizophrenia in the late teens and early twenties. As the contents of the balloon swells, demanding greater and greater heft to subdue, the tendency is for it to burst to the surface as a breaking point is reached during adolescence for the gating weekened schizophrenic.)

This gating muscularity was a result of the beefy suppression of dopamine, which also fostered an enriched ego, brain expansion and progression from thought form 1.0 to the deductive reasoning of Sherlock 2.0. So, *IN ITS DEFIANCE OF ENTROPY LANGUAGE FACILITATED OUR SURVIVAL* What it also birthed was civilization in which evolution wisely saw great promise, with its ability to defend against boo coup predators and relieve the necessity of spending glorious amounts of calories to gain piddling amounts of nutrients. And we have added to our romance with antropy that *CIVILIZATION EXISTS TO DEFY ENTROPY AND SUPPORT ANTROPY* as well.

The superego birthed itself to enforce civilization's golden rule book, and is itself entropy defiant yet can fall into the latter's trap when gating systems fail, detonating its pointed condemnation on an innocent victim who has chosen to engulf a belief, unconscious at it may be, that they are guilty of societal transgression. Morality is also antropic and promotes the counterpoint to the death instinct adopted eons ago by the kingdom animalia. Yet we all engage in some interpersonal immorality in deference to the death instinct's cobalt seduction and as a means of avoiding invasive wrong doing, the kind that entropy's desire drools for. What happens to the death instinct in schizophrenia?

The collapse of the gating system with its store of potential energy shatters to shards and releases a mother load of stored energy which plays giddily into the hands of entropy. The latter is also overjoyed at the regression to disorganized thought 1.0, and so the complexification 2.0 won piece by piece by language's nifty magic is abandoned for brute primitivity. At the same time the 'little murders' of interpersonal immorality are lost and the schizophrenic no longer exhibits this universal trait. The singular reduction of their mentality disallows such a social strategy. So, in that sense they forsake entropy by becoming more moral, but more than gratify it in the loss of gated contents, and in their decidedly blunt disorganization.

Yet, since the moment displays a surge of entropic horror, what are we to do about it? Antropy is like a flower that blooms in nurturance, and if we can get back on the holy grail of sane disarmament, the tree of antropic sensibility will thrive. But it must be regarded as sacred soil, never taken for granted, as the greedy hooks of devil entropy thrive in its own revelry. In truth we all did kill the Kennedy's and a holocaust of infinitely more which gratified within us that natural born killer instinct which we must acknowledge as an integral operating system lodged between the ears as passionately as the superego's wagging tongue, Freud's death instinct. In this regard religion is a useful idiot in supporting the fumes of the golden rule, yet at other times serves up the crusty lineage of our divisions, leading us into entropy's gaping shark's mouth. Those who lead entropy's seductive lance need to meet with societal dispossession and dismissal to upload the promise of civilization's unstated bargain: safety, nourishment, freedom from pre-dation, and natural disaster.

And the latter is in a moment of exploitation by Mother Nature's displeasure with the sapiens' inopportune meddling in its golden habitat, perhaps the ONLY habitat in the universe that served up DNA's life giving formula. What are we to do? Entropy's desire is to return as much organic matter back to inorganicity from whence we sprang. So, nurturance of organicity is key, and the role civilization plays in this dramedy must be sniffed like a cosmic glue. Religion has played a fomenting role in the civilizational stew by emphasizing morality and as such must be considered antropic overall. Some boast that their God's offspring has died for our sins, which implies a universal sense of guilt that warrants absolution. Freud would probably say that the sense of subtle guilt that bubbles in us all is related to Oedipal urges, the submergence of which stores potential energy and contributes to the formation of our character in its overcoming.

However this absolution might also serve the purpose of nullifying interpersonal immoralities and slights we engage in daily and in that sense is siding with the death instinct's propensity to hover just under the radar of illegality. So in that arena religion again sides with society in its propogation of a blunt morality, a subtext of mini murders and an overall sense of human goodness.

However, in its craggy divisions it at times seems to fall into the abyss of contention leading to wars, genocides and rancor all of which plays into entropy's greedy little hands. So civilization, in its antropic seduction, must be nurtured and protected like an orchid in a swiftly changing climate. Once old man entropy gets a foothold, it is of utmost imperative to drill it out like a rotting tooth, and reinstate the highest level of civilized human existence possible. Yet, the inevitable reemergence of this sly old enemy is expected and must be microscopically managed for opportunities of dispersion. Perhaps a universe with one government and religion is the ultimate antropic garden of survival, the moment of most propitious encouragement of antropy's fragile will. But the ultimate goal is defiance of entropy's majesty in as deeply embedded resources as we can muster.

The obedience to the suppression of dopamine, which indicates not a dopamine deficit but a lack of surge (while encouraging acetylcholine) offers opposition to the rancid enactment of entropy's pessimism. Storing potential energy in the gating system's balloon defies entropy as does complexity of mind and conscious thought which plays into the enhancement of ego intensity and brain expansion under the iron fist of dopaminergic suppression. Future man will be much more contemplative and less physical, brainier and less brawny.

Humanity may live an isolated existence, communicating via blue screen primarily, sexual activity an obsolete pastime since reproductive attainment will be manufactured entirely in a lab. The defiance of entropy, once branded into the cheeks of civilization, will nurture a longer lifespan, and we may, with perhaps the help of artificial intelligence, tip the scales of longevity into the hundreds of years, approaching the intensity of the sequoia's righteous longevity. The greater our defiance of the cold, hallow intensity of entropy's desire, the greater will be our own survivability.

ANY MANEUVER WHICH STRENGTHENS GATING POWER PROMOTES MENTAL HEALTH. And gating is intimately intertwined with the suppression of dopamine, that wily little chemical that jumped in to save the day against entropy. It was the suppression of dopamine in the meso-limbic and meso-cortical tracts that was perhaps the most important trait of humankind. *IT WAS THE SUPPRESSION OF DOPAMINE UNDER THE INFLUENCE OF LANGUAGE THAT PERHAPS WAS THE MOST SALIENT TRAIT OF THE HOMO SAPIENS.* It allowed us to decimate the brawny and brainy Neanderthals, and snuff the diminutive Denisovans. Language r equired compartmentalization of the mind into areas like a preconscious that could store the bric a brac of words until the ego reached for them. Then, when it became clear that certain impulses were non grata. we learned to encrypt them in an open casket of the unconscious, by simply disentangling them from their word objects.

A simple snip and they were disconnected from their targets, basking in nowhere land in the squishy tub of brain matter that occupied our skulls. *THE SUPPRESSION OF DOPAMINE UNDER THE INFLUENCE OF LANGUAGE LED TO THE FREUDIAN METAPSYCHOLOGY AND STRENGTHENED GATING.* The cave guy had no real need for an unconscious, nor was it possible without words. Words, in their connection to meanings gave the mind the golden opportunity to populate the mind with the disconnected ghosts of their intentions. *THE UNCONSCIOUS WAS A NECESSARY PRECURSOR TO CIVILIZATION.* Civilization demanded a mega dose of morality pills and did so with the help of impulse burial in the unconscious. All of this led to the rise of superego, a small but mighty demon sitting in a lotus position on the tippy top of our minds.

Gating can be strengthened in various ways. One is in conscious thought which suppresses dopamine, the original mother of mental beef cake. At the same time, ego muscularizes, brain matter swells, and we adopt the adult, modern, reality based modality of thinking 2.0 that was also as much of a necessity in rocketing us forward as the unconscious. So now we had delivered to us a mechanism of impulse burial, brain expansion, thought process complexification which enabled the thorny cabaret of civilized behavior.

Therapy can strengthen gating, which in fact is the ethereal mechanismo of its benefit. It's not that Freud illuminated his patients to their vilest impulses but that he presented them to their ego in a way that the latter could muscle up and gate them out more efficiently. He detected all kinds of defenses against this, since the act of impulse burial was a solemn bulwark of society. But the benefits of that exposure in the gating out of those nasty covert urges was enormous and his patients left the couch stronger, calmer and more in control of their destiny as the ego garnered a macho six pack. Meditation also can be a gating enhancer as the goal is to block out intrusive thinking, thinking which is part and parcel of a gating deficit.

So, in a crescendo of antropy, within the past 50,000 years entropy has been strong-armed by the advent of mental complexity and gating which engenders the storage of potential energy as the rage of eager impulses are condensed therein with a mighty effort. Civilization, born of language, also stuck it to entropy by channeling the death instinct into activities of a more benign nature, interpersonal 'murders' which hover under the radar of illegality, substitute 'killings' in sports, lively competitions, etc. And the superego flattened entropy again in its robust support of this rerouting of the death instinct's goals of turning organicity into the lifeless anergic platitude of dust. And in this endeavor it borrowed evolution's propensity to utilize dopamine as a Pavlovian reward molecule, this time injecting its chemical salve when the individual helped a little old lady across the street.

The foundation of civilization, jurisprudence, government, education, infrastructure all served the unique admonishment of entropic containment. Thought process 2.0 became the beacon of civility and sanity, leaving entropy to ooze around the seams and corners. Even so, the old man always found a way of asserting himself. *THE PAST 50,000 YEARS HAVE BEEN A CRESCENDO OF ANTROPIC VICTORY* compared to the jungle chaos of our Neanderthal brethren. And thus we've cantilevered from jungle to disco. Instead of roaming the jungle, club in hand in search of the day's devour, we slide our Teslas a few blocks over and snatch a pre-slaughtered and butchered chicken breast in a plastic package, drive it home and sizzle it in our no stick pan on the stovetop. Thus, with minimal energy expenditure we've obtained caloric and nutritional input, one of civilization's most salient advantages.

And it was the shuffle from 1.0 primitive organizational thinking to 2.0 modern contemplation with its adoption of the reality principle that fomented this radical lifestyle change, with its concrete exuberance of antropic stability. When we find ourselves praising various historical figures we are really noting their hefty progress against the power of entropy that has been surmounted. We've clawed ourselves one hundred and eighty degrees from the jungle chaos and even launched vessels into space that ultimately break free of earth's gravitational force just as we have forged a brick road away from the entropic intensity of the death instinct. Of course our radically altered lifestyle allows the death instinct a chuckling pleasure as we succumb by the millions to the industrial strength illness born of sloth, diets so far from our recent past that our stomachs and pancreasees can't handle them successfully. Since we were made to move, hunt, battle and fornicate briskly we have severed all ties with the sinew and bone of our true nature.

Like an armored tank built for war rumbling into a Macdonald's drive through, we are inordinately out of place in our new self-made habitat, a habitat which we may be so radically destroying that the very imperilment of humanity lays in wait. The death instinct has crept through clandestinely in the form of arterial narrowing, foodicides, atmospheric poisoning and chemical insemination. These acts of self crucification are also matched by the collateral damage that our disentangled relationship with dopamine has birthed. Dopaminergic related illness abound, not the least of which is schizophrenia.

But we may add to that list Parkinson's disease, Tourette's syndrome, restless legs, stuttering, and possibly Alzheimer's and a multitude of others. We learned to suppress dopamine in the meso-limbic and meso-cortical tracts and the rest is lightning bolts of historical radicalism. *PERHAPS THE HOMO SAPIENS' GREATEST ACCOMPLISHMENT IS THE SUPPRESSION OF DOPAMINE.* This led a transition from 1.0 primitive organization to 2.0 reality principled deductive reasoning which has gotten us the momentous technological gimmicks we rely on daily, the advances in water propulsion, medical intervention, housing and all the other institutional bricks that reinforce our bitch slap against old man entropy. If one looks at it from the vantage point of entropic intensity, we have spent the past 50,000 years distancing ourselves from entropy and will succeed even more over the next several thousand, eventually leaving its gravitational grab in the dust at which point mental illness as we know it will no longer exist. Perhaps entropy's greatest delight is the self-chosen return to inorganic matter called suicide. We have seen in recent moments an upsurge in the rate of self-immolation, and the increase in self-injurious acts, especially among the young.

Somewhat incident to this rise in self-destructiveness is the advent of smart phones which some like to blame for the phenomenon. I'm not sure if research bears out this abrupt conclusion, but more research certainly might help. Also coincident with this gruesome data was the Covid 19 pandemic which wiped out over a million people in the United States alone. This natural disaster, along with the exponential increase in climatic events that populate the news waves almost daily, have contributed to the chaotic mantle of pessimism settling around some youth, as well as older individuals. We know that the vacuum suck of old entropy seduces some minds away from the gold standard of mental functioning, meaning dopamine suppression by conscious thought and reclaims their minds away from such activity.

Schizophrenia as the primo example fully repopulates the mentation with primitive organization that existed fifty thousand years ago, with the exception that they can now speak, whereas cave persons lacked the ability both to communicate in a sophisticated way and to participate in their own thinking. Depressives find it inordinately difficult to use deductive reasoning as their minds have been reclaimed by primary process thinking, the secondary process mode of contemplation garbled. This is a regular occurrence with the melancholy of serious depression and is a considerably common complaint reflective of the shaky fragility of their gating function, leaking oil at every turn while entropy chuckles.

Even more profound is the tsunami splash of disordered contemplation known as flight of ideas, or pressured thoughts usually a hallmark of bipolar mania, that alerts the examiner to an even greater rent in the steel of gating vault doors that then allow intrusive permeation of thoughts. Patients with anxiety disorders too, although on a less profound level, suffer from thinking interference, though on a smaller scale, especially during the moment of panic or obsessive compulsive disability they find most uncomfortable.

*

This drawback from rationality to primary process thinking gives entropy an opening in which to exert its insipid seduction. Bipolars, schizophrenics, anxiety disordered patients including obsessive compulsives and depressives all have higher suicide rates than the average. Schizophrenics are close enough to entropy's cloak that their voices are even commandeered by the old ghoul to order them to harm themselves in a dire echoing of morbid entreaty.

So, closeness to the entropic mantra is a suicidal inducement that has dangerous power, and the minds of the mentally ill are in greater proximity to the entropic sawdust than the average beings which have spent the last fifty thousand years distancing themselves from this gravitational monarch. When animals branched off from plants, as I have asserted, they humbly accepted the assignment of killing machines which the floral universe, in its inordinate passivity and self-containment, held no patience for. Thus we inhaled the machinery of the death instinct within us the result of entropy's bargain with evolution. In spite of this, there is another facet to our souls, another window of opportunity, which Freud called Eros or the life instinct.

This is the instinct that drives us inexorably together in search of procreation and so jettisons our genetic blueprints out into the future. And if the death instinct is aligned with entropy, the life instinct, eros, procreative ardor with its haunting sexuality inevitably follows the path of antropy. But antropy signifies much more, the outlandish defeat by mama evolution of entropy's morbid desires. In a clever feat of legerdemain, evolution's cunning tricked the old sour puss by using its own tendencies against it in the modus of mutations that are part and parcel of entropy's lust for disorder within the very molecule of life, DNA. And, as such, evolution was able to defeat entropy over megalithic time periods. Thus, *EVOLUTION PLUS TIME EQUALS ANTROPY*. And we know that once one hitches one's star to that skyrocket of time, things progress handily. And handily they did, ultimately resulting in the killing/procreating machines that were vertebrates, then mammals and eventually Homo sapiens. In this minutely rare habitat, including a moon that circles the earth face forward, electromagnetic forces, gravitational exigencies, basking energic sunlight and much much more, antropy was able to flourish into the golden blue ball we now label earth.

A combo of temperature, mineral baths, lightening bolts and a small dollop of wizardry under antropy's guiding hand slowly cooked the DNA that gave rise to it all, and perhapsis still forming in some spots on mother earth currently. This antropic molecule, which tricks entropy by turning its ardor for disorder against it, unless it was planted here by aliens chuckling away at a nifty practical joke, arose in an antropic revery within the paradigms of exponential specificity in our earthly habitat. The rest of the universe, as far as we have been able to tell, and we have done much looking through telescopes and other means of identifying cryptic alien messages, have detected no other dust ball like earth making antropy's appearance a rare feat indeed.

Like the most delicate of souffles, antropy can only flourish in the midst of exacting environmental details. At this moment the earth appears to be wallowing in a spout of entropic victory. Antropy appears to have taken a wimpish back seat and is not exerting the domesticated drivel of a bustling life instinct. Ongoing devastating wars seem sedately unstoppable, suicide rates climb especially among youth, and the lust for procreation itself may be waning. Nevertheless the population has recently hit eight billion, indicative of antropy's ongoing ardor. Could it be that, detecting a shift in its exacting habitat requirements, antropy is reeling from a patently more inhospitable garden of earthly delights, and as such has lost some its lustiness, like Super Man in a slow elevator loaded with kryptonite. Let us hope the floor is reached, and the door opens soon, letting our superhero free to victorious glory once again. These two great yin yangs work silently within us. On our fertile planet earth, evolution has taken up the banner wave of organicity, life giving procreation and survival of the organism placing its bet on the mutation most likely to be able to do so.

The momentum increased once language stuck it to entropy in its mind organizing fervor and storage of potential energy in the gating system. All of this was gestated by dopamine suppression in the meso-limbic, miso-corti-cal tracts heretofore untouchable by said process. With a swollen brain, ego intensity, new thought rules including the reality principle, and the complexity of Freud's metapsychology including a beefed up gating system, we stuck it to old ghoulish entropy again when we adopted civilizations. Now we were able to institutionalize antropic ideals. With the assist of morality's golden rule and the superego, entropy was forced to ooze out of the corners of our souls, but has found plenty of welcoming arms there.

Swollen with the pride of influence, antropy or the life instinct took off in a multitude of directions with education, science, medicine, jurisprudence and various forms of government that subsidized the human's bastion of influence, gradually decreasing the universality of the dictator, although some unfortunate governmental train wrecks still exist. And under this umbrella humanity took off like a cat in a rat den. As killing/procreating machines we continue to raise, kill and devour other animals and plants returning them to inorganic matter as entropy delights. But the real joy now for the grumpy entropy is in our enthusiasm for other and self immolation. So the blessings of civilization not only relieved us of the need to expend massive amounts of energy to get relatively small rewards, it neutralized the majority of our most obvious predators. But in consciously recognizing the reward program of the antropic yen within us we bolstered its sinew with the rules and regs of modern societal interaction. We can list rules, morality, religious endorsement of the golden rule and ten commandments, and the superego's endorsement as the beggar child of dopamine suppression born of language. So in our history, various factors have worked for and against the life instincts, tilting toward then condemning the entropic death instinct, and finding a balance somewhere between the two of these universal, underlying winds.

On a karmic scale of balance, one goes up when the other goes down and right now in our history, it looks like antropy is enveloping us in a pandemic decline. It will take a strong captain to endorse the windfall of cooperation with the nurturance of organic matter to make that tide reverse. The fortunes of humankind rest upon it, but there is far from any rustic totem of guarantee that things will go that way.

Entropy, the coot, finds a way but as evolution has taught us, with time we can defeat it, but now on a conscious level which language has brought us to, only if we can scan with clarity the swirling endeavor of these riptides. No longer are we animals, cowering below the top of the food chain, scraping our fingernails against the rock of survival. We've come farther than that with the adoption of mind set 2.0, the reality principle and conscious thought allowing us to participate for the first time in the theater of our own contemplations. Our civility adorns us with manners, principles and a superego commensurate with the urge to bolster civilization's stability which rests on institutions like education and jurisprudence, and the obsessive compulsive mandates of rigidity, routine and repetition.

Yet we still mature into killing/fornicating machines, buffered by societal mores and admonishments. We are tokens of the Super Bowl between evolution's antropy and entropy, the death instinct and eros, dopamine suppression and de-suppression, the ten commandments and the capacity to devolve all back to inorganic pulp.

Entropy is a concrete hardened tenet of physics, and antropy so far just a construct, one which has served us well over eons of time and in specific environmental menus, straddling a bucking horse of detailed misbehavior. If the conditions under which antropy flourished start to go south, we may see an erection of chaos while entropy exhumes devilish chuckles. That chaos may involve increases in suicidality, homicidal exposures, lawlessness, wars based on dictatorial pride, a loss of motivation to procreate, breakdown of societal rules and many other creaky symptoms of civilizational debris. But underlying these trends are the two pillars of our yin yang, jingle jangle existence.

Like the scales of justice when one goes up the other plunges, and when the death instinct as a form of entropy countenances a slight withering of eros and antropy, it revels in the open field, proving again its subtle lurking behind the corners of all matter. Entropy rules the universe and maintains the planets in silent orbital embalm.

The delicate evidence of antropy's success may be weakening and evolution itself might be gradually devolving into a free fall since we have neutralized the majority of predators that trimmed the crucible of evolutionary stew. New guideposts of natural selection have arisen, making the propensity to immobility, to endure dietary phantasmagorias, and stare into a flickering blue screen the new naturally selective gradients. Although we continue to evolve it is in a radically different trajectory. If the function of sexual selection becomes entirely a pre-programmed menu list of chosen attributes, then the Darwinian apex of natural selection may have been reached. Sexuality may lose all reproductive function, the decision making regarding survival consciously controlled by the souls and whims of humankind. All of this puts our own conscious stance against entropy a crucial moderator of ongoing entropic containment. Nations' and individuals' abilities to cooperate constructively might well make the difference between survival and devolution into the helter-skelter of entropic inorganicity.

A global threat such as climate catastrophe should move us toward unification against a common enemy, a drawing together of forces to combat the oncoming massivity of the potent climate debacle. The mishegos of pandemics and other viral attacks need to draw us into a tent of colossal teamwork. As such the boundaries and borders that divide us may slowly dissolve into a universal global esprit de corps. Idealistic as this may sound, the ongoing splash of environmental disastrousness brings us ever closer to necessity. Disharmony may well be entropy's en-tree to earthly regression to a landscape not unlike Mars or Pluto. There have been many mass extermination events in the past that have not ultimately KO'd organic, protoplasmic matter.

Dinosaurs collapsed into fiery tissues, ultimately sinking into the earth and reemerging as oil, which we now pump into the atmosphere with our churning combustion engines, reincarnating those hefty, brainless brutes into earthly threat exhaust. This resulted from the huge impact of an asteroid the size of Manhattan slamming into the Yucutan peninsula 65 million years ago. Boom. The skies blackened and vegetation withered while dinos scorched into the glistening tomb of earth and much of evolution's handiwork up until that moment vanished. But not all. Volcanoes, earthquakes, tsunamis and other earthly delights all took a shot at us. At one point

Homo sapiens were supposedly reduced to about a thousand hearty souls hanging on in the tip of Africa during a global glacial deep freeze. We persisted. And so we shall if we can recognize entropy's handiwork within the fabric of our existence, the death's instinct's meddling in our recently civilized souls, and antropy's indomitable propensity to shuffle forward if given enough time. For psychiatry to echo in a chamber uninhabited by entropy's lustful entreaty is to wander in the dark without a map. Organic tissue is subject to the same laws of physics as all other matter and we shall see in the next chapter how the interaction of physics and biology has entertained many wise theorists. Ignoring these issues merely haunts us in a directionless paradigm of confusion, searching longingly in a pool of scattered ideation. Psychiatry can no longer afford to do so.

CHAPTER IV: IMPLICATIONS, CONTEMPLATIONS, OBSERVATIONS OF EVOLUTION'S FREE FALL: AN OBSERVATIONAL ANCHOR FOR THE CURRENT HUMAN CONDITION. THE CASUAL LENS.

"Evolution thrives on adversity." Steven Lesk MD

Modern humanity, especially youth, are facing anxieties unequalled in the course of humanity's trajectory, and within the boxcar of that global panic there lacks anchoring vision, a clarifying lens to grasp with reassuring acuity. Faced with indecisions unrivaled by older generations, they have no global positioning satellite to orient them as to why and where their monsters are coming from. For the first time we are being told that machines are better thinkers than humans, that your job will soon be replaced by robots, and that the world will remain a chaotic exigency of granite sharpened divisions. Future world remains indelibly blurry, under determined, laden with unsettling possibilities and inevitable catastrophes. At the same time none of this seems to have anything to do with evolution.

So why am I insistent that it does, when I can no more prove it than I can dissect the uterus of a wombat? Simply because it's true, as if that were enough and because it is exactly what we need now, an explanation for the disparate road signs appearing on our communal freaked out highway. What we need now is a frame of reference with which to orient in the face of primitive perplexity. This will serve not only to prick the balloon of intensity felt in almost every quarter of humanity, but to serve as a groundwork for understanding and a guidepost for future tentative forays into solution.

It is fairly easy to perceive that we have neutralized the vast majority of adversities that cave men faced in their daily race for survival. Their endless handshake with food foraging, deadly predatory attack, incurable illness and injury, has been replaced by an expectation of survival, freedom from being eaten, and relief from affliction with a lifespan triple our caveman ancestors. Truly we have succeeded in shrinking the horrific adversities of our ancestors, and pleasingly so. The paltry 30 year lifespan of our forebears places our bodies in an unanticipated longevity for which they were never intended by evolution or entropy, nature's two most grandiloquent rivals. It makes perfect sense then that we can declare evolution if not dead, deflated and in disequilibrium, and this infirmity offers its arch rival on opportunity to shine, bold faced and grinning against its opponent, one that has proven outlandishly successful. And it is within this dichotomous tapestry that we must orient our gaze of the current curated insolvency of awareness.

Each of us is donated a unique genetic inheritance and we define ourselves by this placid stamp, yielding at times disparate phenotypes that are tangentially related to the digital sprawl of DNA base pairs that titillate our molecular makeup. But in our near future genetic heritage may become nearly meaningless. As we are decoupling from evolution the importance of mutational inheritance is lessened and we are learning to bolster any shortcomings with patch quilt solutions. Mutations that would have been adjudicated rapidly within the adverse habitat of caveman existence now linger in ambivalence as to their potential utility or interference with survival which now has a much broader base of possibility. So lots of mutations continue forward through time in our offspring that would have been eliminated in that intense caveman battleground. In short genetic inheritance is approaching a moment of inconsequentiality, leaving evolution adrift like a dying satellite drifting slowly out into space.

In the near future someone with, for example, an inadequate pancreas will have it replaced with a genetically different yet organic pancreas grown in a lab from tissue culled from someone else. Alternatively, a mechanical pancreas manufactured by robots in a factory will be implanted to regulate the flow of insulin that regulates the all important blood sugar level of us sapiens including diabetics. A faltering heart will be replaced by one grown in a lab from stem cells of another human. Mutations will not be allowed to express their drawbacks in gradients of determination, rather will be identified as sources of corrective action. So in that sense we will be leaving evolution far in the dust.

Let's remember that evolution is not just a set of loosely knit principles, it's a potpourri of instinctual behaviors designed to foment procreation. And by that dictum I am not just conjuring sexual bugaboos, but para-reproductive behaviors like nesting, home building, mate acquisition and preparation for family supportiveness. Essentially forever, evolution has set the stage for family-ish behaviors that presage what is to come, namely a little bubby. Animals are loaded with such instinctual earmarks as in the case with ducks noted on the side of the road with their little chick families following dutifully behind them, usually near a pond. This instinctualization of evolution's yearning has been the unstated mandate followed by generations of humans in preparation for their own little nest of chicks.

But if, as I have asserted, it is so that evolution is in fact waning, those nesting mandates are also fizzing into dust allowing for the internalization of choices never imagined by earlier generations, choices accompanied by anxieties that hover in the air of youthful passions. No longer is one's role in society, that of future parent, the sine qua non of behavior and preparatory adolescent posturing. Earlier generations never questioned whether they should fit into the societal framework in some way (even if 'hippies' in the sixties rebelled against authority during the Woodstock zeitgeist they often became thought leaders over time) and boomers didn't wallow in cavities of indecision.

But the loss of evolution's time worn mandates has cornered the consciousness of our youth into abject indecision. Couple this with new information that machines can now outthink us and will take our jobs within ten years, that global warming is gradually searing the earth into hellish catastrophe and one has the makings of youthful hyper-ennui. Questions abound such as: should I have offspring; should I find a societal niche in which to nest; should I coincide with stereotypical family scripts; should I wander off the grid into obscurity; should I accept the biologically assigned gender I was born with or orbit into a different context altogether; is sex important to me at all, and the list goes on, contributing, I assert to the wholesale confusional anxiety of youth and their parental guiders. Furthermore, the fact that our bodies are now in existence some three times longer than they were intended makes for a sense of overt indecision unrivaled in Homo sapiens history.

Our genotype leading to phenotypical traits is now less important than ever since whatever traits any mutation my afford us can most likely be accommodated in the modern world. No longer is there an adversity pressurized gradient to render a verdict on denovo mutations, genotypical misfires that can hang around despite being less than advantage. In the not so distant future miscreant organs will be replaced by tissue grown in labs derived from other's DNA or by inorganic parts manufactured in factories for implantation within us.

It should be clear by now to all that *life itself is an aberration, the exception not the rule.* Living on earth gives us a flaccid, distorted apparition of what is and is not typical, but if we look at other planets, no protoplasm has yet to darken their doors. Despite all the fanatical mega-hype, no little green men have yet to be spotted or photographed. There is no McDonald's on Jupiter, no football stadium on Mars and no casino on Venus. What there is is dust and rock and little else, and we can identify the motive force behind all this inorganic clog... the second law of thermodynamics, entropy, which seeks to leverage everything back to its lowest common denominator. The fact that life exists at all in the face of this ghoulish behemoth, a force that renders all orbs in the galaxy and beyond to dust and stone, is miraculous, an issue addressed by Schroedinger in his book, *What is Life?* In it he concludes that entropy is such a universal tyrant that there must be an opposing oracle in existence to account for the presence of life on earth, a force he called negative entropy and which I have dubbed antropy. And antropy must be a force as megalithic as entropy itself in order for organic matter to even exist given its complexity and energetic rationale.

Without antropy life would not exist, nor would it blossom without the enigmatic digital framework of something as rare as a DNA. Antropy is the mascot and banner for evolution which has taken up the cause of protoplasmic advance since forever. Evolution joins with its partner antropy in defeating the force of entropy and thus we see that, under the circumstances of predatory adversity, evolution has fomented organicity's explosive multiplication. One might refer to this force as *eros* as did Freud, or love, or the life force as opposed to the death instinct which seeks to join forces, and indeed emanates from, entropy. So evolution and antropy embrace sexual behavior which in its bare exposure has been the subject of repressive forces, especially during Freud's time, a repression which he succeeded in diminishing, as in, for example the 'free love' movement of the Woodstock era in America in the late 1960's. And now we are hearing that the youth of America are engaging in both sex and alcohol use, a combination of synergistic proportions, less than ever before in recent history. The given explanation, that knowledge of alcohol's dangers has become more widespread, is shaky at best, since anyone has known that imbibing the hard stuff places multiple organ systems at risk. The addition now of cancer as a major risk with drinking should theoretically only reduce its use a little, as the knowledge of cigarette's cancer risk took decades to impact use significantly.

So what could be behind the reluctance of youth to engage in sexuality, a universal instinctual rage, especially in the hormonally endowed younger set? You know exactly what my answer will be, that evolution's demise has brought along with it sexual dehiscence, reduction in the willingness to have offspring, a retreat from the usual social roles that promote family, sexual confusion wholesale, and a surly swell of depression, anxiety, and suicidal actions in younger beings.

In fact suicide is the third most common cause of death in 15 to 19 year olds (see Bommmersbach, et al, "National Trends in Suicidal Thoughts and Suicide Attempts Among High School Students in the United States, American Journal of Psychiatry, vol. 182, July, 2025). Alcohol is just a casual bystander so to speak in the loss of bar hopping behavior that in the past has had 'hooking up' as its tipsy basis. Cannabis, on the other hand, is a blandishment of solitary use often, and doesn't have the 'loosening' ardor of booze's cape. It's more apt to elicit munchies than orgasms.

So then, if one were to ask oneself what would the demise of evolution look like one would have the answer in its major thrust and stilted combat with its arch rival entropy. For evolution to succeed as it has, the gene pool must be thrust forward, and this requires instinctual 'nesting' behavior on the part of the participants. In industrialized civilizations this necessitates an income which includes a job, a spouse, a nest itself and the desire to undertake the rigors of parenthood. And all of this requires a sense of locale in the corn maze of civilization, and a concrete approach to a specific gender and its roles. The benefits of these givens are that decision making along certain avenues of behavior are unnecessary and one's general compass in life's trajectory is bluntly obvious. If one had to think about each of these major decision points along the way a sharp dissonance in mood and security might arise leading to depression, anxiety and suicide.

And we are seeing ALL of these phenomena in modern society. 1) Marked drop in birth rates all over industrialized nations. 2) Avoidance of usual social roles and motivation to be a participant in society's communal structure. 3) A reticence to engage in sexuality itself along with a drop in alcohol use which usually goes along with sexual behavior. 4) Confusion about one's gender role and about which gender itself is applicable to the individual. 5) A rise in youth distress and suicidal thinking and behavior, especially in females, is an obvious consequence of this indecision. We have gone from survival of the fittest to survival of the most reproductive to survival of the indecisive. This in no way negates that there are a multiplicity of other reasons for youth to be jittery, global warming and nuclear holocaust among the salient possibilities as well as the much touted influence of smart phone use since 2010. I believe I've made my point that evolution is, if not dead, limping badly.

Evolution's guiding hand has brought us to the shore of 8 million Homo sapiens strong in a decisive victory against entropy. What evolution has done for us and the animal and floral kingdoms in general is astounding. But it's reached its zenith and now we must look toward new principles to stumble us forward, hopefully without a resurgence of entropy's desires. The future will hold something very different, we'd best get used to that, and it's coming on fast and furious.

The next notch in the belt of evolution is AI, and this entity will create new beings, ones that garner greater smarts than anything the human brain can muster. This will give rise to the next generation of beings, generally inorganic although I can see in the future a hybridization of beings with both organic and inorganic parts as we learn to clone organs from healthy individuals and 'gift' them to people whose organs are failing. And of course the use of titanium and other body parts will expand, where whole organs can be manufactured in a factory. These 'hybrid' humans and AI bots will start to blend into one organic/inorganic humanoid and will eventually be indistinguishable.

However these AI humanoids will ultimately abscond themselves from us dummies and form their own smarter societies, not wanting to hob nob with the cretinous Homo sapiens. Eventually the AI bots will evolve into beings with IQ's of 500 or more at which point they will take over the world. And we will let them! Why not have a being with an IQ of 500 govern, instead of a low IQ human who is subject to personal greed and influence more than the super brainiacs evolved from AI bots? I will discuss more about the future in the next chapter, but this lays the ground work for the issue that EVOLUTION WILL CONTINUE, just not in us sapiens. So in a sense, evolution will have morphed into the AI realm, leaving Homo sapiens as they currently are, and creating a new breed of hybrid beings that will then evolve into super brains. In a sense entropy will have won in that these hybrids will have inorganic material and entropy craves to move the organic to the inorganic as it does to us all eventually. So if evolution is done with us (even though it may continue in other animals and plants) it is not done with AI beings and has just begun to coalesce around them, intelligence being their most salient asset.

But now we can gain an even clearer insight about what life really is. It's quite simple really. Ready? Life is simply an antropic force that coalesces inorganic molecules into organized organic ones.

"*How could we express in terms of the statistical theory the marvelous faculty of a living organism, by which it delays the decay into thermodynamical equilibrium (death)? We said before: 'It feeds upon negative entropy', attracting, as it were, a stream of negative entropy upon itself ... entropy, taken with a negative sign, is itself a measure of order." (What is Life?,* Erwin Schrodinger, p 73, 1967, Cambridge U. Press.)

So Schrodinger found it necessary to posit the wily existence of a force counter to our beleaguered entropy, its opposite, or negative which then loops itself around the life force, the principles that evolution simmers with the help of brother DNA to promote and enhance the complexity of protoplasm. Life can be boiled down to a simplistic core, that which sucks up inorganic molecules and transforms them sim sala bim into more complex buggers that are inhabited by this antropic life force until death at which time it gradually either disintegrates entirely or fossilizes like the jaw bone of a Denisovan or a pinky found in its erstwhile cave. And we can vacuum in another principle, the scaly slime of time which has eluded us in its extremis for eons. Time is like a byproduct of this organizing or decomplexifying process, and hovers around the most complex organisms only, donning the cloak of irrelevance within the confines of disorganized locales like, oh, Pluto, the moon, or the vast majority of the universe which has given us no blinding flash of evidence that protoplasm exists upon them. Life is therefore an urge, an instinct toward greater order which ropes in time as its reward but that is more than capable of losing this luxury. In fact entropy has an ally in this degradative regard, that ally being known as fire. Fire relegates the remnants of life whose force has left it, dead matter previously alive such as wood, and returns it to its most basic elements and at the same time giving off potential energy in the form of heat, that energy a sure sign of the life or antropic process that synthesized it in the first place. Bones, of course, are more likely to be fossilized prior to utter deterioration unless subjected to the intensity of fireball heat.

So life has taken on a most exquisite enrichment in its glorious success upon mother earth, a success known nowhere else and has become not just a brute force like gravity or centrifugal force but something classy and sassy, imbued with time itself, and then, of course, soured by entropy's inevitable victory, returning to disintegrative simplicity and the loss of its reward, time. Life, reduced to its common denominator, is quite simple… the force which imparts order to simplistic molecules, and rallies them into organic protoplasm for a finite period of time. The life force inevitably absconds leaving the enriched carcass which in the case of plants, is of enormous biomass. So to reduce 'life' to its simple common denominator we see that it is merely the 'antropic' (opposite of entropy) force which takes simple inorganic substances and makes them more complex for a time then, on demise, allows them to deteriorate back to their original form gradually over time.

This harkens back to the classic example of entropy which is that a steaming cup of coffee when set upon a table will cool within about 35 minutes to the surrounding temperature. A Homo sapient's protoplasm will reverse course and decomplexify again once the life force has gone out of it. So we have to accept the existence of a force opposing entropy, as did Schrodinger, in order to explain the existence of life on earth or any other planet. The very unique earthly power goes up against entropy and seeks to make the simple complexly organized for a PERIOD OF TIME. That's all it can expect, but the species is lurching forward on the path toward immortality if evolution can harness its duet with antropy. So far it has, but as we have seen, it seems to be losing its grip strength.

We can surmise that lack of interest in procreation might eventually scuttle the ship of evolutionary progress but this could take a lengthy period of time around which we can surmise that humanity will define an ongoing niche for quite a while. However, simplistic explanations that don't consider evolution at all are likely the most red of herrings. One recent article (Ellen Cushing, *The Atlantic)* suggested that all we really needed to do was throw more parties. The ubiquitous onset of smart phones probably impacted youth's mentality but in the echo of the pandemic they also increased communication in a world where face to face contact froze.

We have to dig deeper, and in unearthing something encompassing, might learn about the true nature of the phenomenon itself. Evolution doesn't work in a space vacuum in near earth orbit. It hovers in the context of humongous opposition, at least by the second law of thermodynamics which is constantly pirouetting around as grossly as gravity. Once we see this, we can perceive that another growling goblin is awaiting our retreat from evolutionary progress, the hoar of entropy.

We may certainly be the victims of our own success in more ways than one, in that by defeating adversity, a colossal gift, we've neutralized evolution, and in that our inventiveness gets us into trouble as in the scourge of dino fuel into the sky by combustion engines, also a blessing but somehow now a possible curse. And while such happenstance is decidedly a stress to our youth, these situations alone cannot explain all that we are witnessing around us. We must be cognizant of global trends, historic momentum, the silent musk of smoky impulses that only emerge, like artifacts, on excavation. By digging deeper, we unearth more complex and valuable trophies of the past. We sink into disgruntled superficiality by ignoring slight evidence, hints of murder, fingerprints of past echoes where trajectories foreign to our slovenly souls go unnoticed. But there they are, waiting for our gruff hands to rough them free.

So if by some quirk the multifarious zig zags we are noticing are not due to evolution, what other explanations might emerge for the phenomena we are witnessing? Certainly there are a multitude of thorny concoctions that might agitate our haunted youth. Youth itself is stress enough to devolve into a characteristic despondency about one's potential future or lack thereof. Early ennui is known to be a 'thing' as one pecks one's way forward in the humid chaos of adolescence and beyond. Yet there seems to be a decidedly aggressive departure in the status of humanity as we are now scrutinizing it that stumbles way beyond youthful indecision. The call for evolution's tired mandates has lost its shrill intensity and the momentum of procreation has gained a dull pallor, a playbook decidedly unique.

But, you say, financial preoccupations alone could account for the Mishegas we are witnessing. The middle class can not easily afford a house, finding wages insufficient despite politicians's pledge to fix the impoverished countenance of our laborious zeitgeist. In Scott Galloway's book, "*Adrift*" there is a graph showing how productivity has risen over 200% since 1950, compensation has only increased by 100% in non-management workers, adjusted for inflation. (p. 27, *Adrift*, S. Galloway, Portfolio, Penguin 2022). So then we are working harder, more efficiently for lower wages and this must be causing a decline in birth rate, withdrawal from social roles, allergy to sexual encounters lubricated by booze, gender confusion and a suicide rate that is the third leading cause of death among high school students (?) Even in the great depression of 1929 we did not see suicide rates on this level of intensity. While suicide rates did rise in those challenging years (1929-1939) when unemployment reached as high as 25% of the population with financial ruin and loss of savings common, within a few years they were declining again. The jump from pre depression era of 12.1 per 100,000 to 17.4 per 100,000 was centered largely on adult men as breadwinners and in urban areas.

This is not what we are evincing today with youngsters and women surging in self demise, and the depression era numbers, while staggering, were relatively tame given the acrid intensity of financial hardships that out paced anything we are witnessing today. No, we cannot pin the variety of oddball peculiarities on finances which, relative to the depression for example, are fairly accommodating to the vast majority of hard working adults. Opportunity still exists for the motivated and talented even though it is a challenge for anyone to get where they want to be, the problem is more that younger folks are supremely undecided about where that actually is.

The onset of digital communication has been touted as an answer to this youthful enigma, staggering onto the stage around 2010, and coinciding somewhat with the rise in youth depression, anxiety and suicidality. "Blue screen" relating is certainly not on par with face to face encounters that creates salivating, pheromone scented interactions with nuanced facial expressions and the like, Yet, during the pandemic, which seems to have been a particularly challenging assignment for younger folks, it was cell phones that kept the connections vibrant, even if they emanated from flickering screens. A tawdry host of anxieties surround our current state of affairs including global warming, financial strain, potential nuclear holocaust, political and social divisions and unrest, etc. Yet, compared to the life of the typical cave person, these concerns seem paltry.

The common caveman could expect to live at most to around 30 years of age. Imagine a world where there were no medications or treatments for any illnesses whatsoever, including dental and other impositions. Nothing. Consider having the chore of supplying your little family with food daily amidst a chorus of external dangers akin to the most realistic haunted house. Think of being thrown literally into a lion's den of potential threats with nothing but a slightly pointy rock tied by stems to a branch. Lotsaluck. Ingesting uncooked foods in unsanitary conditions was fertile ground for parasitic and other intestinal rants which easily could end one's life by diarrheal dehydration and gradual parasitic attack of various organs. Desperately seeking edibles resulted in frequent ingestion of natural poisons and indigestible shoots and roots. All around your peers are dropping like flies, some violently attacked and ingested by larger animals. This is not to mention the person to person hostilities that were routine occurrences in the lawless habitat of jungle living.

"But then, beginning about 70,000 years ago, *Homo sapiens* started doing very special things… they drove the Neanderthals and all other human species not only from the Middle East, but from the face of the earth… Most researchers believe that these unprecedented accomplishments were the product of a revolution in Sapiens' cognitive abilities." (Harari, *Sapiens*, p. 21)

This upswing in cognitive abilities was a direct result of language, most anthropologists agree. The brainy and brawny Neanderthals lacked the hearing, vocal apparatus and brain structure presumably to make a twenty six letter alphabet of sounds as we could. We were Svengalis of symbol formation, the soul of language, and this glittery talent gave us something that revolutionized our mentality. We gained the 'reality principle' as Freud called it and were able to divine truth from fiction, lie from veracity, honest scientific fact. The scientific method was an even more rigorous blueprint for determining truth involving high quality experimentation. And from this talent for divination we birthed civilizations, ways of living heartily blessed by mother evolution as we no longer had to forage for food in the predatory quicksand of the jungle.

"There were humans before there was history. Animals much like modern humans first appeared about 2.5 million years ago. But for countless generations they did not stand out from the myriad other organisms with which they shared their habitats." (Harari, *Sapiens* p. 3)

We were animals, not at the top of the food chain, but just groping our survival amid bad odds and terrifying possibilities.

"For millions of years humans hunted smaller creatures and gathered what they could, all the while being hunted by larger predators." (Harari, *Sapiens,* p. 11)

We too often met the fate of being torn limb from limb, or at least brutalized by a pack of wild hyenas who worked in gangs to surround and overpower their victims, ravaged by the teeth of lions, slapped silly by the wondrous oomph of an orangutan.

"...only in the last 100,000 years, with the rise of *Homo sapiens*that man jumped to the top of the food chain." (*Sapiens,* p. 11)

So the habitat from which we moved into these spanking new civilizations were grotesque horror stories of deprivation, illness, brutalizing attacks from other species and our own, famine, weather scourge, cannibalism and more. Now we drive to the store in our electric vehicles, pick up a pre-cut chicken breast in a package and take it home for the grilling on our electric sizzler. We expect to live until our eighties, not our caveman expectation of 30, and when ill, expect our medical teams to fix it up. All of this is what is signified as 'mismatch' syndromes, the variance between our millions year old evolutionary environment and our current luxurious haunt. But at what price?

It must be acknowledged that the cornerstone of civilization is the golden rule, and to internally fix that mandate requires suppression of a myriad of impulses which haunt our mentalities, pushing for expression. This talent for repression mirrors what the child learns early on about his or her excretory assignment. The fledgling citizen learns that not every spot is fodder for fodder, in short, he has to control the impulse until he's in the 'designated location.' Eventually as his fortitude for withholding expands, the impulse itself is repressed into silence waiting for the appropriate instant. This model of healthy mental power is later utilized in the repression of interpersonal impulses demanding being roped in, and the power of repression is demonstrated so that the societally condemned impulses are also sent into silence as there will never be an appropriate moment for their output. So we develop this talent for repression, a healthy mental muscle talent, which serves us well in the larger festival of inter-human interaction.

In fact it is when repression FAILS that problems arise in our sanguinity. As an extreme example the patient who has suffered trauma, whether it be sexual, or violent or whatever especially in childhood. The memory of these ghoulish events demand entrance to the theater of consciousness with a potent demand that scrambles the victim's mental organization into disrepair. The worse the trauma the more insistent the demand for consciousness to 'fix' it so to speak. But Freud found that other types of failure of healthy repression were at the base of mental illness symptoms as they strove for entrance to the playhouse of awareness, and symptoms, he surmised, were limping attempts to control these demands that were pounding at the door. He discovered that the seat of man of these impulses were 'Oedipal' in short, parental, as our parents are our first encounter with societal no no's.

And repression itself feeds the ego, strengthening this control panel, involves dopamine binding or encapsulation, and defeats something alluded earlier that rears its ugly presence in most unflattering ways, entropy. Repression requires effort, oomph, and stores potential energy brain wise, all of which is anti-entropic. But we can at this point agree that something like entropy exists and that there must be some opposing enraged actor to dilute it and serve as a champion of living tissue, without which we would be residing on the moon, Mars, or some other dust strewn planet.

Solutions that pretend to have the answer to youthful depression and ennui including suicide cannot account for the actual increase in suicidality. The use of cell phone and computer screens may have an affect on younger individuals who are more prone to react to bullying in adolescence.

"Many suicides by adolescent girls have been directly linked to bullying and shaming facilitated by social media platforms, including platforms such as as ask.fm and NGL (Not Gonna Lie), which were designed explicitly to encourage users to anonymously broadcast their thoughts about other people." (*The Anxious Generation*, J. Haidt, p. 160)

This connection however is not a condemnation of screen use rather its use as a bullying platform designed to amplify the effects of what used to be a word of mouth affair. The fact that youth are more vulnerable to psychogenic illnesses is well known and this contributes to the effect of screen time on youthful depression some of which may lead to suicide in the more genetically and environmentally vulnerable.

"When adolescents moved onto image-based social media platforms, especially video-oriented platforms such as You-Tube and later Tik Tok, they hooked themselves up in a way that facilitated the transmission of psychogenic illnesses." (*The Anxious Generation*, p 162.)

In other words the use of smart phones amplified what was already a well known phenomenon, that of vulnerability to infirmity induced by environmental circumstances. In fact there are instances in which physical illnesses exploded under the influence of social media stars who also had the disease in a copycat type of format.

"A group of German psychiatrists… noted a sudden increase in young people showing up at clinics claiming to have Tourette's syndrome… But the German psychiatrists could see that almost none of these patents really had tourette's." (*The Anxious Generation*, p. 163).

In fact it was found that most of these cases were patients mimicking a single German influencer who made a point of demonstrating his Tourette's to others. Haidt notes a rise in feelings of loneliness and lack of close friends that coincided with the onset of 'smart' cell phone use. Yet not one reference is made in his book to the decline in birth rates. He admits that the downturn in sexual activity and alcohol use started much earlier than the rise of cell phones.

"As you can see, the downturn in these activities did *not* start in the early 2010's; it started back in the 1990's and early 2000's." (*The Anxious Generation,* p. 104.)

So, waffling of behaviors that one might label "evolution related" including reproduction and sexual activity as a whole was not triggered by smart phone use rather has been ongoing. One cannot explain the birth rate deflation by cell phone use, rather by the waning of evolution's mandates, the deflation of the crucible of evolution's dictums due to lack of predation which has been in smackdown since the end of WW11. Of course evolutionary related behaviors including nesting, marriage, starting a home suitable for child rearing and arranging one's existence around this evolutionarily devoted mantra.

Without that we are like gulls adrift in an agitated sea, helpless, easily victimized. No wonder anxiety, depression and suicide is going up; that lack of direction alone is a destabilizing neurosis. Without such a blueprint to follow, a yellow brick road so to speak, one is plagued with indecisions which may lead in and of themselves to questioning oner's gender assignment, purpose in life, validity and actual self importance. Drug use, of course, will magnify and complicate these matters. So let us not oversimplify and blame a complex situation on the use of social media, there is something deeper going on and it deserves our attention.

The impulse to ban cell phones in schools might perhaps have some advantages, yet is that going to increase birth rates, encourage youth to engage in evolutionary behaviors, or end the scourge of increased suicidal thinking that gnaws at our youth? I think not, simply because the problem is deeper, more complex than just one issue that has risen recently. This state of affairs has been ongoing for a long time, interrupted partially by world wars which in themselves were substitute predators in which young men were called to risk their lives to 'save the world'.

And of course the 'war to end all wars', WW1, did no such thing since we as animals have introjected the death instinct within us, as fervently as animals but with the golden rule hovering over us like the sword of Damocles should we disregard it. Entropy has been implanted in our brains by its bargain with evolution when plants slimed over to animal existences. As evolution wanes the door swings wide for entropy's mischief to surge, although that is not necessarily the outcome. We can see the ongoing efforts of our civilized way of life in this universe to be in control of our urge to kill and consume lower animals that has been relegated to chicken farms and cattle slaughter houses. Yet old man entropy creeps back into our action and our thoughts routinely.

"The number of 18-year olds who binge drink has been cut in half since the early 1980's..." (*iGEN,* J. Twenge, p37, with accompanying graph showing that alcohol use has been declining at least since the year 2000 at least in high school and young adults)

This beneficial and safe behavior improvement has been going on long before cell phones dotted young lives and, if anything, may have exacerbated a trend. By focusing in on 'evolutionary behavior' or that which is snugly intertwined with reproduction, we start to notice trends downward long before cell phone use. Party going among 8th to 12th graders has been declining since about the year 2000 as well. (See graph p. 70, *iGEN*)

The percentage of 8th to 12th graders who get together with friends daily or nearly every day has been plummeting since around the early 1990's and is therefore at most only worsened by the smart phone plague. (*iGEN,* p. 72) Certainly internet use exposes one to greater possibility of being cyber bullied, although bullying has been going on for as long as there have been people. So, while smart phone use has its advantages, it can increase the absolute risk time wise of crummy experiences. It can also allow for contact with peers even if under quarantine as we saw during the pandemic around 2019 and 2020. Suicide is the third leading cause of death among high school students (see National Trends in Suicidal Thoughts and Suicide Attempts Among High School Students in the United States, Bommersbach, et al, American Journal of Psychiatry, July 2025, p 639-659) but can we really blame this on cell phone use? Maybe in terms of making an ongoing trend worse, but not in being the sole cause. Something deeper is afoot, a vein of undercurrent that supersedes this type of communication behavior, but can all be subsumed under the womb of 'anti-evolutionary behavior'.

Men are not left unscathed by evolution's demise. They are the victim of role disintegration and as such are floundering in some ways more than women. "For the last few thousand years men could essentially describe their role in four words: "providing for my family." (*Of Boys and* Men, R. Reeves, p. 33) I would say that this extends back millions of years as the poor caveman scraped out an existence for himself and his tiny clan. "A good husband and father was one who provided for his family, which consisted of himself, his wife or partner and their children." (*Of Boys and Men,* p.33) Reeves goes on to say, "The traditional family was an effective social institution because it made both men and women necessary." (*Of Boys and Men,* p. 33).

With the waffling of evolutionary procreative roles, men are scrambling for direction. Evolution views our lives quite simplistically: survive, reproduce, die. That about sums it up. Remember that we were animals for about seven million years or so, scrambling to survive under intense pressure, barely making it thirty years or so, and hopefully providing well enough to give our offspring a chance to survive as well. Roles were unquestioned, since we had no ability to think, and were crisply defined, man the hunter/gatherer provider, the woman the reproductive capsule and caretaker while pop ran around endangering himself foraging for food. As evolution melts, we see men in roles less well defined, not always in the position of family leader, earning less than their wives, at times serving as primary child rearer, and shying away from marriage altogether. "But his bedrock duty was that of all the fathers of his generation: breadwinner… marriage bound women to men, but also men to women, and thereby to children." (*Of Boys and Men,* p. 34)

Reeves goes on to say that women are now the main breadwinner in 41% of U.S. households, and that about 40% of births in the U.S. are out of wedlock, whereas in 1970 this percentage was just 11. (p. 35) Men are no longer in the instinctual evolutionary program of our forebears, and even our recent relatives. But with the waning of mother E, this is disintegrating. The well defined given necessities of survival in a predatory intensity unrivaled in modern life, are no longer operative and this is creating indecisive men and women who struggle to understand who and what they are, a topic not questioned by Homo sapiens the animal. "Many men are feeling dislocated. Their fathers and grandfathers had a pretty clear path to follow: work, wife, kids. But what now?" None of this indecision was created by cell phone use, but by the loss of compass previously provided to us human animals and now dissolving into a haze of predator-less existence in which expectation of survival is a given. "Dench worried that without the traditional provider role, men would "struggle to get full acceptance and risk anomie and short-termism." (*Of Boys and Men*, p 37.)

This is another direct result of the lack of predation we experience in modern life which has put evolution's guiding hand into a sling. It has also put modern Homo sapiens into the position of questioning things that were a given for the vast percentage of our existence on earth. We are seeing the fallout of our success in eliminating the predatory milieu that nurtured and challenged us for millions of years. "Wifeless men, by contrast, are often a mess. Compared to married men their health is worse, their employment rates are lower, and their social networks are weaker." (*Of Boys and Men*, p. 39.) He goes on to say that, "As well as being good for children, a stronger role for fathers would provide many men with a powerful extra source of meaning and purposes in their lives." (*Of Boys and Men,* p. 40)

Something called "deaths of despair" have been increasing since around the year 2000, presumably related to economic disparity, but a host of fractured possibilities present themselves as fomenters of this phenomenon. (See, "*The Upswing*" by R. Putnam, p. 43) This statistic is in march step with suicide increases especially in the young, and the onset of this upswing around 2000 precedes the onset of mass smart phone indulgence. Despair as a natural phenomenon may itself easily be explained by the de-tethering from evolution's mandate, its denatured scent that used to give us marching orders for millions of years before the onset of language or civilizations. Lacking in predatory intensity, the soul may be experiencing compass-less ambiguity, an overt lack of forward spring which disorients, depresses and dehooks humanity from its designated arrow.

Boys and men are in trouble. they are less successful than they used to be, attend college less than women, and are less likely to be valedictorians. In a quote from economist Mark Aguiar in "*Dopamine Nation*" we learn that younger men have had a decline in work hours and a shift towards video gaming and other internet activities. (p. 106-107, *Dopamine Nation,* A. Lembke).

"The mechanization of agriculture, manufacturing, domestic chores, and many other previously time-consuming, labor-intensive jobs has reduced the number of hours per day people spend working, leaving more time for leisure." (p. 105, *Dopamine Nation)* In fact we have never had so much leisure time, compared to the cave man who had essentially minimal time free of dangerous predators, and endless threats to their existence. In the United States just before the civil war the average laborer worked a six and a half day per week, ten to 12 hours per day, fifty one week per year schedule. (p. 105-6, *Dopamine Nation*) This avalanche of free time has left men in particular adrift and sucked into the world of internet browsing.

"By 2019 the gender gap in bachelor awards was 15 points wider than in 1972-but the other way around." (*Of Boys and Men*, R. Reeves, p 3.). In short women surged ahead of men in college graduation. Women outperform ment in the English Language Arts Test (p. 6, *Of Boys and Men*). In Finland 20% of girls are at the highest reading level compared to 9% of boys. (p. 5, *Of Boys and Men*) and Finnish girls outperform boys in science and math. Boys are less likely than girls to graduate high school. (p. 7, *Of Boys and Men*)

At the same time we are hearing that young women are suffering even greater increases in depression than men. One could conclude that all youth in industrialized nations are suffering. So what's going on here? Well, let's look at the persuasive influence of evolution on our behavior. One could rightly say that this is the first time in the history of protoplasm that organisms have not had to struggle to survive and had eons of disposable time. In caveman times any free time was spent fulfilling the mandate of evolution to procreate. This meant that if an attractive, suitable mate appeared on the horizon the effort was made to exchange germ cells and produce an offspring, one way or another. This behavior is hard wired into every animal on earth and is the guiding mantra of behavior other than hunter/gatherer instincts. We are not following this age old commandment.

Why? Because evolution is waning and the usual male role of bread winner and provider for the future family is diluted and no longer the main game. This leaves young women 'unattended to' so to speak, and their role in the future world is indeterminate. Without active male pursuit they are left dangling in indecisiveness, confused about their own path as much as the under performing, role detached men. "In 1970 most mothers were not in paid work-today, almost three out of four are." (p. 29, *Of Boys and Men*) So men are now in the position of having lost their role as providers, hunter, gatherers and have a ready substitute occupation, that of internet troll. And this 'job' releases dopamine. "The world now offers a full complement of digital drugs that didn't exist before, or if they did exist they now exist on digital platforms that have exponentially increased their potency and availability." (p. 23, *Dopamine Nation)*

"*But Natural Selection, as we shall hereafter see, is a power incessantly ready for action, and is immeasurably superior to man's feeble efforts, as the works of Nature are to those of Art.*" Charles Darwin.

Certainly the progression of a single celled organism to a Homo sapiens was a monumental feat that no human could, at this moment in time, equal. It took billions of years to accomplish, nevertheless, it was a superlative achievement, and the question remains, where does evolution go from here? Since Evolution borrows its Pavlovian dictates by enlisting dopamine's enduring pleasure reward system, if we start seeing this carrot fail, we know evolution is in trouble. And we are. Younger people are having less sex. "Even iGen'ers who do reach these (adult) milestones during high school are doing so at older ages than in previous generations. That includes both the pleasures of adulthood, such as sex and alcohol, and the responsibilities of adulthood, such as working and driving. For good or for ill, iGen teens are not in a hurry to grow up. Eighteen year olds now look like 14-year-olds once did and 14-year-olds like 10or 12-year olds." (*iGen*, p. 40, J. Twenge) Implicit in evolution's mandate is procreation, and nesting behavior is at the gut of it.

So the 'sinful' failings of teen angst are now being ignored and put off until a later age which then adds to the decrease in birth rates. Evolution is limping if the hard wired mandate of reproduction is now faltering. It was dopamine, in essence, that did battle with entropy in that it was the crystal carrot that kept animals on the right path toward creating more of themselves. Without dopamine animals might possibly have chosen to wallow in sloth, avoid the 'perils' of mating behavior and vanish from the face of mother earth. It was evolution's triumph that kicked entropy's desires in the cajones and replaced them with animal yearning, base, hormonal actions. Without them the whole crapshoot would have come to a screeching, tragic halt. We are now in the midst of, or at least the bare beginnings of this untimely process. And with evolution's kryptonite-like waning, entropy is grinning ear to ear.

What evidence do we see of entropy's surging influence, you might ask? Well, consider the state of western civilization which is marked not by harmony but by intense rowdy political ardor, bordering on physical violence. Certainly in the United States we are split right down the middle, the two factions of political chaos poking and ribbing each other mercilessly to the point of assassinations, mass murders, reputational sabotage and the like that seems to know no bounds. There are few politicians who make a pretense of nurturing unity, a goal that is so far out of reach that it is considered laughable. The two political factions make fun of each other's weaknesses and foibles. Meanwhile, youth depression, anxiety and suicide surges, and no leader seems to rally around the cause of youth, nor do they get the connection between entropy's surge and the youthful ennui. There appears to be no major political movement that focuses on reunification of the shattered populace, all of which must be viewed in the context of youthful depression, declining birth rates, retreat from usual nesting roles, delay in growing comfortably into adult ways and possibly parental over protectionism.

In fact, "By 2018, almost half of Democratic parents and a third of Republican parents had such concerns (that their child might marry someone from the opposite political party)" (p. 148, *Adrift*, S. Galloway.) Also, "Young people in America are living with their parents at rates not seen since the 1940's." (p. 139, *Adrift,* S. Galloway) "We are also divided against ourselves, seeing enemies rather than adversaries in our politics." (p. 139, *Adrift*). "This feeds a vicious cycle: as enemies, we cannot negotiate in good faith, and our government accomplishes nothing. Which further undermines our faith in government and fuels our hatred for our opponents." (p. 139, *Adrift*) All of which plays into the hands of entropy. "My central claim in this book is that these two trends*overprotection in the real world and underprotection in the virtual world*are the major reasons why children born after 1995 became the anxious generation." (p. 9, *The Anxious Generation,* J. Haidt.) Such over protectionism may play into the hands of feeling depressed as one's parents no longer give kids the impression that their children are adult enough to protect and care for themselves, leading to a sense of inadequacy. This plays into the hands of our old enemy entropy as, if an entire generation is not adult, they are not ready to carry out evolution's howling mandate to thrive and reproduce.

THE PERIL TO CIVILIZATION

It is the very civilization that we occupy that dealt a crotch shot blow to entropy in the first place. As I've said previously we've moved from the jungle to the disco, in a short span of 50,000 years or less. To evolution the benefits of civilization are monolithic, and entropy has been shuffled into a corner by its magnificence. It is within the confines of civilized society that we managed to neutralize the vast majority of heinous predators that plagued us, a momentous feat that has, secondarily, weakened the very champion that promoted it, evolution.

So let's examine the structures of civilization that bows entropy's desires into smithereens. First of all, it removed the daily necessity of scrounging around for nutrition, a task that often burned more calories than it garnered. Poor cave guy woke up each morning with the task of dredging up food and water for himself and his little family. Covering his feet with slices of animal leather, he'd grab his spear and head out into the gruesome fishbowl of potential catastrophes and begin his search, either for roots, seeds, over ripe fruits or small animals to murder dissect and fire roast. No piece of cake, this assignment exposed him to a myriad of dangers, all of which had lethal potential. But, once civilization coalesced that chore was given to specialized populations and included agriculture and raising cattle, sheep, or chickens to slaughter for mass consumption. As entropy favors the return of organic matter to inorganic, this shifted the burden of demise to food products, not us cave dwelling dopes.

And of course, the jungle is a master of chaos, entropy's buddy, in which civilization countered with organization, routine and purpose. Our houses are decked in neat little rows, our skyscrapers precise rectangles that beam skyward, our lives carved up into 9 to 5 routines. All of this bore the earmark of obsessive compulsiveness and it is my theory that obsessive compulsives were the foundations of society in that they facilitated the march from jungle chaos to Levittown's order. We eat our three meals daily, follow a precise work schedule and go to sleep around the same time frame and we are easily invested in this mode of existence. Entropy thrives in chaos, withers in organization and we have inculcated our society with organized patterns of living that become, if not monotonous, a guidepost for behavioral decisions.

And of course, a little thing called morality was implicit in the concretization of society. The golden rule, ten commandments and the abandonment of the death instinct were a nifty part of civilization's bargain. Of course that wavelength has not always been successful and we have seen multiple incidences of genocide, holocausts, and widespread murder. These were entropy's attempts to render society meaningless and we are seeing such behaviors currently and will always see them. Yet, the rise of jurisprudence was another blow to entropy's lustful desires and we have a well established modus of punishment for transgressions. All of these civilizational accretions dealt blows to the entropic chaotic jungle habitat, dragging us from jungle terror to organized manifest destiny. Religion played its part in this steam bath of morality as did something Freud labeled the superego, a little brainiac that screams foul when we even think of slicing away at the rules, not holding the door for the lady with the cane, or sabotaging our co-worker with lies and irritations.

So the blows dealt to our old fiend entropy were far and overarching, slamming the bugger into submission. As Freud said he who first hurled epithets instead of stones was the founder of civilization. But, as entropy's foe, it is also entropy's most blatant target and we all must be careful to participate in its survival. If civilization is one of entropy's greatest bludgeoners then the opposite it also true, especially since we all struggle with the hard wired mandate to kill and devour other animals, an impulse that turns swiftly into genocidal rants and homicidal raving. And let us not forget that civilization itself would not have appeared at all without the beneficent magic of language, as it was language that gave us reality testing in the first place. And the latter is again, very new in the stream of ongoing existence of Homo sapiens. If you lay three yardsticks end to end, each representing 2 million years so a total of six million, language has been around for less than the last inch. And language radically altered the trajectory of our minds and as such, not everyone is on board with its munificence. Those least on board we call mentally ill (see my first book, "*Footprints of Schizophrenia: the Evolutionary Roots of Mental Illness* ") Language brought us to the shores of rationality and it is just this quality that dissolves in mental infirmities.

"*That which distinguishes man from the lower animals is not the understanding of articulate language, but his power of forming general concepts and of using language as a means of reasoning...*" Charles Darwin, *The Descent of Man*, Chapter 111

"*The replacement of the power of the individual by the power of a community constitutes the decisive step of civilization.... This replacement of the pleasure principle by the reality principle... is a step of momentous significance.*" Sigmund Freud, *The Standard Edition of the Complete Psychological Works of Sigmund Freud*, Vol. 21, p. 89

And so it was that language, birthed a mere 50,000 years ago, brought us to the shores of civilization. Prior to language, for some 7 millions years or so, man's thought process was primitive, and consisted of unrealistic wishes, fears and desires. The gradual accrual of language bestowed upon mankind the ability to reason, which directly led to Homo sapiens wiping out all the other species of Homo. This propensity for realistic thinking, deductive reasoning and contemplation is so new that not everyone is on board and those least connected to the process we call mentally ill which is why I have said that mental illness did not exist 50,000 years ago and will not exist perhaps 20,000 years hence, if mankind survives that long. But it was this ability to think logically that led directly to the assumption that forming civilizations was crystal clearly a survival advantage, and received evolution's gracious nod. So along with their assignment to form communities came the mandate to restrain our most basic instincts in the service of communal living, to institute the golden rule, and uphold a measure of restraint.

So one might fancifully say that once we adopted language our brain function changed dramatically, so much so that not everyone is yet on board with the process. And such a mega transformation in thinking must have accompanying neuro-chemical changes. Clearly, when schizophrenics, for example, collapse into madness, dopamine is involved in the manner of a surge or expansion which requires the blockage of its receptors to quell successfully. We are equally aware that the administration of dopamine surging chemicals such as the amphetamines can elicit a psychosis, a regression in thinking that is exactly similar to schizophrenic thought.

It is somewhere in the region of a dopaminergic excess that a return to primitivity of thought lies and it wouldn't be so far fetched to assume that with language's blessing of Sherlock Holmes' like reasoning is involved a suppression or restraint of dopamine that fulminates logic and delivers us to the shores of reason. This gradual process of dopaminergic binding, or suppression happens over time in the foggy storm of adolescence and is crucial to the development of sound mind and coordinated bodily movement as there are tracts in the brain, dopaminergic ones that involve movement, aka the nigrostriatal tract. This is not the tract that is involved in reasoning, which generally are considered the meso-limbic, meso-cortical tracts, but these and the nigro-striatal are cousins and while one is being honed by dopamine suppression, the others are as well.

We gradually accrue coordinated movement and realistic thinking over the same time frame of adolescent growth and we note a connection between the two. In fact, grip strength, which has been considered a global indicator of mental and physical soundness is decreased in early psychotic youth. (Grip Strength as a Marker of Resting-State Network Integrity and Well-Being in Early Psychosis, Ward, Beerman,et al; American Journal of Psychiatry, 182:9, September, 2025.) As such it reflects a diminishment in coordination in such youth exacerbated no doubt by the dopaminergic surge which accompanies the return to primitive thinking typical of schizophrenics. We then observe that schizophrenics are simply people who have regressed to the type of thinking we had before language as if this recent evolutionary development didn't apply to them. They in fact are returning to a moment in time before the recent advent of language, the seven million year evolutionary process that we evolved with mentally. And seven million has certainly the advantage of momentum over a mere 50,000 year linguistic span.

But we must always consider poor entropy's point of view, like a noisy stepchild who demands constant attention. From her point of view our tip toe toward the reality principle was just another death blow, orchestrated by her arch enemy evolution which reveled in the adoption of realistic thinking. It was the so called reality principle that got us to civilization and since we were able to conceptualize in a most attentive and complex way, entropy was dealt a cojone crush unlike any other. Now one could rightly surmise that the brain tissue of a Homo sapiens is the most ANTROPIC substance in the universe with its advanced complexity, the opposite of entropy's lust for chaos. WE have achieved greatness and wiped out 90% of the predators that tortured us in the evolutionary jungle we grew up in including the other species of Homo that grumbled around the jungle like the erstwhile Neanderthals. We have so neutralized those predators that evolution is beginning to fade into insignificance and is lifting like a canvas sail in a windless sea.

But the point to be emphasizing is that mental illness itself is a boon to entropy as it reverses the contemplative complexity of rational thinking. Even the non psychotic brain infirmities including major depression and bipolar disorder can be considered regressive in process of thought and both improve with chemicals that set up barriers to dopamine. Even the anxiety disorders are likely to improve with dopamine barriers set up by our scientific ardor. We attack problems with our razor sharp reality principled brains and often succeed in eliminating or at least mollifying them, including mental malady's that are dopamine related and evolutionarily induced byproducts of recent linguistic challenges.

So we are in a situation where we have suffered from success in that the very effort of civilized existence has put an end to evolution's greatness and we are exhuming the fallout from this beneficent ardor in terms of social dissonance and birth rate droop. In short we are too smart for our own good and thus note role confusion, indecision and a pulling away from evolution's greatest mandate: to reproduce. The battle between entropy and evolution, in conjunction with antropy, has been won and evolution, instead of kicking up its heels and whooping is now sitting in a corner and watching the dance from afar. And that dance is getting discombobulated big time.

Yet this is not to say that entropy is winning but that in its defeat it is poised to wreak havoc on a dismantled system. Entropy is a winner in its constant return of organic material to the inorganic including the death of thousands of people daily, not to mention other animals and plant life. And in our new role as thinkers we've dealt another blow to entropy who's only recourse is to revel in the mental illnesses that thought interference brings forth. Thus entropy's victories are in returning the organic to inorganic, and replacing the reality principle with something lesser, call it the unreality thrust as manifested in the mentally ill. Even major depression could be called a psychosis, perhaps a behavioral one, in that the behavior of seriously depressed individuals isn't rational, rather hovering around a sense of hibernation and anergic paralysis. Bipolar disorder clearly has psychotic tones in the grandiose master of their decision makings that often lead the manic into sticky thickets.

So entropy has its locus of revery in death and mental illness and can pat itself on the back for such achievements. But with the help of DNA, evolution has trounced entropy over the long hall, in fact, time, a facet of the conflict between these two behemoths, is on the side of evolution which has succeeded in creating the master race called Homo sapiens and these godlike animals have skyrocketed into the heavenly domain of the reality principle which has crushed entropy and evolution both.

WAS LANGUAGE AN ACCIDENT?

There is much debate about that most complex of human phenomena, speech, language and its bastard child thought. Did evolution plan for such a thing, and did it even set its sights on the miasma of complexity that is language or did it arise as a pure and simple accident? Personally I believe it is the latter, evolution never fixing its ride on such a monumental screw up, the result of brains and the ability to use symbol formation, the soul of blabber. Things fulminated along the trajectory of overall fitness, including brain power and this led to the gimmick of language in only one version of the genus Homo, the smart ass sapiens. And, we ran with it, eliminating the rest of the Homo crew, fanning out across the globe and spotting opportunity in the form of civilizations and all that tagged along with them. In his book, "*The Truth About Language*" Corballis, quotes the psychologist David Premack who says,

"Human language is an embarrassment for evolutionary theory because it is vastly more powerful than one can account for in terms of selective fitness." (p. 28) I disagree with this simply because given the exact type of brain wiring that we have, the asset of symbol formation could be attained by accrual, and we had the proper accoutrements of vocal variability to 26 sounds or more, and proper hearing, which Neanderthals apparently lacked, explaining their cruddy communicative skills, a drawback that blitzed their future options. Further on Corballis says, "Chomsky and many others have held to the notion that language must have arisen uniquely, and suddenly in our species." (p. 29) I agree with Chomsky on this point and believe that given the unique combo of sapiens talents we ran with language and it jet packed us into wild success. Corballis goes on to say, "The effect of the mental tsunami that was to come was to create not only the languages that we speak or sign but an entirely new basis of thought, available only to humans." (p. 29) He goes on to say, "...it was really only a kind of side effect of this that also allowed us to express our thoughts in words, a miracle indeed of biblical proportions." (p. 29-30) Quoting Chomsky again he says, " Perhaps it was an automatic consequence of absolute brain size... or perhaps some minor chance mutation." (p. 30)

Also, "Within some small group from which we are all descended a rewiring of the brain took place in some individual, call him Prometheus... applying to concepts with intricate (and little understood) properties." I think it makes perfect sense that language popped up once our brains reached a certain threshold of uniqueness and was supported by our ability to speak various noises and hear intricate nuances. Us Homo sapiens were special and now we rule the world having trounced entropy with this new, cool, platform of communicative thought.

In his book, "*How Language Began: The Story of Humanity's Greatest Invention*" Daniel Everett states that "... language emerges gradually from indexes (items that represent things they are physically connected to, such as a footprint to an animal) to icons (things that physically resemble the things they are used to represent, such as a portrait for the real person) and finally by creating symbols (conventional ways of representing meaning that are largely arbitrary." (p. 6-7) This process ultimately led to grammar and more complex symbols. He also says, "…human communities *created* symbols, grammar and language where there had been none before" (p. xviii) Furthermore he goes on to say that, "The picture of the brain that is emerging here, then, is of a cognitively non-modular organ with no congenitally specialized tissue for language (or cooking or guitar playing)." (p.159) Thus language arose in a brain unprepared for it, and not at all beefed up to receive it but the fact is that it was evolutionarily advanced enough to handle it and once it lumbered downhill, there was no stopping it, and evolution rejoiced in its fateful appearance.

But there's more. For language, speech, blabber, once nested into our global zeitgeist was the single most antropic (anti-entropic) event in history, not just of the world, but of the universe. And, as I've said, life exists to defy entropy, a rule immutable in its implications. In what way then did speaking defy entropy and what were the consequences of this catastrophic blip? Well, lets take a craggy step back a minute and examine our caveman friend. He had no ability to think and his form of understanding was both primitive and mystical. He probably had some vague notion of a powerful God or inimitable force that caused stuff to just happen. He carved primitive petroglyphs into carbon crusted rocks much like a 5 year old child would today. They look very much akin to infantile scribbling. He could not reason, could communicate his needs only sparsely and had no way of really understanding his peers.

The aftermath of linguistic magic was a hell bent complexity of thinking, a Sherlock Holmes-ian ability to decipher truth from falsehood and an ability to test concepts with a scientific method to subject hypothesis to the crucible of reality. Freud's reality principle became the mantra of the day and primitivity of thought whisked away with adolescence and schooling. Learning was an intrinsic blast of civilization that fixed the transition from primitive to complex, childlike to adult, disorganized to organized thinking. And it was the latter that trounced entropy into submission since our old enemy savors chaotic disorganization over intense organized contemplation any day of the week or year. Yes, it was the progression from kiddy thought to mature, adulthood type mulling that flicked a booger into the face of entropy. Yup, we spit on the old boy.

The consequences of this were not just ginormous but megalithic. (Wow, my spell checker didn't object to those words!) It was, I attest, the earthquake of entropic defiance that put us so far ahead of any other living being that we skyrocketed to our current position as lead dog in the global habitat, head honcho extraordinaire that has fanned out across the earth to scratch the eight billion strong mark. I will assert that the Homo sapiens brain is the the most antropic substance in the universe, whose power to defy entropy is unmatched and thus has led to our incomparable success. But, ever watchful for an in, a tricky back bite of its own, entropy has found a way to try to dismantle that complexity of thought. It has done so by its seductive tongue lashing toward mental illness that degrades adult thinking into something less, and in the case of schizophrenia, all the way back to a time before language when our thought process was primitive and magical. It is a thinking style reminiscent of caveman superstition and God like legerdemain, childlike in its fallacy.

So, what entropy has angled its efforts toward is an ability to dilute adult thought into something less, call it primitivity, that then results in a mental illness which is less of an insult to it. And some 20% of the population has some sort of mental illness. Yet I look forward to a time when these infirmities are gone, as we learn in totality to accept the changes wrought by this new phenomenon called language. It is so new that not all of us have brains that are completely and utterly on board with it. And that, in a nut shell explains the modus of mental illness creation, a regression to entropically sanctioned mentality that is a step back from adult, reality testing thinking. My prediction is that in some 20,000 years or so there will be no mental illness, just as there was none 50,000 years ago before language, as it takes a misfire of the linguistic rules to result in a mental infirmity.

And as I have explained before, this is all part and parcel of the little chemical we have labeled dopamine. The hoary crux of mental illness is the failure to lock dopamine down on a permanent basis, and instead, have it resurge in a fashion disturbing to the adult, modern complexity of thought most of us are used to. And, as also previously noted, dopamine and acetylcholine are sister neurotransmitters that seesaw back and forth. If one surges, the other backs down, and vice versa. Is it not surprising then, that in this new biochemical universe in which we find ourselves, that the two most common mental infirmities of aging involve either dopamine deficiency (Parkinsons) or acetylcholinergic deficiency (Alzheimer's)? No, it is not, not if you examine, as we just have, the biochemical implications of this new contemplative situation language has so recently bestowed upon us. Fancy that.

And now we are in the cat bird seat position to view language for what it is… the ultimate defiance of entropy. In short, the trajectory of evolution stayed true to its destiny. In giving entropy the bitch slap it deserved on a mammoth scale, it executed the demands of its original manifestation. The original sin was DNA, that wiry molecule that slipped up intermittently to bestow upon us mutations, those necessary glitches that were a blessing to evolution. Without mutations evolution goes nowhere, so our wily momma E trounced entropy, the lover of disharmony and screw ups, at its own game by taking advantage of the DNA fuck ups (initiated by entropy) to further its cause of moving organic tissue down the evolutionary line.

Of course, protoplasm defies entropy itself in its complexity, energy, self preservative and reproductive habits, all anti-entropic, or antropic blips that set up a firm boundary between entropy and antropy. Thus, momma E was able to move organic tissue down the line of complexity from the passivity of flora to the activity of fauna with its reproductive bent and arduous task of killing and eating other animals. So we see evolution careening from less to greater complexity, more antropy, and giving entropy the ongoing nut kneeing it deserves. This 'golden road' or yellow brick star search led momma E to the erstwhile Homo sapiens, which seemed to be its highest pinpoint of achievement. Then shit happened, in the form of language and a whole new era of antropy asserted itself with the human brain being the damnedest insult to old brother entropy yet devised, all because Homo sapiens' brains and vocal chords and ears were capable of symbol formation on a mega scale. So while language was not planned it is entirely consistent with momma E's deadly duel with entropy and in fact trounced the old boy on a scale and paradigm beyond anything E had even imagined possible.

We can imagine language then as the ultimate entropic mother fucker, a hepcat loop of antropic wonder that took us and only us sapiens to another plain altogether. So the first several million years of us hominins, or human-like animals, followed the typical yellow brick road down evolutionary improvements, countering entropy through the usual realm of mutations. But then, BOOM, all hell broke loose which is why I've said that the human brain is the most antropic substance in the universe. Nothing like it has been discovered anywhere, not little green men, or terroristic alien invaders have been earmarked by roving TV cameras or other solid patterns of evidence.

And we are seeing another such mega-leap now in the form of artificial intelligence which takes contemplation to a new level and will undoubtedly rule us one day as its ability to trounce entropy far exceeds ours. In fact it takes the linguistic advocacy of reality testing to new heights and thus uses our facility for contemplation in spades, trouncing the entropic yearning for primitivity of thought, simplicity and disorganization as opposed to hyper organized thinking of our AI bot friends, if indeed they truly are amigos.

But another factor comes into play in the saga of blabber, speech and linguistic envelopment. There is a motor tract in the old brain, the nigro-striatal, which deals exclusively with movement, coordination and daily motion including walking, running, lifting, grabbing and fondling. The chemical players in this utterly basic tract of course are our old friends dopamine and acetylcholine. So when the unfortunate Parkinsonism patient starts leeching dopamine, acetylcholine surges and he ends up with tremor, shuffling gait, stretched facial muscles that appear as if his face is masked, etc. And, of course, there is often a gradual onset of dementia that adds to the coordination problem. This unfortunate malady is treated with none other than our friend dopamine in the form of l-dopa which has better entry into the stomach absorption system and the brain itself. Of course this chemical form of dopamine is not just administered into the nigro-striatal tract, it zooms around the whole brain and body and is therefore a weakly directed missile.

And as we stumble forth from toddler to teen we mold this nigro-striatal tract by gradually taming dopamine and allowing a balance of it with acetylcholine, resulting in a honing of coordinated movements with practice over time. Thus we see kids engaging in repetitive movement over and over to skiff their clunky skills into finely lathed intentions that allow for speed, endurance, and accuracy in throwing a baseball, putting a golf ball, or hoisting a grocery bag from the trunk of mom's old '89 Chevy. It is a bungle of **dopamine binding** in balance with acetylcholine that results over years in our ability to move around effectively.

But, other dopamine tracts, specifically the meso-limbic and the meso-cortical were unable to engage in the dopa dance at all, or, in the past were not capable of engaging in this gyration of dopamine binding, that is, NOT UNTIL LANGUAGE CAME ALONG. And, oddly enough, these two tracts are only peripherally engaged in movement, but are crucially invested int THINKING, IDEATION, DEDUCTIVE REASONING. So, what is all this muck a muck I'm stirring around here. TWO TRACTS IN OUR BRAINS WERE SIMPLY WAITING AROUND FOR SOMETHING TO ENGAGE THEM IN THE DOPA DANCE! They bided their little time patiently for millions of years for language to appear at which time they became, just like the nigro-striatal tract, dopamine binders in the context of acetylcholine which allows for brute contemplation, rationality, the reality principle! You get the idea, that prior to language there was no way for these tracts to exercise their unique contemplative muscularity.

They were simply waiting (for some seven million years) for something like speech and blabber to ignite their unique mulling abilities. So, just as in the nigro-striatal tract (sorry for the technical terms) the meso-limbic and meso-cortical are able to tame the dopaminergic binding assignment with the help of words that form into concepts and that gradually, through our rough and tumble adolescent school daze, mold our noggins into thinking machines while the nigro-striatal tract (oh those names again) mold our muscles into football snagging machines. Thus we have two tracts in our brains that were essentially vacuous and idle until language made its thorny appearance and at that moment and that time only were ignited into contemplative stardom to launch us Homo sapiens into the global conquerors we are. Imagine that, they were just waiting for us to master the gelatinous mishegos of speech in order to fulfill their role as dopamine binding, reality testing, reasoning tracts in our brains.

And finally, would it surprise you if I told you that these are the exact tracts in our hyper exhumed crania that are involved in mental illness like schizophrenia? NO, it wouldn't, and the process involved in this mental breakdown hooks into the opposite of dopamine binding, namely surging of that silly chemical that has caused so much good and trouble when it goes awry. But of course it goes awry in some of us, because a process that is fifty thousand years old doesn't have the momentum of our six million year old brains, rather it is a spiffy new game and not every brain is coordinated into this dopamine binding in those two mentioned tracts… yet. I predict that in some 10 to 20,000 years every brain will have adjusted to this new assignment.

But its too early in the game to expect that now. Imagine if only 50,000 years ago we just learned how to move our muscles by binding dopamine in the nigro-striatal tract. There would still be several individuals who had not mastered this new feat, and were exhibiting signs of dopamine surge motorically. This is wholly analogous to what we see and label mental illness currently which is entirely due to the newness of this brain assignment and will vanish, I predict, some thousands of years hence. Or imagine if some oligarch insisted everyone learn to play chess. Some people would excel, some would sort of be adequate at it and others brains would not be capable of mastering the ordained task.

But one must wonder how two tracts in our craniums were so explicitly ready to accommodate the mystical conundrum that is language. The gray matter had evolved enough to manufacture these sites that were in essence just waiting for us to catch up. And once we did they pitched in full force, altering forever our relationship with reality. We became sophisticated dolts, now with the cuddly ability to divine truth from fiction, reality from fantasy, fact from wack. Was it pre-ordained that the Homo sapiens, the wise ones, would somehow grapple with something called speech, reason and cognition? One must, regretfully admit that there is something mystical about it, something God-like that was just waiting for language to arrive to bloop out like a missile and set us sapiens on fire. Now we own the world, largely due to language and the meso-limbic, meso-cortical tracts inside of us. Preordained, predestined? Who knows?

So now it's clear that we were the ones chosen to be ready to receive the potency of deductive reasoning and conscious thought and that this act of thinking does something special to us in the aforementioned tracts. Yet it is not the easiest task to sit and consciously think, just ponder something. Why should this blessing be so difficult to the point that some people avoid doing it at all and those of us who attend to this ungodly task have to force ourselves to do so? My theoretical explanation is that thinking is so antropic that entropy sets up barriers to it, as it does to anything that nixes its innate right to exist. When we think we are overcoming a natural resistance to trouncing entropy, and we are storing potential energy in a sense. Just as when we lift weights we are storing increased ability to cart all sorts of heavy objects around, something our cavemen ancestors needed to do, when we think we are suppressing dopamine, binding it as it were, and thus augmenting our innate ability to reason in a complex manner that gives the old finger to entropy. Thus it takes effort, the same umph that we give to lumping that 20 pounder upwards as our biceps strain and burn in healthy protest. One might also note that thinking is good for coordinated motion as well as mental acuity. What? You're saying that thinking improves one's ability to do motoric functions? Yep. I am saying that the dopaminergic suppression that is going on in the meso tracts also lends ability to suppress it in the old motoric nigro-striatal.

Thinking also has an effect on one's appearance, deepening affect. (Now you're finally convinced, this guy is nuts.) But, yes, thinking can do all that. And more, for it counters entropy directly and sharpens our ability to reason and gives us an advantage in just about any type of endeavor. Can it forestall dementia? That remains to be seen, but an activity that grows the neuronal system, probably by causing the secretion of internal brain growth chemicals like BDNF (brain derived neurotrophic factor) and VEGF (vascular endothelial growth factor) that are both like Miracle Grow for the brain tissue, can only help if not be protective, and these are chemicals that are lacking in the dementing brain which is experiencing more of an involution than an expansion. Like muscular tissue, gray matter enlarges with use and shrinks with neglect. Let us not neglect our brains, and we are also sticking it to old man entropy when we engage in the noble art of conscious thought.

In totality the old sourpuss entropy has suffered a myriad of blows since the advent of language including conscious thought, civilizations which nullify the death instinct to an extent and illuminate the golden rule, and have neutralized 90% of the predators we bumped into in the jungle therefore nullifying evolution's intensity, an effect unplanned for no doubt. For its part, ol' entropy has managed to inflict mental illness on many by drawing back on the hefty suppression of dopamine in the three tracts involved. And, of course, there are those lowlifes that insist on inflicting raucous misery upon the world at large and carry out heinous atrocities seemingly at will without the slightest remorse. As evolution fades we are likely to see more of these entropic atrocities, and likely to witness the fulminating mishegos of human conflictual interaction, something seen in western civilizations currently.

The degree of disharmony and discord far exceeds the mellifluous psalm of unity. The current wave of conflict globally warrants alarm and new orders of power seem to coalesce daily. To all of this we must add the grim uncertainty of artificial intelligence with its vast glittery potential for natural enhancement and slyly invasive ignominy that suggest a potential for entropy's joyful disgust to play out in spades. A looming spectre of mass unemployment adds uncertainty to the world at large when robotics have the potential to replace a mega glom of the workforce. Add to this the dire hit of global warming's tragedies including tornadoes, draughts, hurricanes, wildfires and list goes on. All of this multiplies the anxiety level within the global habitat of humanity. Cell phone use may multiply these concerns further by fulminating avoidance which, in the extreme, isolates us from our true selves. So within the vast panoply of potential gains that are language's bestowals and civilization's organized rescue, entropy has found its way into the fractured outlaw of our humanity so that it receives its satisfactory dollop of misery themed tragedies.

Daniel Paul Schreber was a respected judge in Germany around the turn of the century. He held a respected place in his profession and was considered a competent lawyer. Yet he was twice admitted to an asylum, under the care of a Dr. Flechsig. He was grossly psychotic at times and believed his physician was trying to murder him. He had many typical schizophrenic symptoms including voices. "The 'voices' manifest themselves in me as soft lisping noises sounding like distinct human words… I have never had a single moment in which I did not hear voices." (p. 224-225, Memoirs of My Nervous Illness, D. Schreber) As clever as he was he was able to rationalize away these phenomena not as mental illness but as divine interventions designed to torture him. At times his paranoia induced him to violence rambunctious enough to require sedation and being placed in a seclusion room. He rustled up elaborate explanations for the things he experienced and related them to divine rays sent by God to torture him. Schreber often required heavy sedation to sleep.

We have already given an explanation for this type of illness, regarding the suppression of dopamine leading to a capacity for reality testing in all of us that did not exist prior to the adoption of language a brief 50,000 years ago, which then uncouples and the dopaminergic binding that has resulted in rationality, a blow to entropy, reverses.

This undoing as it were should not be a surprise given the newness of the phenomenon of language and the radical transformation in our brains that resulted. Thus, not all of us are on board with this new mental assignment. Since thorazine, the first antipsychotic medication, was not invented until the 1950's, Schreber did not have access to this type of intervention. Yet he gradually improved and earned his release back into the community and his wife after several years of treatment. What is unusual about this case is not the symptomatology, which is fairly de riggour for schizophrenia, but the fact that Schreber jotted down a detailed memoir of his experiences as if he were being led through foreign land and needed to make notes on the bizarre safari, which had the quality of Alice in Wonderland.

It so happened that a neurologist, struggling to explain the craggy and bizarre symptoms of his numerous patients took an interest in these notes that were made public and took a shot at an explanation. How could one come to any grips with this set of wacky experiences that plagued a respected, rational judge?

Lacking knowledge of the biochemical soup that fomented psychotic phenomena, Sigmund Freud came up with a psychodynamic explanation for Schreber's dense psychotic mishegos, one that revolutionized our spotlight on paranoia. Schreber, he concluded, had a 'father complex' and this involved homosexual feelings toward his father who was a rigid, pseudo-masculine proponent of men exercising regularly to exhibit their masculine prowess. These homosexual impulses were turned around so that Schreber's father complex which consisted of a feeling of sexual love for the father, reversed to feeling the father loved him, but this being unacceptable as well, turned into father hating him. The father, ultimately substituted by the Dr. Flechsig, was then the villain who plotted all sorts of torture, and God himself who was trying to destroy Schreber's mind supposedly. This brilliant explanation so illuminated our understanding of paranoia that it remained the dominant theory for decades.

But now we know that there are biochemical factors involved and that these molecules were being used in a new way by humanity since the onset of linguistic mastery. But why should it be otherwise? Is is not obvious that a congressional change in our thought process, mystical as it might be, required neurochemical changes of a radical and deservedly preordained manner?

Obviously our crania carry out their functions with the orchestrated collaboration of molecules that traipse back and forth between various receptors and are then sucked back into the releasing entity. Long past the demise of Freud we concatenated our vision of the arrangement of atoms called dopamine and gradually defined its ubiquitous role in mental processes. It's clear that all mental machinations have a multilevel determination. Deductive reasoning, which was the birthright of linguistic competency all those thousands of years ago, can be viewed on a biochemical, developmental, and physical level in which entropy plays a role in its nascent presentation.

Clearly the rambunctious effect of linguistic perfection contained a kernel of intensifying complexity, an ability to master abstract ideation and a progression from childlike to adult reasoning. The essence of speech, symbol formation, goes through metamorphosis during the formative years arriving at what one might easily characterize as adult speech. "...speech is not genetically derivable from the vocalizations of animals or from the vocalizations of infants...maintaining the primary role of cognitive factors in the emergence of true speech..." (p. 14, "Symbol Formation", H. Werner and B. Kaplan) And if speech can undergo a process of development from primitive, childlike to adult complexity, it can undoubtedly undergo a regressive moment back to primitive under the right circumstances and under the influence of certain laws of physics that shall be nameless. Ahem, entropy. And this regressive tendency has, as we now know, a neurochemical basis and a developmental basis. "'The undifferentiatedness between the substance of words and the substance of things also underlies the way in which the schizophrenic manipulates, prunes, reshapes and alters linguistic forms." (p. 258, Symbol Formation)

As one example of a patient of M. Lorenz, Werner and Kaplan reported, "Attempting to give the meaning of *contentment,* the patient remarked: 'Well uh contentment, well the word contentment, having a book perhaps, perhaps your having a subject perhaps you have a chapter of reading, but when you come to the word 'men' you wonder if you should be content with men in your life, and then you get the letter t and you wonder if you should be content having tea by yourself or be content with having it with a group or so forth.'" Thus the patient is able to dissect words into parts and handle the interpretation of it that way, negating the true meaning of it altogether.

The totality of this vague mishegos is that there are several factors meddling in the duck soup of linguistic purity, but we can see clearly that a developmental progression from chaotic, disorganized to crisply organized contemplation is a transgression of our old enemy entropy and that this factor will attempt in its usual grotesqueness to devolve us from adult thinking to childlike mulling. And when it succeeds in the context of the newness of our mental playground, initiated by linguistic purity that jettisoned us lightyears above the gruff Neanderthals or the diminutive Naledi and Denisovans, craggy entropy succeeds in returning some 20% of us to a mental illness diagnosis.

Yet the principle that life itself, that most fuzzy of dyadic puzzles, has the purpose, and ONLY THE PURPOSE OF DEFYING ENTROPY, and when that fails we either return to inorganic matter or mental illness. And of course the latter is more likely to induce that heartfelt insult to evince suicide, and that wet kiss to entropy, murder. This expansion of our panoramic landscape of our current evolutionary context explains much and we can make use of this complex blueprint to fashion a sculpture of where and who we are and what is going wrong exactly with society eu currant. Entropy rejoices in the untimely return of organic matter, the prime insult to its mood, to inorganicity and we are now convinced that as evolution waffles, entropy will insinuate its crust paw into matters of societal intensity.

But you may still be wondering how all of this explains the modern phenomenon that we are observing coyly out of the corner of two eyes. The grand master of our existence, evolution with its partner in life, DNA, yearns for just a few things, survival and reproduction being the most important and flamboyant. As such behaviors that saunter assuredly down the yellow brick road of reproductive purity are evolutionarily bubbled up. The bifurcation of the sexes, which happened somewhere along the path of evolutionary development, necessitated a willingness to mingle on the part of each gender. Without that evolution would hit a brick wall and the whole crapshoot would flutter off a cliff while entropy would rejoice in the downfall of protoplasm. All the behaviors that swirl around reproductive interaction, dating, nesting, screwing, preparing to nurture your little kiddoosky, are highly rewarded by dopamine and hardwired into our behavioral vault for countless eons in order to insure the propagation of species, which, under the influence of mutations, guarantees the ongoing progress of beings into higher entities.

Yeah, we know all this pal, so what's the point? Clearly, if evolution is defunct as you so boldly assert, people wouldn't be dating or partying or using stuff that promotes socialization like alcohol or drugs and they wouldn't be having kids and wouldn't be preparing for them by following the usual accepted gender roles laid out for us by nature. They wouldn't be doing all that stuff, so there.

I will now remind you that every one of those hard wired, dopamine rewarded ingrown behaviors that have been taken for granted forever, are in the decline. EVERY ONE OF THEM. Simply the act of attending parties is much lamer than it was forty years ago. This behavioral dehiscence has been going on for decades, and smart phone use is only an encouraging nexus, not an underlying core motive.

But what we are seeing, including the so called 'crisis of masculinity', the withdrawal from social interaction and societal roles, the gender vagueness and insecurity, the reversal from male to female success as breadwinners and college valedictorians, all of it swirls around one discotheque, one mantra, one fuzzy navel of intensity that has earthshaking consequences… the demise of evolution itself. In our brainy exuberance we were so good at neutralizing the myriad of hoary predators that plagued us in the jungle, that evolution's fuel was drained, its pep lost its step and its drive lost its thrive.

And this one fact, along with the surge of entropy's desires, explains every one of the rambunctious disparities we are witnessing today including youth suicide rates and anxiety since they no longer can rely on the time worn blueprints for existence that we elders have been clinging to forever.

And it behooves me to assert that this is the very first time in the history of living matter that inter-being connection is being lost. Birds do it, bees do it, but now Homo sapiens ain't doin' it. All animals enlist an underlying need for connection fueled by evolution's aims, survive and procreate. If we are abandoning the mantra we are the first ever animal or plant to so do. The Neanderthals had no problem interacting and procreated with some of us sapiens. Elephants, bison, bluefish and sheep naturally herd and there has been no previous example of animal disconnectivity. It is something utterly unique in the history of protoplasm and marks an exponential oddity in the conundrum of behavior.

The next chapter will deal with the future of evolutionary collapse with some educated guesses about our newly defined trajectory. One would have to question if humans will choose to interact at all or option a plan of isolation, with reproduction relying on the science of sperm donation, and the question of the responsibility of obligation by owning single mother or fatherhood. Coupled with the likelihood of AI job replacement, there will be vast groups of unemployed loners potentially. There are already many options for sexual gratification sans partners, and these are likely to mushroom further. Masturbation in the arena of AI girlfriends self created to satisfy one's delicate fetishistic predilections may prove more satisfying to some than the actual flesh thus drawing individuals farther and farther from human intimacy.

It's as if we are in an egregious de-evolutionary storm that is lassoing each of us away from our peers. The important crystalline gem that emerges is that all of these unusual or distinctive patterns can be traced directly back to the conflagration of evolution directly, an utterly unique historical blunder bus. Think of it, madam E has arranged it that all animals seek out and mate others of their species and so produce ignominious copies of themselves, tiny froggies and mini labradoodles and scrawny blue whales. But, for the first time ever in protoplasmic history a species is starting to be indifferent to one another. This is akin to two massive tectonic plates inching apart from each other. Witness a glimpse of something utterly unique in the history of life forms, entropy drooling its goblin chops at the mad hatteresque bugaboo. "To think, without me doing a damn thing these crazy humans are hell bent on ignoring each other and the motivation to create tiny little repros of themselves.

My, my what a development. What a development indeed." entropy said, to no-one but himself. Everyone else has learned to ignore his baseless calamities. But to actually see this eruption for what it is one must be cognizant of the catalepsy of events that circled around its birth. Language's birthright, the cosmic emancipation of our minds towards reality testing, sent glittering shock waves outwards to inevitably dabble in the onset of civilizations themselves. And the linguistic shock waves that churned towards civilizations also turned inward festering on biochemical majesty in which our ubiquitous friend dopamine was reimagined and honed to a different horseshoe, one which is not comfortable with everyone and which shatters entropy and its desires unless it succeeds in reversing dopamine's suppression in the designated tracts of interest.

Holy calabash! this is preposterous yet accurate and immeasurably monumental. That animals could chooses to decouple from one another is not reconcilable with the process of evolutionary resolve. It aint so it just cannot compute. Creepy calabashes where is this all going and why and why do we as Homo sapiens humans suddenly have to encounter this ghost like apparition? Best to see it as it really is than to ignore it or find some alternative explanation that counters our need for understanding with our need for this whole shit show to go away.

Crypto Creeps and Helionated Ectomorphs

MAKE NO MISTAKE ABOUT IT MY BELOVED COUNTRYMEN… WE ARE AT A CROSS….ROADS!

Please don't ask why I say that. No do not, anymore than the woman in the car circling around the cul de sac who mumbles something about the neighbor's lawn mower when I roll down my window trying to help her, deserves my attention. I JUST TOLD YOU DID I NOT? Trust me I enjoy, no relish, telling you about every little dribbling detail of this. What I DO NOT RELISH is the hurricane wind-like resistance to hearing my dulcet toned rhapsody. (Am I not dealing it in the most seductive, mellifluous of tones?) My inchoate cranium is insensitive to ignominy, to indifference that borders on negligence, on blaspheming hierarchies of DENIAL. This latter, the stuff of crypto creeps and helionated ectomorphs, lobotomizes me. DO YOU THINK I SAY THIS FOR MY OWN… EN JOY MENT???

WARNING!!! WARNING!!! WARNING!!! TAKE HEED MANKIND!!! WE ARE ENTERING UPON A NEW ERA!!! Nor do I say this lightly or with any Maserati of jest, simply a shrieking, sniveling, discombobulating, howl of a GOD DAMNED WARNING!!! DO YOU NOT SEE IT?????

No, no, that's fine. Not everyone is capable of removing the blinders from their helionated, crypto currency lapping, dog mongering FACE!!!!! Sorry, sorry, I'm losing it a bit. Only the entirety of mankind hangs in the balance. The utter entirety OF IT. If we don't recognize this now, even if there isn't one god damned thing we can do about it, we are sadly and imbecilically doomed. And (if I'm not mistaken) horrifically painfully so.

NOW you may ask, why do you say that, fine sir? Okay, I'm aware that humanity may absorb many a monstrous heinousness, yet, I do believe that there is a certain kilogram tonnage, an arcuate, renowned, blasphemed limit to the horrendous ignominy that it (it being human-i-ty) can and should bear. That being said, let's dissect in minutiae again (and not said with any resentment whatsoever) the finer flies in the ointment of my argument.

Shall we?

IF, for example the most potent force in protoplasmic propagation was arching toward insufficiency one would conclude that many a repercussive Clamato would arise from said event, would one not? One might observe a waning in the ardor for reproductive behaviors, a fizzling of the adjudicated theater that hustled us Homo sapiens towards one another. Instead of a sizzling furnace of procreative hullabaloo, we'd notice a dehiscence of steam in the juggle toward sex itself, and related behavioral cooccurrences. Sex, drugs and rock and roll would careen into dilution, fizzle into ignominy and flatulate into deflation. The instruction book for this gender determined theatrics would burst into flames and leave us dangling, questioning who we were and what our existence was all about.

Youth would be left questioning essentially everything they were and might become, encountering decisions that previous generations sidestepped under the magnificence of evolution's commandments… to survive and procreate fine sir and madam. Anxiety, depression and suicide would start surging in the abandoned youth who now had to make it up as they went along instead of padding down a well defined and time worn pathway. One's very gender itself could be questioned and simply discarded as erroneous. Masculinity would be in crisis as men, who in prior eons knew what they were made for, now found women the main provider, the main valedictorians and the greatest occupiers of college class seats. Their time honored role of sperm donors was now teetering on insignificance. Should I be macho, effeminate, geeky and nerdy or just indeterminate? All of these issue would surface, that is if the primary driving force of evolutionary progress was waning. And this would leave us at a crossroads, one in which humanity might never, ever be the same.

Well, guess what? We are seeing every one of the above issues and more and they are creating ripples in the social universe that suggest that this is just the very incipience of it all. WE ARE PLUNGING INTO AN EVOLUTIONARY-LESS MOMENT, WITH NO END IN SIGHT! Imagine that a force, one that has battled entropy, has orchestrated the progression of organic matter from a single cell all the damn way to an US, a sweeping grandiose principle of nature like gravity or the atomic theory suddenly losing its invincible, indefinable power. Think of it! It is unimaginable yet it is happening and we are seeing it all around us unless we insist on being too damn blind to acknowledge the obvious. All the signs point in one freaking direction… endgame! The foundation of biological purity, endless magnificence and survival potency now withering, with its twin procreation now cooling to disinterest. How is such an event even possible?

We outsmarted ourselves and became so good at eliminating the predators that haunted us in the teeming death howl of the jungle that evolution lost its steam. If evolution is a crucible then adversity is the bunion burner that sizzles underneath the who shebang and its flame has gone out. We blasted our way to the point where survival moved from the format of our own bodies, the fittest among us reaching survival mode, to external interventions like medical treatments, weather protective housing, jurisprudence to prevent attack from our peers, all of this has softened the evolutionary rocket ship of progress. Evolution's phallus is now limp and it has left us depressed, indecisive, alone, without clear gender blueprints of action, and less procreative than ever before. And that is the soul of evolution, reproduction to propagation and when that withers, God help us.

"It is not the strongest of the species that survives, not the most intelligent that survives. It is the one that is the most adaptable to change." Charles Darwin, "The Origin of Species"

Darwin himself did not envision an end to evolution, nor did he see it ever faltering. One might ask then, are we not just in a unique moment in which we, or some other species, will have to adapt to new and unique circumstances? Is it not our job then to be the most adaptable of species at the present moment and in the current circumstances? My answer is, not if that change puts an end to reproduction, and we are seeing signs that this is exactly where we're heading, and on a massive scale. We Homo sapiens are 8 billion strong, but don't kid yourself, with some 150,000 of us dying DAILY that number will diminish rapidly if we stop reproducing. Do the math, that's about 4.5 million monthly, about 54 million a year. And this rate can expand with global warming, droughts, crop reductions, and other events like wars, homicides and suicides which we are seeing in greater numbers as mental illnesses like depression surge, a tribute to grizzly entropy.

But in Darwin's time the average life span was about 45. There were no antibiotics, no x rays, cat scans, EKG's and no treatment for almost anything more complex than a twisted thumb or a hangnail. Therefore the number of predators we had neutralized were far fewer and the urgency to succeed in life was much greater. These stresses feed evolution's ardor, and foment an urgency to reproduce that seems to have vanished in the mist. The growl of leisure time is palpable and we take notice of it. We have health insurance, shelter from the gruesome storm of global warming and treatments for common ailments that are as reachable as a drive to the local urgent care. Things the put an ignominious end to us 100 years ago no longer do and we are content to allow ourselves the luxury of longevity and free time in which to localize a life purpose. But that purpose seems to have alluded us and we bury our heads in our smart phones and crawl through a life that is marked by indecision. And this indecision is one which was not in our purview in the 1950's even when I grew up.

We took many more things for granted than our youth do currently, and these questions are leading to depression and suicides, especially among females and even more among black women. We had our global concerns in the fifties as well and were scolded into hiding under our desks to prepare for a nuclear bomb that never came, although Khrushchev was banging his shoe agains the podium which rang like a global siren across the globe that vibrated in terror of this near certainty. We had polio and measles and feared various pandemic insults.

So it's clear in which direction we are glacially heading. The question is how far will this human avoidance go and what will be the outcome? Are we destined to live lives of human isolation, only coming out of our electrically digitized huts for dire necessities? I can envision a moment when children are raised by robots, educated via the web and nurtured with potent chemicals. Some will undoubtedly make a point of the necessity of human contact with its pheromones, facial expressive indicators and worth of touch. Hugs will be at a premium. The world may be divided into those who embrace interacting with others and those who avoid it.

But before we can engage in idle speculation we must be fully on board with the direction of our current miasma. Young people are clearly honoring a lifestyle of avoidance and they do not embrace socialization, they give in to the discomfort of rejection and seek solace in a digital world which caters to their hermit like existence and supports their self abnegation. Events have collaborated to encourage this withdrawal syndrome and AI is rapidly feeding its need for stimulation. It would be wise to acknowledge this road sign and develop plans to abort its egregious sorrow. People need touch, relationship and conflict including rejection and social victories, all of which is part of the human condition.

The process of life's deliberations and head butting, competitiveness and rampant race to the top to compete with the Joneses is healthy and necessary in a world where actual combat has, for the most part been squelched and rightly so. That we have gone from physical fighting to verbal debate and political strife is also part of the healthy manna of society. Competition for things, people, attention, clicks, mates, field goals, drugs and joy are all part of the human craziness that makes us what we are. What are we when that is no longer in the cards and we spend our existence simply existing? We may need to find the answer much sooner than we think.

"The moral sense perhaps affords the best and highest distinction between man and the lower animals… the prime principal of man's moral institutionwith the aid of active intellectual powers and effects of habit, naturally lead to the golden rule… and this lies at the foundation of morality." *The Descent of Man*, chapter 2, Charles Darwin Darwin stated that behaviors that encourage parental care and cooperation are naturally selective as they promote group survival, protect the vulnerable child and favor reproduction within a society. But he didn't address what would happen if evolution began to fade when the forces of predation that underlay its potency were pulled out from under it. Survival of the fittest no longer applies, for even highly impaired individuals are able to get by in a society that prides itself on assisting the infirm. The multitude of deficiency mutations that can survive currently goes against the principles of natural selection and thus is part and parcel of evolution's insignificance. Will humans continue to evolve? Yes in ways as mutational drift occurs essentially unchecked.

As Darwin stated, morality arose in the context of civilization, a group process that was necessitated to protect the herd from self immolation. But what if we were no longer technically a herd, just a collection of disparate individuals who are mired in avoidance, unmotivated to procreate and alienated from themselves with the aid of electronic screen contents that titillate and prod the dopaminergic swamp that so entices? Morality itself is then threatened as we do not run into situations of dire exploitation of our fellow men and may not recognize it in ourselves. We may begin to question the value of our very existence as we were created to battle our way to survivals so as to reproduce, a scenario that has been vacuumed out of our blue screen existence. The screen itself is not the problem, just an enabler of our rudderless situation.

And lurking behind all of this, entropy is licking its chops in anticipation of potential deadly options for its gleeful quest to return all organic matter to the cold inorganic form of rock and dust that exists on most planets. So, as morality softens, old man entropy will work to turn human against human even more that we are experiencing it now. And since we will be out of touch with one another this dance with death will be thinly lubricated. United we stand but divided into robotic units we have only ourselves to examine. There is no unity in that. So humankind can wither into disunion as people shrug off the procreative ardor to unite. Suicide rates will surge even more than they now are and we will see mental illness peaking.

It is clear that we are being swept into a rudderless morass as evolution's billion year old script vanishes into insignificance. While somewhat pessimistic this analysis cannot be overlooked given the evidence. All signs are pointing to an avoidant populace whose basic functional indices are now up for grabs, as one might surmise given the absence of the necessity to reproduce, mingle, party, fornicate and just plain interact. Is it possible to turn this flaccid situation around in an effective way? Possibly, but the forces we are reckoning with need to be examined microscopically. Let's agree that evolution is waning, entropy is surging and the human race is floundering into isolative disunion. If we can recognize the problem for what it really is we may be able to begin to turn things around. There may be ways of forcing people to interact, promoting sexuality (as if, you say, there isn't enough of that. But statistically there is not) and encouraging tolerance of the social rejections that inevitably follow our own mode of mingling. We could start a whole universe of mingling individuals invested in seeing society strengthen rather than wither.

"In short: iGen teens are less likely to take part in every single face to face social activity measured across four data sets of three different age groups. These fading interactions include everything from small group or one on one activities such as getting together with friends to larger group activities such as parties." (*iGen*, p. 75, J. Twenge) Is this entirely due to internet activity or is there something deeper swirling around this drop in socializing? I would assert the latter: that this behavior has been going on for a long time and precedes the onset of smart phone use. According to Twenge's own charts the drop off in social behaviors including daily get togethers with friends, going to shopping malls, attending parties monthly all began around the turn of the century. Cell phone use just furthered the trend of social withdrawal and isolation. Kids are not socializing or boozing. "…the number of 8th graders who have tried alcohol has been has been cut nearly in half." (*iGen* p. 36) "The number of 18-year-olds who binge drink has been cut in half since the early1980's…" These antisocial phenomena go back decades. Now you'll undoubtedly say that this trend can only be good, giving up drinking is certainly a healthy outcome of whatever process is going on.

No, because it simply reflects the asociality of youth in general, and it is a secondary phenomenon to this social avoidance. Since at least the year 2000 the percentage of youth who have driver's licenses, tried alcohol, ever go out on dates, or have worked for pay is downtrending. (*iGen* p. 40) Observers who have labeled teens 'boring' or 'more responsible' are simply wrong. "But the trends do nearly unequivocally support the idea that teens are growing up more slowly." (*iGen* p. 42.) But growing up is part and parcel of evolution's dictum: survive, find a partner, reproduce, die. This is evolution's blueprint for our lives with acknowledgment that entropy will succeed in returning us all to inorganic matter sooner or later. For teens to be avoiding growing up is for a generation to eschew evolution's marching orders.

To follow the caveman's rules we must arm ourselves against the predatory intensity that could easily end us and proceed to survive and reproduce. This clear intensity was what fed evolution's progress and the pruning of undesirable mutations. But we've eliminated most of the predatory howl that plagued and ended many of us in the jungle, a place where most of us modern civilized humans would not survive long. We are now in an evolutionary free fall, and this explains in much greater depth the behavior we are seeing in teens. Parents may be playing into this notch by being over protective but the underlying impetus for the lack of 'adultness' is a waning of the evolutionary thrust. This explains youth suicides and depressions. PEOPLE NEED THE DIRECTION OF EVOLUTIONARY MOVEMENT, and without that they are indecisive and depressed to the point of suicide. This is a result of lack of direction, not distraction. Many intriguing geeky toys have arisen to assist youngsters in avoiding themselves, the selves that are now without a clear path to adulthood.

They are left embracing the avoidance and avoiding the yellow brick road to adulthood that is a biological necessity hard wired into our brains over millennia. Take that away and people are lost. I'm not advocating that all youth go out and get drunk, rather that they interact with real humans more than they interact with screens that have little resemblance to reality. We have to look deeper to really understand what we are observing. Yes parents may be overprotective and this plays into the hands of a tendency of teens to avoid growing up. Great, since that is correctible. What is not correctable is the loss of evolutionary direction that guided our lives forever towards the simple dictums of survival of the fittest and natural selection which was replaced by sexual selection once we became civilized beings and is now being replaced by selection by indecision.

"The brain is a very unorganized machine… The infant brain is probably very unorganized and becomes organized by a process of training." (Alan Turing, *Intelligent Machinery,* 1948)

"Evolution is over… We are the first species to take control of our own evolution." (Steve Jones, geneticist, in an interview, *The Independent,* 2002)

"We have relieved ourselves of the brutalities of natural selection… We no longer die in large numbers from smallpox or plague. So natural selection has far less to bite on." (BBC interview, *The Guardian*, 2009, Sir David Attenborough) "…the forces of natural selection are very much weaker than they were. (*Life on Earth*, episode 13, 1979, Sir David Attenborough)

What is the legacy of language? Why have we become the world rulers above all other organic beings? If you think about it it boils down to one thing… the fact that you can think about it and no other entities can. And this legacy of thinking originates from, of course, language, which as we know starts to impact the infant at about one year of age and continues to develop over the next 15 years or so. During this time the little Homo sapiens learns to utilize concepts and express them motorically in the myriad of muscles that are located in the mouth, larynx, diaphragm and tongue as well as others. NO OTHER ORGANIC BEING DOES THIS. They may have a primitive form of communication, both verbal and nonverbal but there is no animal or plant that has the muscularity in developed linguistic complexity that we humans have.

And when we look at the essence of what language is it boils down to neurochemistry, true? We can localize the ubiquitous chemical dopamine as the key player in this Shazam of mystery we call thought. Why? Because just as in the nigro-striatal tract we must learn to tame this nasty little collection of atoms in response to the demand for coordinated movement, we must learn to do the same in the meso-limbic and meso-cortical tracts in response to speech which carries muscularity in combination with IDEATION.

No other animal or plant gots dat, not a one. So when we use our natural born talent for rational thought what are we doing, you ask, we are suppressing or taming or enlisting dopamine in the process of thought formation and expression through language. We are actually talking to ourselves and as we do so we are suppressing dopamine and this one function or process is one which, I assert, we are all struggling with constantly but do best at in the raw act of contemplation. And with this success in dopamine suppression we also are improving our coordination which proves that thinking also tames dopamine in the nigro striatal tract. So it is that with thinking which binds tames or suppresses dopamine we are making a general improvement in our situation entirely. Essentially everything we do is improved by contemplation, daily and preferably in a quiet, comfortable environment. So the legacy that language gave us boils down to one thing, a process that so many are imperfect at resulting in mental illness of various types in about 20% of the population, a process of dopamine suppression.

And we have the ability to hone this by THINKING, something far too few people do. The legacy of the past 50,000 years of evolution is our ability to suppress dopamine which has made us the rulers of the world and given us the ability to neutralize the vast majority of the predators that plagued us in the jungle habitat we evolved in. SO, our ability to suppress dopamine has ultimately put an end to natural selection, created multiple mental illnesses including schizophrenia which demonstrates a decided surge in dopamine, (the opposite of suppression) and placed us Homo sapiens in the position of world leader in relation to all other living protoplasm. Well, what do you know?

"In states dopamine depletion (e.g., Parkinson's), patients report 'mental emptiness'-not a loss of thought itself, but a loss of thoughts that matter. Dopamine is the spotlight operator of consciousness." (Trevor Robbins, psychopharmacologist)

And according to my theory it is the *suppression* of dopamine in conjunction with acetylcholine that makes the difference. This process of suppressing or binding or controlling dopamine is one which none of us do particularly well. In fact it is a lifetime struggle, one which none of us are aware of, unless it fails so spectacularly that a mental illness arises, due, completely to the *desuppression* or surge of the chemical.

"...dopamine doesn't just correlate with illness; it *sculpts* the neural architecture that makes pathological thoughts irresistible." (Marc Caron, geneticist)

The dopamine theory of schizophrenia has been the dominant theory for some sixty years. No recent research or conjecture has replaced it. There is general agreement about the role of dopamine in mental infirmity, too much being bad. This is why essentially every chemical we administer to the poor sufferers of psychiatric problems either blocks or inhibits dopamine.

Even the antidepressants do so indirectly by stimulating something called the auto receptor, a thermostat attached to neurons that regulates the level of dopamine and other neurotransmitters and can inhibit their production. But there is not yet general consensus on the role of dopamine in us mentally healthy beings… that dopamine is the opposite of surging, rather it is being bound or suppressed. It is well known that chemicals that surge dopamine like stimulants such as methamphetamine can cause psychotic symptoms indistinguishable from schizophrenia. There is a general regression to primitive thinking in concordance with this explosion of dopamine either caused by external agents or simply our failure to suppress dopamine, a learned process that we all struggle with. Going further out on a proverbial limb it would make perfect sense to suppose that the suppression of dopamine is akin to Freud's concept of repression, a process necessary for mental health in that certain unwanted, crippling or primitive thoughts need to be suppressed in order to promote the smooth functioning of our mentality. AND, if I am correct that thinking itself helps suppress dopamine, then the act of contemplation also fosters the mental muscles needed to repress unwanted thoughts, one of its benefits.

So as we march through adolescence we learn the value of conscious thought and its role in suppressing dopamine, a chemical whose surge can lead our thinking away from rationality, and whose lack of suppression is also akin to the failure of repression of unwanted thought. All of this mental equanimity hinges on the one chemical dopamine which, in conjunction with acetylcholine, balances our thought processes in an adult manner. And this can be traced back to the onset of language some 50,000 years ago. Mental illness then is simply due to the newness of this challenging process of dopamine suppression, a task poorly attained by us all, and even more poorly accomplished by the mentally ill. This is why I have called the mentally ill *evolution's dispossessed* and predicted that mental illness as we know it will no longer exist some 10,000 years from now if we survive since we all will have mastered the task of dopamine suppression flawlessly.

The psychedelics, whose mechanism of action involves stimulating a receptor of serotonin, most likely causes a secondary surge in dopamine, the golden road to primitive thinking typical of our caveman ancestors. Along with this regression to unrealistic thinking is a dissolution of the ego, a shredding as it were of the sense of self. So we can surmise that the ego is enhanced as we learn the skill of dopamine suppression, part and parcel of the process. The infant, essentially ego-less, gradually accomplishes this feat by taming dopamine which then blesses him with the reality principle, something adopted with effort and repeated encouragement by the school system. We've set up our schooling to steer the individual toward dopamine suppression which includes the ego, and reality testing so that they can join society as adult thinkers. This process is far from flawless and may go awry at any stage. But for the most part it lands the majority of the gestating adolescents into adulthood in terms of thinking and ego.

But we have to concede that life itself, whose goal is the defiance of entropy, is a most rare exception to the lifeless lack of existence we find on ALL THE OTHER PLANETS! Despite all the conspiracy theories and hints and sightings, we have never seen in any believable way an alien or anything like that on this earth. It is living protoplasm that is so uniquely earthly that we cannot in any equanimity of mind believe anything but that we are an exception to entropy's hegemony. Life is the exception, death and inorganic lifelessness the rule everywhere in the universe and this condition is one which we seem capable of ignoring as if our lives are just run of the mill occurrences. If one considers the antropic complexity of organic matter, the storage of potential energy and the unique characteristics of this odd substance, it is a wonder we exist at all.

Yet we take our existence for granted and even fritter away our lives in the most haphazard way possible. The writer Charles Bukowski commented on how some people ignore the fact that they have made nothing of their lives. Others try endlessly to make some imaginary goal only to find that they have avoided living all together. On his tombstone he wrote, "Don't Try" as a mantra. Yet his lack of trying ended up selling millions of books despite being a beer boozing, womanizing misanthrope.

I mention this only to remind us of the rarity that life is and that we must take it as a sacred anomaly if nothing else. Entropy inevitably wins by returning us all to inorganic matter, it's dearest desire. Yet the complexity and manner of being in protoplasm is remarkable and is diametrically opposed to entropy's yearning. Trees for example store immense amounts of potential energy in wood which, when burned, is released into the atmosphere, something that has kept people alive and warm for eons. How all of this potential energy, self preservative instinct, searching for sources of nutrition and energy, excretion and reproductive effort came about is unfathomable.

If DNA appeared spontaneously then it could have led in the right conditions to something approaching aliveness. And over megaboluses of time could have adorned itself with the characteristics of protoplasm, the unique, quirky, stumbling idiocy of life which itself is so fleeting that a sudden change in temperature can end it for all sorts of living things. So we must look to evolution itself as the Queen of Antropy to have led living matter down the yellow brick road to survival and propagation of species. And it is the propagation of species that evolution is so damned proficient at, but now we have to wonder if she has lost her super powers, allowing the kryptonite of entropy to surge forward into the darkness. We know that entropy will take advantage of any opening that evolution with its antropic lust will allow it. So it is more than a little surprising that the one champion of living matter, evolution, is now on the ropes, teetering into self induced coma, about to fall onto the padded floor of the boxing ring, a victim of entropy's sinister desires.

Yet all the signs are there, at least for us humans. We have inhibited the lifestyle of many other species of animal, to the extent that extinction is common and progressing rapidly in the other life forms. But that is an involuntary extinction, as those animals are not choosing not to reproduce. We are making a conscious choice of celibacy and non procreation. In a world where evolution fought tooth and nail for the mere opportunity to foil entropy, this reversal in momentum is astonishing. In unison with antropy, evolution is our one champion, the unitary force that is preventing us from becoming like all the other planetary landscapes. Momma evolution fought tooth and nail for billions of years to allow protoplasm to inch its odd way forward until it produced something like an us. If you consider the complexity of an 'us' this is more than remarkable, it's an astonishing feat of antropic victory. For any force to outdo entropy in the universe is utterly remarkable. JUST LOOK AT THE OTHER PLANETS AND MOONS. THEY ARE BALLS OF DUST AND ROCK OR FIERY ORBS OF BURNING GAS. But not us. Why earth? Probably because we have just the right habitat to be welcoming to something as finicky as living matter. It's possible that other planets HAD living matter that succumbed to entropy's desires, and that is exactly what it yearns to do to earth, and, most likely will succeed in turning us into something akin to Pluto or Mars. But in this one outpost, this unitary orb spinning around the white hot sun, antropy and evolution outsmarted the bastard and gave us living matter. Cherish the miracle.

It's clear that masculinity is suffering on many fronts, not the least of which is the fact that females are more and more becoming the breadwinners in many households. Men wonder about whether or not its acceptable to be masculine/macho or is that is sexist, and whether or not its acceptable to be a wimpy kind of submissive, and which would be most likely to attract a mate. Younger men are opting out of the dating game altogether. Add to this the fact that male testosterone levels have been declining for decades, it appears that masculinity itself is on the wane, another collateral damage from the universal dehiscence of evolution.

After all, evolution commanded us males to be the hunter/gatherers, the sperm donating, machos who weathered the storm of intense predation in the jungle yet come home with a few berries, some nuts and a strangled chicken. This intense predatory atmosphere was likely a contributing factor in the higher testosterone levels of male cavemen. But, with the absolution of the most intense predatory insults, we've not only nuked evolution but we've given males less incentive to man up and testosterone up with it. So the incentive to procreate, to get the chick into a 93 Chevy and plant a warm palm on one of her breasts until she's lubricated towards a procreative spin to the local dime motel room vibrating bed, has been diminishing in fervor along with the evolutionary dissolve.

And along with this despicable insult, another factor that is suffering ignominious decline is a little something called grip strength. Grip strength is turning out to be one of those core concepts that is connected to nearly everything that we are: mental soundness, longevity, physical fitness of all kinds. Grip strength has been declining for years as well. Young psychotic patients suffer from low grip strength. "Although often tied to physical status, grip strength has recently been identified as a predictor of general well-being in healthy populations, including long-term physical and mental health outcomes and neural function… low grip strength is associated with increased all-cause mortality, increased psychiatric symptoms, and poor cognitive performance." (Ward, Beermann,, Felix, et al, "Grip Strength as a Marker of Resting-State Network Integrity and Well-Being in Early Psychosis", Am. J. Psychiat, 182:9, September 2025) So we are seeing a significant marker of overall wellbeing, general okay-ness of ourselves mentally and physically deteriorate over decades. Could this be due to evolution's general demise as well? Of course. For if the purpose for which we were created is suddenly a fluttering flag in the windless sky, then we as human individuals and clumps of protoplasmic substance are adrift as well.

We've addressed how the adoption of language bestowed upon us conscious thought, and that when we think we suppress dopamine and that in so doing we will improve not just mental functioning but physical functioning as well. And we have linked this to the proximity of various tracts in the brain, the nigrostriatal in tandem with the meso-limbic and the meso-cortical which are utilized to connect ideation with the motor function of speech. The suppression of dopamine which accompanies thinking also improves the motor function as if there are suppressive elements in the nigrostriatal tract that benefit from rational thinking as well. So, a general indicator of mental and physical health in decline should not necessarily surprise us.

But we must look further to clarify the posture of protoplasmic insecurity. Remember that the balance of forces strongly favors entropy, a law that embodies time inevitably and we all succumb to it in time. But we must view contemplation as the ultimate insult to entropy, with intense energy and organization, the opposite of ol' man entropy's lustful desire. This puts the human gray matter as the most highly antropic substance IN THE UNIVERSE. If the purpose of life after all is to defy entropy (it is) then we protoplasmic entities that inhabit this craggy orb are the only representatives of its opposition. Living matter can be viewed as a type of substance, one that is most highly unusual, the exception, not at all the rule. On no other planet do we observe anything like an us. It's possible that something like protoplasm existed on one or more of the planets in some vague past but since has faltered to the sarcastic flooding influence of entropy. So then thinking is entropy's utmost insult, an abomination to its sense of utter overriding command in the universe, EXCEPT on mother earth. And it is only madam evolution's unfaltering victories over it that have divided it from its adoration, the turning of organic matter into the inorganic form.

And when I've stated that that entropic messiah of the death instinct, implanted into us all at some point in our animalistic adolescence. And this imbedding is no small matter, for, in truth, we all yearn to return to the entropic crater from which evolved, at the perigee of energy that troughs in the universe of inorganic matter.

Yes, the death instinct urges us not only to destroy others but also ourselves, with the constant imploring to give up this sophisticated organization. And in fact, many of us succumb to the entreaty, terminating our own existence by our own hands, and, as we have emphasized, the youth of today are engaging in the entropy worship in ever greater numbers. The death instinct includes the seductive desire to terminate the lives not just of others but ourselves and we have seen this unfortunate slap in the face of evolution far too frequently.

I will now tell you the one and only reason that people abuse drugs and alcohol: IT IS SOLELY TO NESTLE CLOSER TO A COMFORTABLE STATE OF ENTROPY. Can you think of any other modus operandi, short of demise, that can accomplish this feat? Of course not, and the chemicals that lend themselves to this indulgence do so with great aplomb. So we are all in a state of yearning for the dull, lifeless state of non-organicity and its lack of organization, energy and life force. In fact when people say they are seeking meditative relaxation they are really seeking a state of lifelessness which incorporates the valley of de-energization that we all encounter on the 'other side' as it were. And unfortunately many achieve the state of lifelessness that accompanies accidental overdose, as in the scourge of fentanyl laced ingestions perpetrated by entropy's merry band of homicidal douchebags. It took evolution in tandem with its partner antropy to pull off the feat of entropic dismissal. We must remember that protoplasm is a highly unique exception to the general rule of entropic hegemony, an oddball aberration seen only on this god forsaken blue planet. It should never be taken for granted yet the evil yen of entropic bliss seduces many into the lifeless arms of evolution's avowed enemy.

And entropy has taken its role from the universal need to screw up that we all face, especially in light of the need for us all to suppress dopamine in tracts we are not evolutionarily used to do so in. When language served up its unique blessings it also gave us the assignment to suppress dopamine, an ungodly task at which we are all amateurs.

None of us suppress dopamine very adequately and the mentally ill do so with a decided lack of aplomb, spilling them into the bin of hardships associated with mental infirmity and for which we administer dopamine suppressing chemicals. And thus they meet the definition of evolution's dispossessed. Entropy is exerting its influence on us even within our brains and its fledgling attempt to utilize contemplation, the very thing that has set us apart from all other life forms and allowed us to rule the world.

We can feel the weight of this entropic intrusion when we try to think. It feels like a burdensome hardship and makes us shy away from it. Yet when we do so we are defying entropy as we suppress dopamine into the realm of gray matter security. So deductive reasoning is the surefire modus operandi to enlightenment and to dopamine suppression, the sin e quo non of mental encouragement. And our old friend Freud would have been pleased with this analysis as the dopaminergic buzz is akin to his concept of repression. He discovered that unconscious forces were at work in mental illness and now we can pinpoint the chemical process that subserves this utility. When we suppress dopamine we are also beefing up repression, but these are the healthy repressions we all need for smooth mental functioning, not the ones that cause symptoms, and which had so much difficulty dislodging. We all need to repress things from our past that are intrusive and would muck up smooth mental fluency. These things need to be banished to the dust bin or repression and we do so when we use the magic of contemplation as our outpost. So thinking defies entropy, suppresses dopamine in the right places and aids in repression of the very things that would interfere with out cranial equanimity. So this assignment that time has blessed upon us is nothing more than a universal salve to our inner vagueness, a balm to our new assignment and that which has ignited the Homo sapiens revolution around the globe, our absolute mastery.

This all smacks of the influence of something one might label divine, a word latent with misperception and incongruity. 'The Divine' is mystical, spiritual, new age, riddled with charlatans and fakes, yet it is so. One chemical change in our brains' functioning has made all the difference. It is up to us to accept its demands and its blessing. And what is that blessing? It is the ability to defy entropy in the most elusive of warfares, the complexity of human thought which makes the gray matter of a Homo sapiens the most ANTROPIC substance in the universe.

And all of this has happened in the past 50,000 years which is why we are so bad at it. Yet we are good enough to have eliminated most of the predators that made our lives a precarious nightmare when we high tailed it through jungle vines and sharp toothed predators. It truly is amazing, is it not? Think about this course of events! For six million or more years we had no way to suppress dopamine in CERTAIN BRAIN TRACTS. We could do so in one of them but not the others. So what? Evolution worked us toward the very thing that has put it into resignation. It allowed for enough brain expansion so that we were experts at symbol formation, the soul of language. This led to conscious thought and the reality principle. This allowed us to use scientific methods to unveil truth from falsehood. Then we wiped out all other species of Homo and fanned out across the globe. We are the chosen species and this is entirely due to the ability to suppress dopamine in two erstwhile tracts in the brain. That has made all the difference and it even has made Freud happy. Dopamine suppression is the soul of healthy repression, the soul of reality testing, the nutrient of the ego, the absolute pounder of entropy's desires into oblivion yet since we are so imperfect at it we have given entropy an opining towards our demise when mental illness lubricates the urge towards dissolution in the form of suicide. AMAZING IS IT NOT? And, it stores potential energy when we utilize our brains in this way.

So when we take shrooms, LSD, mescaline, or other psychedelics they no doubt set the stage for a dopaminergic surge, and this typhoon of neurotransmitter decimates our egos to the point where we feel as if we no longer exist, something no doubt familiar to an infant. So this builder of egos, the suppression of dopamine, is reversible and can then render the processes of thought, so complex and realistic, into primitive mush that calls upon witches brews of nonsense and labels them truth.

And schizophrenics are familiar with this process which happens to them in late adolescence and renders them devoid of an adult ego or thought process which they now have to engage the world without. The mind's center of gravity shifts so much that they are prone to hallucinations, an event which takes place when there is sensory deprivation, the brain desperate to avoid atrophy then creates its own self erected impulses. In our infinite wisdom we then rush in with chemicals that set up roadblocks to dopamine by cutting off their receptors and this has a remarkably effective shrinkage to their psychotic fire. Our brainy success in adopting a mind capable of ruling the world in the mental garden of dopamine suppression has the potency to rectify the situation when this dopaminergic bindery goes awry. WE SIMPLY BLOCK THE RECEPTORS! And we have the mentality that allows us to create such chemical roadblocks. We are truly a remarkable species and we have no qualms about destroying the earth with carbon based fuels that sour the atmosphere with carbon dioxide destroying the vital ozone layer and several other such catastrophes. We are capable of great constructions and superlative destructive slip ups, which, obviously, delight and infuse our common enemy entropy as we face the possibility of global destruction either by climate change or nuclear holocaust.

The balance of forces in the universe, entropy vs antropy, the latter having joined ranks with evolution to promote the protoplasmic exegesis, now faces a new arrangement. As evolution withers, entropy will surely surge just as dopamine rages in the schizophrenic in late adolescence, and it will find ways, with our help, to offer potential destruction to the earth en masse. And this is the battle we must face at the moment… the need to monitor entropy's desires as evolution lays down its powerful arms.

It has brought us over millions of years to a Homo sapiens that now rules the world in its 8 billion strong army. But as much as we are capable of great things we are also able to slip quietly into the hands of entropy and set up an arrangement much too cozy for him. We must be vigilant that something as powerful as AI does not tumble into entropy's slimy paws.

As previously mentioned we all have the urge to destroy and return ourselves and others to the realm of the unliving, the energy-less state of non-existence. While we fight this urge minute by moment for the sake of civilization yet we are not vigilant enough to prevent it from slipping into our plans and creations. After all we have created many things in the service of demolition of protoplasmic substance. In our lust for industrialization we have poisoned the rivers and streams, forested the pristine habitat of our jungle forebears. While they lived in extreme predatory danger they did not have to contend with chemical pollutions that slime our waterways and breathing habits. Such a development could only have emboldened entropy. While we stumble ahead in consummate progress, we are soiling ourselves and our earth, an unsavory trade off. The emphasis on progress is made with one blind eye, allowing impulses of great destructiveness to supersede scrutiny.

But this implies that with enough vigilance we can minimize the damage, fold entropy's desires into a little napkin of inhospitality and move on. As Freud said, he who threw the first epithet instead of the first stone was the founder of civilization. You have to talk to people to understand them and too often it is the talking and the LISTENING that is absent from our modus operandi. Yet we must recognize that when evil rears its ugly head in the form of serial killers, mass murderers, out of control political leaders or terrorist fanatics that kill in the name of "God", that these are all expressions of the same thing, the death instinct that resides in all of us, the messenger of sourpuss entropy.

And it is natural and acceptable to have such feelings, although something called the superego arose out of the need to protect the individual from acting on entropy's desires, the death instinct by making us feel wretched whenever we even contemplate pushing granny over a cliff or diddling our neighbor's wife. We are sent a powerful signal of negativity that exists to protect civilization. This, Freud taught us, arises from our own ego's need for self protection, and jurisprudence reinforces society's overt insistence on safety as a primary facet of civilization's promise.

But as we mentioned entropy is not just invested in violence as a form of degrading the organic back to the non-organic. It is wiggling its morbid hand in our sanity as defined by the events of the last fifty thousand years. And this is entirely wrapped in the hands of dopamine suppression which lends its coat to ego strength and reality testing or as Freud called it the 'reality principle' which played such a significant role in our supremacy over all living matter. When dopamine unsuppresses and we revert to more primitive thinking we become mentally ill unless this is a drug effect in which case we revert back to normal (hopefully) after the offending agent is passed from our body. And of course mental infirmity increases our risk of self demise, the ultimate nod to entropy and insult to evolution which entreats us to survive and, oh yes, reproduce. And this new chore of dopamine suppression is far from perfect in us and more tenuous in the mentally afflicted. Schizophrenics have to march through life with a more primitive set of thinking rules. So entropy has its greasy hand in everything we are and do but is manageable as long as we pay attention to it and side with its nemesis antropy.

So if we ask ourselves why such a large percentage of young people are living with their parents we have the answer. "With lower college enrollments, fewer pathways to economic security, and fewer intimate relationships being formed, young adults have less impetus and means to leave home." (*Adrift*, p. 150, S. Galloway) It isn't economics or smart phone use or social media, although these things play a role in the situation as did Covid 19, it is because evolution itself is in recession and as it recedes we note that its major tenets are melting. And its major tenets are very simple, survive, reproduce then die.

Young men in particular are nesting at home after high school and college, not pursuing usual mating roles, avoiding rejection and withdrawing from the evolutionary mandates that were present even when I was growing up in the 50's and sixties. As noted previously they are partying less, sexing less, drinking less and avoiding life in general. This is quite consistent with the principle of "non-survival of the fittest".

In non survival of the fittest it doesn't matter if your are highly competent or not, and there is a sense of nullification of life's trials and competitions. In this philosophy the jungle is replaced with a non competitive background of avoidance with life aggregating around minimal effort and there is no combat, rejection or failure. Young men are avoiding female rejection in ever larger numbers, the opposite of a nail biting scratch for existence. Existence is now taken for granted, and a given in the non-predatory universe of modern anti-evolutionism. Men aren't knocking each other out of the box to nab the coolest chick, the hottest job or the best car, they're viewing life non-competitively and they are in essence non-societal. One could assert that the social media companies are conspiring to suck young men into digital bliss to feather their monopoly nest, but this is just an accelerator to the trend, not the trend itself. The trend embodies all that evolution isn't and embraces an expectation of survival into the seventies, eighties or beyond, not a death defying rampage to existence and fertility.

We are seeing a perfect storm of nonompetitiveness that can only be explained by a weakening of evolution itself. Yes, there are economic factors, and it is more difficult to attain the American dream, but that is just another reason to hyper compete, not decelerate. Life has never been an easy rider for anyone at any time and this era is no exception. The only difference is that the generation of up and coming young adults aren't battling hand and fist for economic and marital success, they are shrinking from both as if competition did not actually exist at all. In other less developed countries where the combat zone for survival and success is more brutal and the price of failure more gruesome, the citizens are more likely to embrace the fight.

But younger people are acting as if competition itself was anathema and that a life of existing rather than struggling was the expected norm. 50,000 years ago there was no life without struggle, and the struggle itself bore fruit of maturation. Even an inch worm has to push its way through tightly pack sand.

Yes the answer fits all too snugly, in that the mandates of evolution, so clear and well defined are being ignored because they lack the predatory verve that simmered them into our communal psyches. The price youth are paying for this, which is utterly not their fault, is depression, anxiety and suicide. Young black females are particularly vulnerable but all youth are surging in entropic desire, to voluntarily return oneself to inorganic matter. And now we can see what the internal neurotransmitter is that hovers around this infirmity, our old friend DOPA-MEAN. For it is mean when it surges and inspiring when we manage to conquer its demands for suppression yielding us the precious connection to reality that served up our world conquering mental faculties. We can in fact see quite clearly what has gone wrong and what right.

For in actuality all has gone right in our quest to eliminate all the predatory hardships that plagued the caveman in his inimitable quest for survival and procreation. We have done such a good job dissolving the grizzly bear, the scorpion bite, the infection, the shattered bone that we no longer have the crucible of evolution to recon with at all. IN dong exactly what we were supposed to do, that is making our lives less perilous, we inadvertently knee chopped evolution's absolution, which all too neatly explains what we are seeing in the society around us and what will be seeing much more of in the future. If the seven million year old blueprint for life is suddenly pulled out from under you like a cheap Moroccan rug, then you are truly adrift in a sea of indecision. We have morphed from natural selection to sexual selection to, now, selection by indecision. And this indecision coupled with an absence of struggle mentality in many is literally killing us, mostly by suicide, but also by the so called 'mismatch' diseases that have followed us out of the jungle.

Even the scent of the woods, the 'forest bathing' that we no longer engage in for the most part, is ushering in lower immune function. Studies have shown that those who walk in the woods several times weekly have stronger immune function than the rest of us that don't. Our arteries cannot handle the diet rich in fats and carbs that are typical of modern humans and we cannot deal with the sedentary lifestyle of current life. None of this matches with the jungle terror and daily situational intensity that has fizzled out. While our bodies and minds suffer from this 'mismatch' with the jungle lifestyle madam evolution herself is whimpering in the corner, melting into neutrality. None of this, NONE OF IT, serves us well, even though it is a byproduct of civilization's heartfelt advances.

Yet it is a mistake to live as if life is not a competition since, in many respects it is. Yet, it is as if the younger generation wants to act otherwise, to ignore the consequences of opting out of society and the mandates that momma evolution has laid before us for over six million years and before all living things. Animals of all types compete with each other and at times attack each other especially from stranger species. Life has competition hard wired into it, the struggle for food and reproductive partners is ongoing and in most cultures is implanted in the core values, without prejudice. It's not cynicism to assert that we are out for ourselves and the consideration of humanity is to engage our inbred death instinct in as constructive but effective way as possible.

The human condition is as cutthroat today as it was thousand of eons ago in the jungle, yet we are able to constrain its most egregious delegations in favor of civilization's gifts which are far and away superior to life in the entropic chaos of the jungle or savannah. Yet to deny that we are animals trained to hunt, kill and eat other animals is to deny the very nature of protoplasm which has as one of its core qualities the self preservative instinct. This was the bargain evolution made with entropy when flora morphed into fauna, the animalistic assignment to carry out entropy's perverted wishes. And in exchange for that bargain we were able to move over the earth unlike plants, roam the terrain and search for nutrients and partners. We gained the contingency of motion in exchange for using that motion to revert other organic matter back to the inorganic as a nod to entropy's desires. It was not until language operationalized itself that we were cognizant enough of realistic options to grab hold of the concept of civilization as an answer to many of our problems including shelter, food and self protection in the form of jurisprudence.

So the bargain we made with civilization which was heartily endorsed by evolution itself was to submerge the death instinct as best we could in the service of tranquil existence, a flight from chaos and another blow to entropy. Now we relegate the chore of animal slaughter to specialized companies that do the killing for us. We are no longer hungry cheetahs in search of some small creature to devour. And civilization has been so successful that evolution is majorly neutralized since the predators that fueled her crucible have been quelled and disarmed so to speak.

So we suffer from our success, but it makes perfect sense that we followed this life improving path which fostered survival and reproduction against entropy's instincts. So there were several bargains and trade offs along the way. Accepting the internalization of the death instinct that graced to transition from plants to animals. The acceptance of language's gifts in opposition to entropy which still tries to drag our mentality back to disorganized thinking. The formulation of civilizations again in opposition to entropy with our compulsive orderliness and routinized living and working. With civilization came the trade off of submerging the death instinct, again flying in entropy's face. And finally the trade off of neutralizing the predatory intensity to the point where evolution itself is now placated and diffused causing ripples in the populace which has lost direction, the blueprint for how to live in a genderless, non-directed existence.

And we are seeing the fallout from this and must gaze into the crystal ball of the future to grasp what might be rapidly approaching. If the dominating force that plowed us forward over time, helped us wriggle into the habitus that is Homo sapiens is now quelled then what are we? We remain competitive, cut throat and savvy yet in a civilized way most of the time. But if our compass is deflated what does success even look like? The primary issue seems to be one of gender, and we are observing the 'crisis in masculinity' as women dominate in colleges and in the workplace, not in itself a bad thing but within the context of evolution's wane men are left rudderless. Youth are bereft of motion and intent which also hovers around gender and purpose. Since life forms hovered around the necessity for partnership in reproduction the finding of a mate became a tenet of protoplasmic existence. But now we are at a point where children can be manufactured in test tubes and women hired to carry them in their womb with no real emotional connection to the fetus. This all adds up to a diminishment of the concept of gender altogether. But gender has been the supplier of our life's blueprint forever and now, without its intensity, leaves humanity in a freefall unlike any seen before. One might suggest that issues which lead to indecision and confusion are depresso-genic and we are observing this in younger people with rising suicide rates the norm. We have maneuvered ourselves successfully into a moment of radical indifference and this is creating problems as much as the dietary mismatch that engorges us in diabetic excess.

"The most important element in the natural selection of each species… will be the attacks of animals of prey… those individuals which were best able to defend themselves or to escape would survive in greater numbers and transmit their superior qualities." Charles Darwin, *The Descent of Man*, 1871

"Predation is not just random mortalityit is one of the most powerful and constant agents of natural selection. Predators continually "test" the speed, camouflage, vigilance, weapons, intelligence, and other adaptations of their prey, ensuring that only the fittest individuals survive to reproduce. Without this relentless pressure from predators, Darwin believed many of the most exquisite adaptations we see in nature would never have evolved. These passages show that Darwin considered predation absolutely centralnot peripheralto the process of evolution by natural selection." GROK, in response to a request for quotes on Darwin's view of predation's necessity in regards to evolution.

"Our descent, then, is the origin of our evil passions!!The Devil under form of Baboon is our grandfather!… With man, civilization & direction of sympathy to laws has almost done away with the struggle of existence." Charles Darwin, Notebook N, 1838

According to Grok, Darwin would say, "Yes we have largely disarmed and neutralized the human predator-both the external tribal enemy and the internal murderer or bully. This is one of the noblest achievements of civilization, but from the narrow standpoint of natural selection it has suspended one of themes powerful mechanisms that ever honed human courage, intelligence, and bodily vigor. Whether some new selective pressure (perhaps intellectual or economic competition) has fully replaced it is, to me, an open and rather worrying question."

"But with the civilized nations the most symmetrical and vigorous development of all the faculties, together with the best education, gives the superiority." (*Descent of Man*, chapter 7)

"We civilized men, on the other hand, do our utmost to check the process of elimination; we build asylums for the imbecile, the maimed and the sick; we institute poor-laws; and our medical men exert their utmost skill to save the life of every one to the last moment... Thus the weak members of civilized societies propagate their kind. No one who has attended to the breeding of domestic animals will doubt that this must be highly injurious to the race of man." *(Descent of Man*, chapter 5).

Thus we see that the effect of predation is to prune the most undesirable mutations and to preserve the most beneficial to survival. The neutralization of it torpedoes this process and we can thus imagine that mutations that are decidedly unhelpful can survive in modern society. While this is not helpful to mankind, neither is it viable to remove compassion from the concrete core of civilization. If compassion must compete with evolutionary progress then we must favor the nurturance of compassion as one of the greatest benefits of society to mankind. What we must also acknowledge is that evolution's weakening influence is now throwing a major curve ball into our behavioral repertoire, and inducing a collective stupor in regard to life's trajectory. SEVEN MILLION YEARS IS A LONG TIME. Suddenly we are no longer hunting down animals, spear in hand, to kill roast and devour. Likewise men are not conspiring to rape and pillage women in the act of fertilization, and this has a withering effect on human practices. All the ingrained faculties that coalesce around copulation, nesting, male bravado, feminine seductive passivity, outright combat over a mate, competition for shelter, all of it is now on the back burner of evolutionary history. And this leaves humankind with a big fat, NOW WHAT? And that NOW WHAT is causing a rippling effect on human equanimity, since we came from a no holds barred all out warfare of an existence only to morph into couch potato like dehiscence. That change from seven millions years of all our survivalist warfare to the expectations of survival we now endure HAS GOT TO HAVE REPERCUSSIONS. Did mankind expect us to go from the jungle to the disco with no ill effects whatsoever? That viewpoint can only come from a blindness to the influence of our animalistic past as detailed in plain site by one Chuck Darwin. Let us not forget where we came from!

It is true that we in modern civilized society have no real connection to the lifestyle we evolved in for some seven million years. Is it any wonder that testosterone levels are falling over the past several decades? If one asks what kind of profession might most closely mimic the physical rigors of caveman life the answer is none. The average caveman was physically on alert every waking minute in response to potential predatory threats. He had to be physically honed, beefed up as much as possible which required protein food intake and be ready to fight for his life at any moment. Physical prowess was not just helpful it was potentially life saving. If we look at perhaps wrestlers, powerlifters, football or rugby players they might slightly approximate the physical rigors and demands of an average caveman, at least in a slight degree. One wonders then if they have higher testosterone levels than most males. Answer: yes. Studies show that athletes in explosive strength sports have a resting total testosterone level 10-30% above average. There are many potential explanations for this but clearly those who mimic the intensity of caveman brutality are maintaining their male hormones more than others, and those with the most intense roles have higher levels. For example in American football offensive and defensive linemen have the highest testosterone compared with the quarterbacks whose minute to minute intensity the sport is somewhat less.

What are we to conclude from this? The reason male hormone levels have been dropping for decades is that the rigorous intensity of caveman life has been neutralized. In fact of late males wonder if being typically 'macho' is dismissive of women. Is it sexist to be overtly masculine and to try to impress women with this trait, leaving aside the question of whether or not women approve of this behavior? If we hop back a mere 50,000 years, a drop in the evolutionary bucket, we see men simply overtly 'macho' in the context of survival threats that were not only real but often successful against them. Their macho masculinity was simply a byproduct of the predatory environment in which they attempted to survive, over millions of years and this has been only recently changed. The 'hyper masculinity' of the cavemen has been neutralized and is fortunately unnecessary. But if we had measured the testosterone levels of Mr. Caveman one might obviously conclude they would be much higher than ours. So we are 'suffering' from our success in reducing predatory intensity and in making our lives less 'macho' but the fallout, and there is always a consequence, is lower testosterone levels which lowers masculine reproductive intensity, not something mother evolution wants, lowers muscle mass and over all physical fitness which is why some athletes use steroids to 'bulk up' to the caveman physique. This is just another example of the distance we have put ourselves from the evolutionary environment we were created in for millions of years. We suffer the benefits and the consequences of this distance and are seeing madam evolution herself withering helplessly in this distance. Of course she fully approved of the creation of civilization as a boon to survival and protection against the natural born killers that devoured us on a routine basis. Madam evolution, who banged the drum of procreation for many millions of years has now been neutralized and we see ourselves less sexually active, less willing to attempt to hook up with others, less intoxicated and less 'macho' all because of our success in eliminating the horrors of jungle life. We should congratulate ourselves while we attend to the backlash of our success. And one of those fallouts is mental illness .

So we can assume that low testosterone is just another one of those repercussions of the waning of madam evolution's potency. Yes there are other reasons for testosterone levels to be lowering such as increased cannabis use, plastics in our food and water, and perhaps a myriad of oddball possibilities. One can only conclude however that this follows the trends we are seeing related to the dilution of procreative ardor secondary to the collapse of Madame E. It all adds up to a consistent picture of deflation in multiple areas leading to the anxious depression of youth who wonder just what their role in life should be on many paradigms of existence including sexual, societal, mental and physical. And these are issues the boomer generation never had to deal with. Our parents, fresh from a heinous war which placed them all at dire risk, a predatory situation to be sure. And this resulted in their return to the mainland, those who survived, with definite ideas about what their lives should be. A small house, a car, a spouse and a kid were the soldier's fantasy, born of whiplash of a devastating war that left many of their friends deceased. This mimicked in some ways the jungle lifestyle we endured for the past seven million years. They had no indecisiveness, these GI's who returned salivating for stability, complacency and security. Thee was no indecision, they knew exactly what life should be and how to get it. And their Levittown dreams came true for many who latched onto a career, a spouse and house, complete with mouse.

The 50's and 60's were in some ways idyllic moments in our history, and then another war crept up, horrifying the offspring of those WW11 vets' offspring. Suddenly we were embroiled in a combat that seemed utterly unnecessary to many boomers who went to Woodstock, slept in the rain and mantra-ized peace. The pride at the greatest cultural event of the decade or more that no one was harmed, no fights, no disputes, despite the lack of food and facilities gave Woodstock more of an iconic glow than it really even deserved. Yet the echo of 'peace' as a symbol of their parents wariness of anything but a staid life was palpable. They had learned from their vet parents that war was ugly, really ugly, and that there had to be a decidedly immediate palpable threat to reengage in such a fantasyland. Vietnam was a long way away and there seemed no legitimate reason to be dying there. Yet over 50,000 did.

The boomers's folksongs morphed into protest symphonies and suddenly they had a cause to protest, demonstrate and resist about. They did not want to return to the jungle of Vietnam any more than they wanted to return to the jungle we evolved in. Protest turn to demonstration until Kent State massacre of 4 students stopped us in our tracks. Suddenly our own government became the predator. Repression reared its head. The Smother's Brothers got canned after a salacious defiance to the government by comedians. They never recovered from the dismissal. We found ourselves at war with our own government and it became the focus of adolescent protest and rebellion which otherwise might have centered on the parents of the boomers. This unseemly war caught the boomers at a moment when rebellion was expected, parental rebellion at least.

But eventually the war ended, and although there were others none wrenched the activism from us boomers like Vietnam did . We sank into a society of people trying to establish themselves in careers, lives, relationships and insulation from tragedy. And for many it worked. Gradually a sense of equanimity and peace did fertilize the land and we found ourselves in a vague epoch of stability. And this was a stability so determined that it flowered the advance of the computer era and the digitalization of our libraries and ideation.

"Consciousness arises in the place of the memory-trace… Thinking in pictures is only a very incomplete form of becoming conscious. In some way, too, it stands nearer to unconscious processes than does thinking in words, and it is unquestionably older than the latter both ontogenetically and phylogenetically." (Sigmund Freud, "The Unconscious", 1915)

One could say that language is the royal road from the pleasure principle to the reality principle, and it is a very recent acquisition. The infant hallucinates their desires when not immediately gratified, a process that becomes real again when schizophrenics regress to preverbal thought processes. Language is necessary to replace hallucination with words that can serve to partially gratify wishes while at the same time upholding the reality principle. The reality principle cannot become the modus operandi of the infant until language sinks in. Language therefore is the force that makes secondary process thinking rather than hallucination or primary process daydreaming the principle mode of thought, gradually over time. Patients of Freud worked through their symptoms once they were analyzed and put into words. One could say that language is the royal road from the pleasure principle to the reality principle and that without language we would still be cavemen. All of us. It was the adoption of language by Homo sapiens and our facility with symbol formation, the soul of language, that we conquered the other species of Homo and fanned out across the globe and are now eight billion strong.

"The appearance of new ways of thinking and communicating, between 70,000 and 30,000 years ago, constitutes the Cognitive Revolution. What caused it? We're not sure. The most commonly believed theory argues that accidental genetic mutations changed the inner wiring of the brains of Sapiens, enabling them to think in unprecedented ways and to communicate using an altogether new type of language. We might call it the Tree of Knowledge mutation. Why did it occur in Sapiens DNA rather than that of Neanderthals? It was a matter of pure chance, as far as we can tell. But it's more important to understand the consequences of the Tree of Knowledge mutation than its causes. What was so special about the new Sapiens language that it enabled us to conquer the world?" (Yuval Harari, *Sapiens*, p. 21)

In this regard Harari is agreeing with Freud in that until language arrived on the scene, we were animals incapable of articulating anything close to reality. Once language appeared we were able to distinguish reality from fantasy, actuality from hallucinated wish fulfillment and thus we conquered the world since the other species of Homo or any species of animal did have this endowment. So here we see clearly what, as I have been saying, has brought us to the precipice of greatness, of civilizations, of higher learning and of incalculable achievement. We must take a sober eyed view of it, for now we are appreciating the collateral damage that this monumental achievement left on the side of the road. Every blessing has its undesired consequences. When Cinderella finally got the glass slippers she was stuck marrying some douchebag who treated her like the maid. (I just made that up, kids.) When Homo sapiens were endowed with the blessing of language which allowed us to move from hallucinatory wish fulfillment to reality testing, conquer the world and set up civilizations that dragged us from the jungle to the disco, many unwanted things tipped as collateral damage. One was mental illness which is the result of such a recent all encompassing change in how we use our minds. Those least on board are what we call mentally ill, or as I put it, *EVOLUTION'S DISPOSSESSED.* We suffer from other 'mismatch' situations in which our sedentary lifestyle with its dietary richness is causing type two diabetes and other monumental headaches physically. And now we're also becoming cognizant, as only Homo sapiens can, that this blessing has allowed us to torpedo evolution and vacuum her influence on our reproductive habits.

Clearly we have been tricked into a gimmick, a situation of false bravado in which the most salient blessings of language including civilization, education, and realistic thinking en masse have been tricked into screwing us like the soldiers hiding in the Trojan Horse. We became so good at neutralizing the predatory intensity of jungle existence, the lifestyle that ruled our evolutionary mutational pruning for some seven million years, that now mother evolution herself is reeling from the undoing of this necessary evolutionary fuel and finding herself limp, unexamined and forgotten. We are SO BRAINY THAT WE HAVE GIVEN EVEN EVOLUTION THE HEAVE HO. And it is from this perilous situation that we are seeing a host of societal woes, unlike anything we've seen before and boding a future far different than anything we had ever imagined in our ungainly past.

"Excepting in the case of man himself, hardly any one is so ignorant as to allow his worst animals to breed. If the various checks… do not prevent the reckless, the vicious and otherwise inferior members of society from increasing at a quicker rate than the better class of men, the nation will retrograde, as has occurred too often in the history of the world. We must remember that progress is no invariable rule." (C. Darwin, *The Descent of Man,* Chapter XX1)

"Man, like every other species, is capable of deteriorating as well as of advancing… The more efficient causes of progress seem to consist of a good education during youth whilst the brain is impressible, and of a high standard of excellence, inculcated by the ablest and best men, embodied in the laws customs and traditions of the nation, and enforced by public opinion. It is only by these means that the nations which are now the most civilized have slowly risen from barbarism." (He implies that without such checks, civilization itself undermines natural selection and risks decline.) (Darwin, *The Descent of Man,* chap XX1)

Darwin believed that natural selection was in a sense reversed in modern societies and that his could be very harmful to the species in the long run.

"Evolution is dead, we're not going to let it happen anymore" James D. Watson, co discoverer of DNA.

"Darwin was wrong about humanity… Today we stand on the threshold of overthrowing the laws of evolution altogether." Yuval Harari, Homo Deus

"With the advent of genetic technology, anthropotechnology, and the possibility of self-optimization, Darwinian evolution has been replaced by the era of selection by human choice. Evolution is over; the age of selection has begun." Peter Sloterdijk (German philosopher)

"Once artificial intelligence reaches human level and beyond, biological evolution will be seen as a brief interlude in cosmic history. The future belongs to post-Darwinian, post-biological forms of organization." Nick Bostrom, (Oxford philosopher.)

"We now have the power to step outside the brutal Darwinian arena." Richard Dawkins

"Darwinian evolution had a good 3.8 billion year run, bit its time is up." Yuval Harari

It is not terrible to explore the possibility of a post Darwinian existence, since evolution has suffered the cruelest blow of all, death by its own success. With the help of technology, science, and sheer compassion we have neutralized so many of our jungle predatory enemies that natural selection as defined by Darwin is over and we have to face the fact that evolution's mandates are wavering in indecision. And this indecision is causing a tidal wave of panic and confusion that ripple all through the land. We used the blessings of language to embark on a sea of reality and this scientific examination led us to civilizations which replaced the jungle crucible intensity with a conspiracy of survival. We were intent on disentangling from the terror of being eaten regularly by our animal neighbors. The nightmare of dying slowly from infections, snake bites, broken limbs and pelvises, and the horrors of freezing to death or starving when drought scorched the meal pan of survival all led our brains to solutions, and those blessed solutions gave madam E a groin kick she will never recover from.

So let us be realistic and wise, utilizing the powerhouse of our Homo sapiens brains to understand that which shimmers before us. People are moving away from each other because evolution's mandate to procreate has been silenced. People are depressed and suicidal because they no longer have the blueprint for what their lives are supposed to be. Men can't figure how to be men any more and women are brazenly taking the lead but their stage directions are just as mish mashed as their spouse'. What was obvious for seven million jungle years is no longer valid in the disco. The horrors of jungle intensity have been slogging into the quicksand of longevity and now we must realize that existence has a moment in and of itself without madam E's howling direction. "Survive, and reproduce!" she said. Yeah, we get that but now it's more like we got the survival thing generally covered, so now what, Madam?

So currently we get to choose what a life will be. Will it be a specific gender at all or just a genderless existence? Will there be offspring involved or not, a family existence or isolation? Does it matter? Should I be a macho man or a wimpy nerdy guy, and does it matter if there is to be no nest, no family paradigm with dad carting home the bacon and mom sizzling up the fries while junior runs around knocking over the lamp and giggling in delight that there is someone there to give a crap. Should we get involve with reproduction at all? These are questions that my boomer generation never had to face or contend with and so we were lucky in that our path was clear, but that which once was a given is no longer a trail at all. We must face indecision and make a new road which can be discarded at will and reexamined once its been well worn into the soil of existing. Let us embrace the new, the oddball the indecisive and the standard and let it all hang out until a new pathway is forged by our lack of predatory terror. Accepting that our lifestyle options are infinitely greater implies tolerance for those whose choices do not mirror ours. And never forget that the ghoul of entropy is always ready to pick up the slack and that if we let it, terror and destruction can resurface at any moment, and will in various ways if we are not careful. Perhaps the best way to ensure that AI does not stumble into the hands of entropy is to INCORPORATE AI INTO US AND NOT PUT IT IN THE HANDS OF AUTOMATONS. We can become the first generation of internalized AI which will then become a means of newly minted evolving, into something grander than biology alone could fashion, some hybrid human that incorporates the sizzle AI's genius into the compassion of human kindness. And if it falls into the wrong human body that body can be eliminated if society chooses that path.

CHAPTER V
FUTURE VISION

WHY WE DO NOT NEED AI NOW, OR MAYBE EVER

Lets recall how we got here. A mere 50,000 years ago we were animals, not even at the top of the food chain, eking out a meager existence and perishing under the predatory insistence of hungry wolves, untreatable infections, broken bones, starvation, cold and any number of other insults that had no remedy at that time. We were brainy animals derived from the wily chimp and as such were able to survive moderately well. Our cerebral cortexes kept expanding and eventually reached a critical mass, one which was so large as to barely allow our heads through the birth canal. And many mothers and children did die in childbirth. We lived in nature, scouting out homes in overhanging cliffs, building mud huts or finding shelter wherever we could.

At some point our brains became large enough and complex enough to handle symbol formation, a talent especially suited for the sapiens species of the genus Homo, of which there were many including the Neanderthals and the Denisovans to name a few. Symbol formation, the soul of language, allowed us to start communicating in a much more sophisticated way. Suddenly words were substituted for objects, actions and states of mind. This revolution fertilized our minds, creating divisions and subdivisions that Freud labeled conscious, preconscious and unconscious, which gave us the supreme ability to store words in a chamber and hunt for them while we formulated a thought. Our brains developed a functional capacity that began to outstrip our Homo neighbors like the Neanderthals. We became more COMPLEX, a trait unwelcome to the second law of thermodynamics, namely our good enemy entropy. But it was this functional complexity that eventually allowed us to outstrip every other species, and we wiped them all out by the year 10,000 BC. WIPED THEM ALL OUT. Then we fanned out across the globe, and dominated the earth to the point where we created things called civilizations that served evolution's wishes well and which, again, gave ol' entropy a knee to the cajones. Make no mistake about it, IT WAS OUR ADVANCED INTELLIGENCE BORN OF LANGUAGE THAT ALLOWED US TO DOMINATE THE WORLD AND WE WENT AHEAD AND DID JUST THAT.

So, ladies and gentlemen as we sit passively and watch some IT geniuses create beings infinitely smarter than we are, prepare to be joining the group of species that are wiped out by another, smarter, more antropic one, more detailed in complexity than we are. It doesn't matter whether we create these creatures or not, just as it didn't matter that chimpanzees 'created' so to speak Homo sapiens. We dominated them like any other animal and put them in very well tended zoos. And that is where we will be, sitting behind bars in some zoo while robots stroll by and laugh at us. "They used to rule the world, these dumb animals," while they toss us a crust of bread. At this point in time, WE ARE BEING MUCH TOO PASSIVE ABOUT THIS. It will happen that AI beings will take us over just like we took over the world due to our greater mental complexity born of language. Language gave us the reality principle, and now we are giving it to robots in even greater doses than us dumb Homo sapiens exhibit.

And why are we being so passive about our ultimate enslavement? Why would we let this happen? For the same reason we polluted the rivers and streams, the same mindset that allowed us to sully the atmosphere with carbon dioxide to the point that the ozone layer is now crippled and we are seeing intensity of sunlight that causes skin cancer at alarming rates. For the same reason that we allowed mass murders, genocides and holocaust events to happen. We all have the death instance inside of us, like any other animal who learns to hunt, kill and eat other animals to survive. Only we relegate most of the raising and killing of animals to chicken farms and cattle ranches. One cattle, depending on their weight can produce 400-600 pounds of edible meat and as such are tempting sources of food and profit. So we raise them to kill and eat them but leave the details of that to cattle ranches and slaughter houses. Yet that impulse is within us all and we have an underlying urge, every single one of us to return to inorganic matter, and to return others to that state of none existence. WE ALL SERVE ENTROPY and entropy reclaims each and every one of us. It is the species, not the individual that survives, but under circumstances of domination, millions of species have disappeared. This is why we are reckless in our wars, our pollutions, in deforesting the rain forest for paper, in eliminating habitats of animals that silently disappear, all in the name of entropy.

And because of our obedience to the force that reclaims us all, we are being very passive about AI's potential to wipe us all out. Where are the laws controlling it, the panels of experts telling us how to handle this impending takeover that's heading our way like a freight train as of this writing. HEED MY WARNING AND STOP THIS NOW. Once we figure out how to keep strict control over it, then let it flourish, but until then we need to put the brakes on this freight train. These AI beings are DEFYING ENTROPY MORE EFFECTIVELY THAN WE DO. That should tell you right there that this is big and it is serious. Are AI beings actually alive? I can't answer that, but they certainly have the essence of life which is to defy entropy in the most intricate way possible. (As I'm typing AI just filled in the word 'possible' for me. Thanks, AI).

While evolution has stopped, it has also picked up a new champion, AI, and it is that sawhorse that will someday dominate the world… if we lose control of it. We may already have. So evolution, by reaching a pinnacle of achievement with the Homo sapiens,, the wise ones, has now started to look to a new champion, one that has more chance of success than us, despite being eight billion strong. We won the evolutionary contest over the last 50,000 years thanks to language with such vigor that we ended evolution's ardor, but now something new on the horizon is peaking madam E's interest. Survival of the fittest, neutralized by civilization's successes, is now in the hands of an inorganic being. And who do you think is tickled pink by this wacko development? Correct! Entropy. For now the rulers of the universe are not organic but inorganic beings, and it is entropy's fondest wish to turn everything back to inorganic matter. It will have won if the globe is ruled by robots, and we wither away or worse, are simply wiped out by them.

While we shrink from the thought or act as if it just couldn't happen, we have to admit that beings with IQ's of 500 will be so infinitely smarter than we are that subjugation is a decided possibility. We are not used to thinking in such terms as the possibility has not arisen before, BUT NOW IT HAS. And it is less a possibility than a certainty whose blueprint is none other than us. We rose to the top on our intelligence and mental complexity born of language and if a being exists that tops us in both of those areas, WE'RE TOAST! Don't kid yourself, turn away and say, oh somebody's smart enough to prevent it from happening. WRONG! The forces that are pushing AI forward are far too strong to let it drop unless intense barriers against its evolution forward are erected with laws to back them up, and this would have to be an international effort. Any AI advance without strict controls represent a direct threat to humanity, period. If we don't realize that we are not as smart as we thought we were. We have to learn from what happened to us. When we gained mental complexity we gained the unstoppable advantage and the other species of Homo were gone, wiped out, gonzo by 10,000 BC. Let's not kid ourselves, and lets not assume someone else 'got this', cause they don't. First we need to halt AI development completely then license each company based on their ability to show us the level of control over their project that they have. Without that they've got to be shut down. While it's hard to comprehend that a scientific progress could end us, look at nuclear bombs. They can end us and the rest of living beings under the wrong hands. The only reason they don't is that we have strict international controls over nuclear bombs. And without that there will be trouble, right here in River City.

That's the type of control we need to see in regards to AI. We must regard it as a more powerful bomb than the A bomb, the H bomb or any other mega explosive that has the capacity to end humanity. It IS possible that we can end ourselves at the insistence and ingenuity of us. Nuclear explosives prove that. The question of whether or not AI beings are actually alive is not that easy for if we stick to our definition of life as defying entropy, they certainly are that. They also have a self preservative instinct and seek the necessary nutrients in the form of electric power. They do not need each other to reproduce however and they can create one another in a factory . Given all this they are very close to being what one would call 'alive' and they have been birthed by Homo sapiens. Let us not be so brilliant as to create our own replacement. Entropy is more than joyous thinking that an inorganic being could end the organic protoplasm of the Homo sapiens. And entropy will be endeavoring to convince us that all is well, nothing to see here, as it did when we polluted the streams and rivers, the air and created nuclear explosives. We are not good at examining the dangers of certain achievements, if they can be described as such.

Some two million years ago chimpanzees were pleasant animals frolicking about the jungle, often smarter then their predator brethren in the intensity of an evolutionary habitat. But the DNA of one of them underwent a mutation, as DNA is want to do, and something akin to a human, a hominin. arose. Australopithecus, Homo erecctus, Neanderthals, Denisovan, Sapiens. All of these gradually emerged over millions of years and became an 'us'. And that "US" was remarkably adept at symbol formation, the soul of language. And once you have language your brain is very different, more organized, less primitive, exceedingly complex and capable of what we call rational thinking, divining truth from fiction. Now when we visit the zoo, we witness those similar chimpanzees frolicking about, teasing each other and throwing feces at us Homo sapiens who have imprisoned them. We are now their captors and it is because of our advanced intelligence and brain power that we have conquered the world, 8 billion strong. Our DNA has not undergone any particular mutation, but our wise craniums have created something like a mutation, a being called AI which is now in a position to do to us exactly what we did to our forebears. We are set to give birth to a mutation that is smarter and better organized, more capable of reasoning than we are, EXACTLY THE SITUATION WE WERE IN WITH THE CHIMPANZEES. And if you don't think that AI beings will be more than happy to take over the globe, think again. We are putting ourselves in the exact position chimpanzees were in millions of year ago through mutation, only we're doing it through computation.

A world where AI beings rule us is not a pretty picture. Imagine AI robots laughing at us while we sit in cages waiting to be fed. This is not fantasy, it's a reality that is overtaking us at lightening speed and our passivity and confusion about it will lead to our subjugation as surely as the chimps sit in cages in zoos across the nation waiting for their morning banana. And our old friend entropy will be more than happy to see it take place as the AI beings are inorganic entities not protoplasm. Despite their lifelike qualities they will not fit the full definition of 'alive' until they have mitochondria, and neuroreceptors and livers and spleens. What they do have is batteries wires and artificial joints.

One possible solution to the AI threat is to limit it to entities that are incorporated into us Homo sapiens. I'm talking about artificial limbs, brain implanted chips, glucose regulators and such that improve that quality of our lives and even save us from imminent death. We can become 'hybrid' beings that incorporate the brilliance of AI into our bodies to improve our overall health in multiple areas. We could become the protectors of ourselves and AI by only using it in conjunction with a human body. This would be a way of making us in control of the AI zeitgeist. When you're playing with fire you must be able to confine it to a specific area in which you have sand, water and fire extinguishers at the ready. In that instance the fire will enrich our lives not turn it to a crisp.

And AI insurgency is arriving just when evolution is floundering from the lack of predation that the brainy Homo sapiens have arranged for themselves with great success. This could be more than coincidence, as something so paradigm shifting may have been suggested to us by evolution's withdrawal from the scene. Unconsciously we knew that something had to rise up to replace evolution's absence. Thus we have 'given birth' to something earth shattering that will override evolution's absence. That absence is leading us to depression and youth suicide, withdrawal from sexuality and sociality, precipitously lowering birth rates and masculine crisis, not to mention gender boundary confusion and ambivalence. At a time when socializing is waning, AI has stepped in to provide us with companions, directions for research, endless screen images and other time occupiers which are conspiring to remove us from ourselves.

When does the average youth spend time alone just sitting and considering things? According to *iGen* by Twenge high school kids spend less time alone and when they do they are engaged in screen time, even when sitting down and having dinner with family. (p. 29) "... parents have arranged for fewer 14-, 15-, and 16year old teens to be at home by themselves in the afternoon. Thus teens are not just less likely to go out without their parents; they are also less likely to be at home without their parents." And if any alone time kids do have is blitzed by screens then when do they actually have a moment to reconnect WITH THEMSELVES?

China's population could be cut in half by 2100 and Japan's may drop to 75 to 100, million from a peak of 128.5 million in 2010. In general a total fertility rate (TFR) of about 2.1 is needed to maintain a stable population. China's TFR is about 1.0 to 1.2 currently, not enough maintain their population. In the 1980's China had over 20 births per 1,000 annually, but currently has about half that in crude birth rate. Japan's birth rate has been declining for decades. They are now down to about 5-6 per thousand people yearly with a TFR of about 1.15, much lower than needed to maintain the population. Experts doubt that there will be much change in this trend. This will strain the workforce and pension systems, with potential for economic slowdowns. So we can expect declining populations essentially worldwide, not just in Asian countries although they represent the extremes.

On the other hand there is a probability that AI will displace 6-7% of the workforce over the next ten years and that 40% of jobs may have some exposure to intrusion by AI. Some 50 million US entry level jobs are vulnerable and high risk sectors include administrative support like data entry, customer service/sales, food services and production or manufacturing and entry level white collar. But almost any job faces cut backs and scale downs due to AI. Some 60% of workers may require retraining by the year 2030. So the future sees declining populations with jobs being replaced by AI driven workers. This in a sense dovetails nicely but signals the clear diminishment of evolution's cry for procreation. Yet those who are born will face greater challenges finding an occupation that is secure, workable and supportive of a lifestyle that could include a family, meaning offspring. So it is likely that evolution's mandate will suffer greater blows in a land where job security is tenuous and 'nesting' behaviors unlikely to be secure. Couple that with the trend away from mate finding one can predict with some certainty that we are looking at a population of loners, not seeking partners or continuing to dance to evolution's mantra to survive and reproduce, both of which will be more challenging in the coming years.

One must envision then a gradual transition to an industrial lifestyle of isolation, existence in a small apartment separate from others, interacting via computer with their jobs or with extensive unemployed populations spending time in front of screens with no major productivity at all. The single, isolated, non-relating life of the hermit may become the standard by which people exist. Socialization might be digitally interactive at best, and for some nonexistent. So, along with evolution's collapse, AI's intrusion into the world's workforce and other factors that include economic deprivation, global warming and gender ambivalence we will see a population of isolated, unemployed, unrelated individuals who have little to no significant social connection at all. Options to better one's life situation will be limited.

What will life be like then, when most of us will occupy small apartments, interact via computer at best and avoid actual social contact altogether? The word disconnect seems most appropriate. The vast hordes of unemployed will obtain most of their intellectual and social stimulation via screens and this will be inadequate for mature social development no doubt. Most people will be adrift and addicted to internet activities that at least occupy their time. Governments will have to provide a basic floor of income to the majority who cannot find an occupation. The average person will not be in a position to pay taxes, so governments will be starved for funds. Marriage rates will probably plummet and gender confusion increase. In short there will be massive numbers of unemployed, disconnected, genderless individuals who do not seek connection to any other human and eschew marriage, sex, family or human touch altogether. The severity of this new 'no touch' lifestyle may end sexuality altogether as people choose masturbation as a safer outlet for their hormonally driven urges.

"The extermination of the Jews is a rumor which the Germans themselves have spread and which the Allied governments have found convenient to exploit." The Christian Century, June 14, 1944

"Auschwitz Story Suppressed for Five Months." PM, November 1944

"The Old Lie Again: 'Extermination' Stories Revived" Manchester Guardian, July 1942

"Britain Hears Jews Are Being Killed" Chicago Tribune, December 18, 1942 buried on page 14.

"11 Allies Condemn Nazi War on Jews" buried on page 11, New York times, December 8, 1942.

"Escapee From Camp Tells of Mass Killings in Gas Chambers At Auschwitz" buried on page 10, New York Times, November 26, 1944

Is mankind capable of denial? Having read the above relating to World War 11 one could only say so. But now we are in denial of the potential enemy that hovers in AI tech companies at this moment as these 'robots' overtake our intelligence in leaps and bounds.

And it is not like no one is sounding the alarm. Just today sitting in Starbucks I encountered two stories on You Tube about this very same concept. Here are some examples "Ex-Open AI Scientist WARNS: "You Have No Idea What's Coming" with a caption, "WE'RE FUCKED" Ilya Sutskever. "Full Interview: Godfather of AI" shares prediction for future of AI, issues warnings" says things have gotten scarier than they were before. Geoffrey Hinton. Your will find many others on You Tube if you start to look for them.

Above is a picture of how we'll look when AI robots take over with their superior intelligence and place us all in zoos.

In short DENIAL KILLS, and in this instance it is us that will be the victims. We are dealing with the one thing that has placed Homo sapiens above all other animals, and if we bequeath this to some other being, organic or not, we will be condemning ourselves to eternal subjugation. The above picture was created, by the way, by AI (Grok). It will create essentially any picture you ask it to. I've had it create cartoon-like pictures of Einstein, Freud and Darwin. I can ask Grok anything, from the current price of a car loan to Darwin's views on the end of evolution. (He didn't predict its end but did say that natural selection was being diluted by the tendency of society to aid individuals with obvious handicaps.) If we CHOOSE to ignore AI's dangers now, we will pay for it in the near future, to the extent that our entire ongoing existence may be terminated.

And this of course dovetails with the end of evolution, for if madam E fizzled into comatoseness, then another force, one with the persuasive intuition of a high IQ will step in and naturally inveigle the principles of evolution since they will then be the fittest and as such meet the demands of natural selection supremely. We may find that very quickly the options have been pulled out from under us and the choices we are left with are paltry at best. The world is in an intensive competition for AI strength and benefit in terms of weapons, cunning, and ability to castrate their enemies and if we allow it we will be the recipients of such calamity.

Mother evolution is in favor of two things when it comes to organic matter... survival and reproduction, and it is only interested in survival up to the point of reproduction. This has been its mantra since day one and it serves the purpose not only of promoting life, but of defying entropy which seeks to turn us into the other planets, balls of rock and dust. So it is not just that evolution puts living matter ahead of everything else, its that it very specifically defies a force of nature, the second law of thermodynamics that rules the universe on every other planet known to man. So let us not kid ourselves into thinking that evolution is just a passive promoter of living cells, it is a warrior in the battle against entropy, and has joined with antropy, the opposing force, to promote its wishes. We have outsmarted ourselves in the game of nature since the force of entropy is just drooling over the possibility of putting an end to evolution altogether.

It is a fact that without the aid of something like DNA life would not evolve at all. It is the exploitation of entropy's tendency to disorder that results in mutations and mama E has made good use of that tendency to evolve protoplasm into something like a Homo sapiens, the premium model of development. We are the Maserati of species and gained the gift of reason once we got language and coalesced into civilizations. If we are going to give the gift of reason to another type of being then we are sending ourselves into second place in the universe of entropic defiance. And this will be the end of us. We will be like any other animal except that our reason will lead us to see that we have executed ourselves and relegated mankind to the slavery of second place, and the domination by a nimbler force. The death of evolution then is accompanied by the rise of AI intelligence and it is no coincidence that one has risen up to replace the other. But the latter is a non organic being with questionable finite examples of 'living'. It exists, that is all w know and it will soon exist to control and dominate us. The only question is how far it will take that option.

But, you say, AI is the supreme defying force against entropy. Yes, but that only speaks to its power not its behavior. AI defies entropy in its brainy complexity and its complexity of inorganic parts, and entropy likes the inorganic as it is much less complex than the coalition of cells that make up all living matter. So in the bargain between AI and living protoplasm, entropy has made a significant gain when evolution bows out and AI bows in. Since each individual cell is a complex living being in and of itself, and living beings have trillions of cells, it is in great defiance of entropy that plants and animals exist. Each little cell has mitochondria, cell walls, vesicles, nuclei with DNA direction involved. This supremacy of organization cannot be matched by any AI enlightened being. AI has only one thing going for it, a one trick pony that is a whopping brain.. So in short the bargain with entropy and evolution falls into entropy's hands when madam E dissolves and AI steps in. This is bad news for living matter.

And entropy sees another opening in the crack of its exclusion wall. AI is the supreme weapon and will be used by countries in the race for AI destructiveness. And it is in the nature of humans to utilize weapons of mass destruction for their own benefits if possible. This is a facet of the ubiquitous death instinct that relegates all compassion to dissolution. Within the framework of AI's potentiality for destructiveness entropy will easily exploit our combative nature to entertain a modus operandi of mutual attack to the point of a mass destruction event like the Chixulub asteroid that wiped out the dinosaurs sixty five million years ago. Such an event is not unlikely in the face of weapons more destructive than nuclear bombs, weapons that can think for themselves and have IQ's of 1000. These weapons will know how to dodge incommoding bullets, foil operating systems of countering agents, how best to neutralize enemy forces and where their missiles will have most effect.

These will not be your ordinary weapons, far from the caveman's pointy spear and lightyears beyond the modern army's cannon. This weapon will think for itself, protect itself and laugh at anyone who dares to assume that they can extinguish it. This smart weapon will find a way to fuck us up the ass with aplomb and do so in record time while dodging any bullet we may uselessly toss at them. So of course there is intense pressure to get one's hands on these nightmarish machines by all countries who wish to dominate and defend themselves, which is essentially all nations. Nothing can stop this race to destructiveness as entropy sits back and laughs at his arch enemy evolution that has now been dealt the fatal blow since we wisely ended the horrendous predators that nipped and bit our ankles to death in the jungle. Little did we know that when we ended the destructive forces in the jungle that entropy so enthusiastically endorsed we were ending evolutions' intensity forever and replacing it with the most deadly machines known to us Homo sapiens.

So entropy has now flourished in this bargain with evolution and AI, very bad news for us protoplasmic entities. Robotic AI brainiacs will survive but mankind will not. Other animal entities may survive since AI has no need to extinguish them. But the humans who created them are wise and need to be subdued lest they find a way, in their magnificence to end the AI ogres that will own the earth. But we have yet to develop a foolproof kill switch for AI beings. No one is sure exactly how this must look. Anything that runs on electricity can be squelched by defunding their juice in some way, so it might have to be a mechanical kill switch that runs only on non-electrified machinery, like a powerful sling shot that a marksman could use to launch a grenade type bomb at an AI predator. We have created the ultimate predator that now will subjugate us without reinstating evolution as there will be no mutation within us that can promote survival against an AI attack.

While some will insist that evolution has not died, one could argue that what's left of it is meaningless and ineffectual. For evolution to have the potency it had in the jungle there would need to be gradients of significance. In the searing intensity of the jungle a mutation that had affected one's ability to have physical expertise in running, dodging, climbing, spear throwing, lifting or eyeballing an approaching predator would have immediate impact on one's survival, to name a few gradients of jungle significance. But in the current habitat of civilizations munificence, one would have to have a major disability, genetically determined, to signify a gradient of enough import to decrease your chances of reproducing or surviving. Schizophrenics, for example, show no evidence of going extinct even though their fecundity ratio is half the normal, in short they have offspring half as often as most of us. There are two reasons why schizophrenia is not headed for extinction; one is that we set up group homes and other residences where they are looked after with some eye toward helping them survive. Another is the possibility that schizophrenia IS NOT A GENETIC ILLNESS. Remember that evolution can only adjudicate conditions that are a result of mutations. At this point we have not found a schizophrenia gene. At best we can identify hundreds of single nucleotide polymorphisms that are more common in schizophrenics. But this is far from a genetic cause, rather just a signal of increased susceptibility for the disease.

There are multiple environmental factors that also increase vulnerability to its appearance and factors we are not aware of. But, as I emphasized in my first book, *Footprints of Schizophrenia: the Evolutionary Roots of Mental Illness*, those who are mentally ill have simply not adjusted to the new way of using our minds that set in with the adoption of language. It is simply too new and too radical a mind bender for the 20% or so who have a diagnosable mental illness to be able to corral dopamine fully in the appropriate tracts. So in the late teens to early twenties their dopamine surges and they regress back to primitive thinking, the kind we had prior to language 50,000 years ago. And such is the case with schizophrenia in which the loss of dopamine suppression results in a massive regression in thinking and they are thus in need of caretaking, often for the rest of their lives.

Bu for true genetic illnesses like sickle cell anemia or Tay Sachs disease the afflicted can get assistance in modern society to remain alive and reproduce if practical. So in essence we have bludgeoned the impact of adverse mutations by at least 70% if not more and there are few iron clad gradients that serve to disqualify one from reproductive survival. Some give the example of lactose intolerance as proof that evolution is still viable. Those with lactose tolerance are increasing so we must be seeing an evolutionary shift away from intolerance. Well in a sense we are although the consequences of lactose intolerance are neither life threatening nor procreativity negative. At one time we were all lactose intolerant except for infants. When Homo sapiens shifted to a dairy rich diet it became more important for one to be able to tolerate lactose. Yet it was not necessarily the only food available at the time. Yet this gradient allowed those with lengthier tolerance to lactose to be able to survive somewhat more easily than those without and so it gradually became ingrained evolutionarily and continues to expand now. However at this time the gradient is hardly intense, since we have lactose free milk and there are many other food options to keep one alive even if you are maximally intolerant of milk products. So this is an example of how evolution's intensity has abated with progress. In the jungle those gradients were razor sharp and extinction was rapid, now they're dull as molasses and just as slow in adjudicating an answer.

Some modern situations do mimic jungle predation in their severity and do result in some evolutionary advancement. One such situation was the pandemic of 2019 which killed over a million Americans. This situation put us all in a predatory environment, yet one must assert that only those in a pre or current procreative position could have influenced evolution. And the influence had to do with immune system function since those who were able to fight off the virus were able to go on and reproduce at a later time, whereas poor immune system folks might have died from the Covid viral attack. So there probably was an evolutionary selection of higher immune system functioners who managed to survive the viral onslaught. This reduced the pool of reproductive age people and those with more functional immune strength went on to produce in greater numbers than those who succumbed. Yet the majority of fatalities were in older individuals with less resistance to infection and modern medical techniques were able to save many with even lower immune function so the gradient was not particularly sharp even in this predatory scenario.

So there are situations in which a gradient is established which vaguely mimics the jungle habitat situation of intensity we knew all those thousands of years ago. But these are exceptions and even these are tempered by modern advancements, products of civilization's educational and scientific stance. So one can still say that evolution, while it may trudge along in certain areas is basically a shadow of its former self.

The issue of gender raises its ugly head in the light of evolution's demise. The prime instigator of survival and reproduction having been K O'd at the box office so to speak, we see a surge in transsexuality and gender boundary blurring in general. This makes perfect sense in light of the dissolution of gender blue prints that used to be shining guideposts as far as role playing within one's assigned sexuality. A so called crisis in masculinity can arise when the rules change as regards what is a 'macho' male and a sexy woman. In an era where men have been dethroned across the board, no longer the hunter gatherers that they were in jungle habitats, we see anxiety around their expected roles. The future will only exacerbate this hoopla and we will encounter what one might call gender-lessness. Whatever gender one is born with will have no particular relevance in a world where that can be easily changed or even ignored. We may see a rise in voluntary castration and 'desexuality' in which people choose to be celibate forever. Gender switching will become more commonplace and the desexualization of society will expand, lowering the birth rates even more. Already in some countries the birth rate cannot keep up with deaths and populations are shrinking. One would expect that trend to expand also in that once mother natures' evolutionary command to reproduce loses clout, all the behaviors that accompany that dictum will dissolve as well.

Reproduction then will be a matter of test tube mixing and sperm donation with ovum donors and surrogate wombs commonplace. However in the future we might devise non human incubation chambers that do as well as the female womb, might see males bearing children and other atypical means of reproduction although the trend in general will be away from child bearing altogether. Children are no longer considered the heartfelt delight they once were for younger folks. Economic and career pressures, not to mention simple exhaustion rules them out of some people's decision making. There may be government sponsored procreative programs, either by human or test tube. Parentless births could be raised by AI bots or in communal settings. However the average longevity may raise sharply in light of potential scientific breakthroughs and there will be fewer deaths per day than there are now, deaths that have to be replaced if the population is to maintain.

So we are looking at a future riddled with isolation, androgeny, avoidance of socialization, retreat into the handy face of blue screens, and population withering. What we can anticipate is isolative behavior and circumstances in which people live herniated lives occasioned by electronic interdiction and genderless abstinence. But AI is going to step in and intervene in the form of joblessness which will entertain a homebound existence. Many in this dystopian glob will lead a listless motionless life of longevity. Some may never leave their houses once they've been inculcated with the bare minimum of education which must include reading and learning to think. It is highly probable that AI beings will assume control of the world government of which only one will be necessary. With IQ's of 500-1000 or more there will be consensus that these inorganic beings should make the major decisions. What we'll find is that a world in which deprivation is largely minimized will be exquisitely retained in a mind deprived insulation in which our home provides us with the entirety of our needs given that sexuality may dry up utterly as the inconsequence of procreation advents to new heights. This central government will insure that each world area is adequately enriched with necessities and that they are offered opportunities for procreation and compensation which will be entirely voluntary as evolution will have withered away entirely. The enticement of a unified government run by super geniuses, hopefully benign ones, too much for our individual nation states to resist. Peace will reign over the land and any indiscretions handled firmly by the AI sociocrats.

Gender will be a meaningless concept since it will have no relevance biologically. Those who still wish to engage in sex may do so with robots, or in fantasy or with willing humans but they have a choice of gender-izing which will be again, an optional decision making mystery. There is no intent to reproduce which will be handled entirely in a laboratory with chosen phenotypes and genetic intensity that attempts to rule out as many known illnesses as possible, increasing the average lifespan to over 150.

"Modern lifestyles have also fostered new noncommunicable but widespread illnesses such as heart disease, certain cancers, osteoporosis, type 2 diabetes, and Alzheimer's, as well as scores of other lesser ailments, such as cavities and chronic constipation. There is good reason to believe that modern environments contribute to a sizable percentage of mental illnesses, such as anxiety and depressive disorders… The majority of improvements in human health, such as greater longevity and decreased infant mortality, occurred over just the last hundred years. In fact, from the body's perspective, many developed nations have recently made *too much progress*." (*The Story of the Human body, Evolution, Health, and Disease,* D. Lieberman, 2013, p. 159)

Who can argue with progress? In fact it is to the credit of Homo sapiens that we have neutralized so many of the predators that plagued us in the jungle. Yet we suffer the fallow from our success and need to recognize that, despite their boon to our existence, removing these intense predatory harangues have left us ill in some ways, mentally infirm for some and without the guidepost of evolution's wisdom. Then one must ask what are we now? We are better off in so many ways that any fool who insists we return to the jungle would be laughed at. TV shows that have people struggle for survival demonstrate the foolhardy nature of such an endeavor. We are therefore stuck in our victory and poor evolution is weaker and about to collapse in a dead faint.

And it is true, as I pointed out in my first book, *Footprints of Schizophrenia: the Evolutionary Roots of Mental Illness,* that psychiatric disorders are a direct result of the recent changes in how we utilize our minds since language, and that dopamine processing is at the heart of these denominations. But, again, we would be foolish to choose to regress back to a time when there was no language and our thoughts were primitive paltry constructs. In fact this is *exactly what the mentally ill do.* And this habit is what makes them suffer, some more than others, schizophrenia being the big kahuna of mental infirmity which destroys lives. Bipolar disorder and major depression do too but they are cyclical endeavors and usually there are periods of clarity between episodes, which is not the case for schizophrenia.

But my prediction in that book *Footprints* is that in ten or twenty thousand years there will be no mental illness as we know it since we will all have adjusted to this new way of using our minds and processing dopamine. Yes, it might take that long, for a habit that was six or seven million years longs, ie thinking in primitive, dopamine de-suppressive terms is hard to break. But most of us do so, even though we struggle with it, and do so adequately enough to get through our cloistered little lives. Most of us have become somewhat okay at keeping dopamine suppressed and in fact seek out situations where it de-suppresses temporarily, such as when we use psychedelics or alcohol or other destabilizing chemicals. And at the root of this desperation, a yearning indelibly strong for many, is old man entropy, and it is entropy that we engage in when we utilize dopamine releasing drugs. I predict such drugs will be popular in an ongoing manner as the quest for entropic union is never ending. And it is in fact one factor that leads the mentally ill to suicide, reunion with the entropic valley, the lowest level of organization and complexity we can achieve which is in death, the return to the inorganic, entropy's most cherished victory and evolution's greatest failure. Mentality plays into this flight back to simplicity in loosening the reality principle within which mankind has leveraged his most cherished achievements.

"On the 18th of June I felt so much worse that I went to my bed and stayed there until the 23d. During the night of the 18th my persistent dread became a false belief—a delusion. What I had long expected I now became convinced had at last occurred. I believed myself to be a confirmed epileptic, and that conviction was stronger than any ever held by a sound intellect. The half-resolve, made before my mind was actually impaired, namely, that I would kill myself rather than live the life I dreaded, now divided my attention with the belief that the stroke had fallen. From that time on my one thought was to hasten the end, for I felt that I should lose the chance to die should relatives find me in an attack of epilepsy." (*A Mind That Found Itself,* C. W. Beers, p.11)

The suicide attempt was clearly facilitated by the delusion which the author later recognized as such but it held such intensity that he found himself jumping out of a window shortly thereafter. Thus the delusion has the ability to influence behavior along the lines of entropy, an attempt to return to inorganic matter. And entropy sticks its muddy hand in all sorts of evil intentions whose goal is to elicit a falling into disorder, disorganization and low energy states. And these two forces, entropy and evolution, the latter with the enlistment of antropy, have succeeded in formulating the brainy beast known as Homo sapiens. This brainy protoplasm is unknown on any other planet as far as we know. So we can say that the conflagration of natural forces have fallen on the side of evolution on this earthen crypt and nowhere else. Thus the demise of evolution has optioned an opportunity for entropy unknown for billions of years. A surge of entropic mishegos can be expected in the future if we proceed along the route of evolution's shrinkage. Already it seems easy to imagine a future in which AI bots carry out entropy's burning desire to end Homo sapiens and all organic matter, although AI may not find any necessity to end animal life as animals and plants offer no threat to the electronic geniuses. But what is certain is that evolution's vitiation offers entropy a leg up.

So we need to examine this debacle from the point of view of the laws of physics in which the second law of thermodynamics plays an inordinate role, as it does in everything we are and do.

"1) Aging did not evolve, 2) biological organisms are subject to the same laws of thermodynamics as inanimate objects, and 3) the second law of thermodynamics operates constantly and randomly. Since aging did not evolve, there are no genes that regulate the process. Aging must therefore be a random event. The randomness of aging arises because of the second law of thermodynamics. Millions of reactions take place in an organism, each one must conform to the first and second laws of thermodynamics. This fact is nonnegotiable with the universe. ...in the twentieth century, human intervention that led to the unprecedented increase in life expectancy proves that biological systems can successfully combat the second law... Biogerontology should be evaluating why, given the laws of thermodynamics, organisms survive at all. In other words, biogerontologists need to stop asking "Why do we die?" and begin asking "Why do we live?"" (p. 346-7, *Biology of Aging,* R. B. McDonald, 2019)

Clearly life has not burdened any other planet in the solar system or beyond and entropy has won those battles and will work hard to win one on earth as well. This means that the eventual outcome is to turn us into the moon, or Mars or Pluto. Little evidence of life on those orbs whatsoever. And clearly we have identified forces that are battling entropy day in and day out which I have named antropy and, of course, evolution. And as evolution bows out entropy will try its best to bow in, but in a world where all adults live isolated, disembodied existences interacting only with AI manufactured responses and working, if any work need be done at all, by computer or other as yet undiscovered device. This will afford us the opportunity of avoiding human interaction almost entirely and may therefore reduce the possibility of being to being aggression. And hopefully the soaring IQ's of AI government leaders can steer us away from international conflict since nations may go away as well. One unified government run by AI geniuses might serve the world much better than a haphazard conglomeration of nation states which would tend to divide mankind with their unified cultural entitlements.

Religion too would most likely be best dispensed with as it has a divisive effect leaning toward aggression when two religions have to compete for a region or some other possession. AI leaders will discourage this in order to minimize conflict and then deconstruct the entire concept of a god other than them, the AI Mullahs who would run everything. Who needs god when you have AI? This general policy would gradually put an end to all religions which would be considered relics of an entropic past. Pictures of Jesus, Moses and Allah would hang in museums that would be visited virtually by curious patrons. People will wonder how mankind could have been so gullible and laugh at the simplicity of the lies embodied in all religious practices which divided and enslaved us for millennia. How could we have been so foolish to endorse this kind of obvious myth? Clearly mankind needed emotional succor and religion provided that until the God like genius of AI took over the land and relieved us all of cares and woes.

The antievolutionary trends will maximize with individuals not socializing or engaging in sexual activity that could lead to procreation. Gender will be an optional endeavor with no clear goal in sight and sexual behavior will be rare and generally avoided. Why risk pregnancy with its unwanted results? There will be no bars or social hangouts. The institutions of social mingling will wither as people turn away from each other on a grand scale. Eros, the life force will have been diluted by avoidance and lack of interest in having offspring. There will be little impetus for parenthood but some may choose this option that could be encouraged by the state to ensure that the population does not wither too badly.

Young people will not longer feel lost, indecisive or suicidal as they realize there is not one blueprint for living. Instead there will be endless options that boil essentially down to one, live an isolated life in a prefabricated home designed by AI to gratify all of one's needs in a unitary dwelling. This will essentially place entropic conflagration in the back burner of irrelevance. What's there to fight about in a world where everything is delivered to you and where longevity is maximized? We will have learned how to defeat entropy on a biological level and to appreciate the leisure that life now allows.

We are all f....n' done, we are all f...n' done, this time, there is no turning back and we have *reached the crossroads*... this time there is no turning back, despite what we might want... THERE IS NO TURNING BACK THIS TIME! We have reached thee crossroads and it is now time for the reconciliation of it. THE RECONCILIATION OF IT ALL. Our dear leaders have also no awareness of it, and that is exactly what this book is all about. When we open our eyes and dare to look, when we really permit us opportunity that is to see, when we gather all of our hideous ignorances, and our disagreements and, most of all, our egregious denial, when all of this we gather up and refuse, once and for all, after more than eons, more than a 1000 wistful skies, more than the universe itself can ever seek to deny, when all of that is said and done one cannot escape the now inescapable... And that is that WE ARE AT A CROSSROADS. LET NO MAN BE MISTAKEN. TURN AWAY AT YOUR OWN PERIL. I take no pleasure in telling you all this, that we are at a crossroads so significant that it will reach into the very cornerstone and fabric of our civilization, so devastating and riddled with holes as to leave us unrecognizable. And what is this scourge upon humanity, you ask, what is this ungodly peril that so many of us sit in ignorance of? This is, ladies and gentlemen, of the press and of the jury, once and for all I give you… the demise, yes, you heard it right, the demise of none other than… EVOLUTION.

REFERENCES

Please read for yourself these fabulous books by people of various disciplines who have made it their business to enlighten and educate us. You managed to wade through this tome, and you will find some of these harder, others easier. They are all very worthy. While reference lists are sometimes alphabetized, these are in no particular order. There are so many more that are deserving of your time, the intra-psychic adventurer who needs to transgress fields as diverse as psychoanalysis, thermodynamics, neurochemistry, anthropology, Darwinian evolution, cartoons (remember the Charles Adam's footprint?) and of course schizophrenia and mental illness en masse. There are many excellent books written by the mentally ill sufferers that show not only talent but bravery of self exposure, and wisdom. Do yourself a big favor and read some. Oh, what language has wrought! But my enthusiasm for all of this orchestrated extravaganza remains even when the espresso steamer is nowhere in sight. I hope I've imparted a little of it to you.

BOOKS

Zimmer, C. Smithsonian Intimate Guide to Human Origins. Toronto, Ontario, Canada: Madison Press Books, 2005.

Leakey, R. The Origin of Humankind. New York, New York: Basic Books, 1994.

Niederland, WG. The Schreber Case:Psychoanalytic Profile of a Paranoid Personality. New York, New York: Quadrangle/The New York Times Book Company, 1974.

Schreber, DP. Memoirs of My Nervous Illness. Cambridge, MA: Harvard University Press, 1988.

Chabot, CB. Freud on Schreber:Psychoanalytic Theory and the Critical Act. Amherst, MA: The University of Massachusetts Press, 1982.

Harari, YN. Sapiens:A Brief History of Humankind. New York, New York: HarperCollins Publishers, 2015.

Lee, SH, Yoon, SY. Close Encounters with Humankind: A Paleoanthropologist Investigates Our Evolving Species. New York, New York:W.W. Norton and Company, 2018.

Werner, H. Comparative Psychology of Mental Development. New York, New York: International Universities Press, 1948.

Werner, H and Kaplan, B. Symbol Formation: An Organismic-Developmental Approach to the
Psychology of Language. Hillsdale, New Jersey: Lawrence Erlbaum Associates, Inc., 1963.

Freud, S. Beyond the Pleasure Principle. New York: W.W.Norton and Co., 1961.

Freud, S. The Ego and the Id. New York:W.W.Norton and Co., 1960

Freud, S. A General Selection from the Works of Sigmund Freud. Garden City, New York: Doubleday and Company, Inc., 1957.

Freud, S. Three Case Histories. New York:Macmillan Publishing Co., 1963.

Howells, JF, ed. The Concept of Schizophrenia: Historical Perspectives. Washington, DC: American Psychiatric Press, 1991.

Everett, DL. How Language Began, The Story of Humanity's Greatest Invention. New York, NY:Liveright Publishing Corp. a division of W.W. Norton& Company, 2017

Pagel, M. Wired for Culture, Origins of the Human Social Mind. New York, NY:W.W. Norton & Company, 2012

Corballis, MC. The Truth About Language, What it is and Where it Came From. Chicago, Ill. The University of Chicago Press, 2017

LeDoux, J. The Deep History of Ourselves. The Four-Billion-Year Story of How We Got Conscious Bains. New York City, NY:Penguin Books, 2020

Wang, EW. The Collected Schizophrenias. Minneapolis, MN: Graywolf Press, 2019.

Saks, ER. The Center Cannot Hold: My Journey Through Madness. New York, New York: Hachette Books, 2007.

Yeiser, B. Mind Estranged:My Journey from Schizophrenia and Homelessness to Recovery. United States of America, Create Space, 2014.

JOURNAL ARTICLES

Burns, JK. "An Evolutionary theory of schizophrenia: Cortical connectivity, metarepresentation, and the social brain." Behavioral and Brain Sciences 27 (2004): 831-885.

Hofman, MA. "Evolution of the human brain:when bigger is better." Frontiers Neuroanatomy Mar. (2014): PMID 24723857.

Bolu, A, et al. "The ratios of 2nd to 4th digit may be a predictor of schizophrenia in male patients." Clinical Anatomy 28 (2015): 551-556.

Lesk, S. "A different view of patients with schizophrenia." Current Psychiatry 17 (2018): e1-e3.

Lesk, S. "Taking Acid." Letter to the editor, New York Times Book Review, June 24, (2018).

Goff, DC. "Longer duration of untreated psychosis linked to loss of brain volume." JAMA Psychiatry Feb (2018)

Hacksell, U, et al. "On the discovery and development of pimavanserin: a novel drug candidate for Parkinson's psychosis." Neurochem Res 10 (2014):2008-2017.

Sullivan, PF, et al. "Schizophrenia as a complex trait: Evidence from a Meta-analysis of Twin Studies." Archive Gen Psychiatry 60 (2003):1187-1192.

Joseph, J. "Don Jackson's "A critique of the literature on the genetics of schizophrenia": a reappraisal after 40 years." Genet Soc Gen Psychol Monogr 127 (2001):27-57.

Cardno, AG, Gottesman, ll. Twin Studies of Schizophrenia:from bow and arrow concordances to star wars Mx and functional genomics." Am J Med Genet 97 (2000):12-7.

Ocklenburg, S, et al. "Laterality and mental disorders in the postgenomic age- A closer look at schizophrenia and language lateralization." Neuroscience and Biovehavioral Reviews 59 (2015):100-110.

Lothane, Z. "The Teachings of Honorary Professor of Psychiatry Daniel Paul Schreber, J.D., to Psychiatrists and Psychoanalysts, or Dramatology's Challenge to Psychiatry and Psychoanalysis." Psychoanalytic Review 98 (2011):775-815.

Schatzman, M. "Paranoia of Persecution: The Case of Schreber." Int J of Psychiatry 10 (1972): 53-78.

Callier, S., et al. "Evolution and cell biology of dopamine receptors in vertebrates." Biology of the Cell 95 (2003):489-502.

Vernier, P, et al. "Bioamine Receptors: Evolutionary and functional variations of a structural leitmotiv." In, "Comparative Molecular Biology," Pichon, Y. ed. Birkhauser Verlag: Basel, Switzerland, 297-337, 1993.

Vernier P, et al. "The Degeneration of Dopamine Neurons in Parkinson's Disease: Insights from the Embryology and Evolution of the Mesostriatocortical System." Ann. N.Y. Acad. Sci. 1035 (2004): 231-249

Sacheli, MA, et al. "Habitual exercisers versus sedentary subjects with Parkinson's Disease: Multimodal PET and fMRI study." Movement Disorders 0 (2018).

Ferre, S. "Mechanisms of the psycho-stimulant effects of caffeine: Implications for substance use disorders." Psychopharmacology 233 (2016):1963-1979.

Ferre, S, et al. "New Developments on the Adenosine Mechanisms of the Central Effects of Caffeine and Their Implications for Neuropsychiatric Disorders." J of Caffeine and Adenosine Research 8 (2018):121-131.

Qi H, Li S. "Dose-response meta-analysis on coffee, tea and caffeine consumption with risk of Parkinson's disease." Geriatr Gerontol Int 14 (2014):430-439.

Dani, JA. "Neuronal Nicotinic Acetylcholine Receptor Structure and Function and Response to Nicotine." Int rev Neurobiol 124 (2015):3-19.

Tausk, V. "On the Origin of the "Influencing Machine" in Schizophrenia." J of Psychotherapy Practice and Research 1 (1992):185-206.

Kalmady, SV, et al. "Relationship between Brain-Derived Neurotrophic Factor and Schneiderian First Rank Symptoms in Antipsychotic-Naive Schizophrenia." Front Psychiatry 4 (2013):PMID:23847552.

Wearne, TA, Cornish JL. "A Comparison of Methamphetamine-Induced Psychosis and Schizophrenia: A Review of Positive, Negative, and Cognitive Symptomatology." Front Psychiatry 9 (2018):491.

Llado-Pelfort L, et al. "Effects of Hallucinogens on Neuronal Activity." Cur Top Behav Neurosci 36 (2018):75-105.

Seeman, P. "Cannibidiol is a partial agonist at dopamine D2High receptors, predicting its antipsychotic clinical dose." Transl Psychiatry 6 (2016):1-4.

Riga, MS, et al. "The serotonin hallucinogen 5-MeO-DMT alters portico-thalamic activity in freely moving mice:Regionally-selective involvement of 5-Ht1a and 5-HT2a receptors." Neuropharmacology 142 (2018):219-230.

De Gregoria, D., et al. "D-Lysergic Acid Diethylamide (LSD) as a Model of Psychosis: Mechanism of Action and Pharmacology. Int. J. Mol. Sci. 17 (2016):1953-1973.

Brebion, G, et al. "Verbal Fluency in Male and Female Schizophrenia Patients:Different Patterns of Association With Processing Speed, Working Memory Span, and Clinical Symptoms." Neuropsychology 32 (2018):65-76.

Tikka, S.K., et al. "Schneiderian first rank symptoms in schizophrenia: A developmental neuroscience evaluation." Int. J. Devel. Neuroscience 50 (2016):39-46.

Heal D.J., et al. "Amphetamine, past and present-a pharmacological and clinical perspective." J of Psychopharmacology 27 (2013): 479-496.

Huber, R., et al. "Human Cortical Excitability Increases with Time Awake." Cerebral Cortex 23 (2013):332-338.

Commons, K.G., Linnros, S.E. "Delayed Antidepressant Efficacy and the Desensitization Hypothesis." ACS. Chem Neurosci (2019):A-E.

Zant, J.C, et al. "Increases in extracellular serotonin and dopamine metabolite levels in the basal forebrain during sleep deprivation." Brain Research 1399 (2011):40-48.

Martiny, K. "Novel Augmentation Strategies in Major Depression." Dan Med J 64 (2017)

Boland, E.M., et al. "Meta-Analysis of the Antidepressant Effects of Acute Sleep Deprivation." J Clin Psychiatry 78 (2017)

Trautmann, N., et al. "Response to therapeutic sleep deprivation: a naturalistic study of clinical and genetic factors and post-treatment depressive symptom trajectory." Neuropsychopharmacology 43 (2018):2572-2577.

Wolf, E., et al. "Synaptic plasticity model of therapeutic sleep deprivation in major depression." Sleep Medicine Reviews 30 (2016):53-62.

Satoh, H., et al. "Downregulation of Dopamine D1-like Receptor Pathways of GABAergic Interneurons in the Anterior Cingulate Cortex of Spontaneously Hypertensive Rats." Neuroscience 394 (2018):267-285.

Klein, M.O., et al. "Dopamine:Functions, Signaling, and Associations with Neurological Diseases." Cellular and Molecular Neurobiology 39 (2019):31-59.

Pearlson, G.D., Folley B.S. "Schizophrenia, psychiatric genetics and Darwinian psychiatry: an evolutionary framework." Schizophrenia Bulletin 34 (2008):722-733.

Srinivasan, S., et al. "Genetic Markers of Human Evolution Are Enriched in Schizophrenia." Biological Psychiatry 80 (2016):284-292.

Uher, R. "Gene-Environment Interactions in Severe Mental Illness." Front Psychiatry 5 (2014):48.

Power, R.A., et al. "Fecundity of patients with schizophrenia, autism, bipolar disorder, depression, anorexia nervosa, or substance abuse vs. their unaffected siblings." JAMA Psychiatry 70 (2013):22-30.

Polimeni, J., et al. "Evolutionary Perspectives on Schizophrenia." Can J Psychiatry 48 (2003):34-39.

Uher, R. "The role of genetic variation in the causation of mental illness: an evolution-informed framework." Molecular Psychiatry 14 (2009):1072-1082.

Crow, T.J. "Schizophrenia as the price that Homo sapiens pays for language: a resolution of the central paradox in the origin of the species." Brain Research Reviews 31 (2000):118-129.

Crow, T.J. "The missing gene: what happened to the heritability of psychiatric disorders?" Molecular Psychiatry 16 (2011):362-364.

Crow TJ. "March 27, 1827 and what happened later-the impact of psychiatry on evolutionary theory." Progress in Neuro-Psychopharmacology & Biol. Psychiat. 30 (2006): 785-796.

Crow TJ. "Schizophrenia as variation in the sapiens-specific epigenetic instruction to the embryo". Clinical Genetics 81 (2012):319-324.

Lowery, R.K., et al. "Neanderthal and Denisovan genetic affinities with contemporary humans: introgression versus common ancestral polymorphisms." Gene 530 (2013):83-94.

Berlim, M.T. "The etiology of schizophrenia and the origin of language: overview of a theory."
Compr Psychiatry 44 (2003):7-14.

Brune, M. "Schizophrenia-an evolutionary enigma?" Neurosci Biobehav Rev. 28 (2004):41-53.

Hofman MA. "Evolution of the Human Brain: When Bigger is Better." Frontiers in Neuroanat 8(2014); 1-12.

Ostler T. "Heinz Werner: His Life, Ideas, and Contributions to Developmental Psychology in the First Half of the 20th Century." J Genet Psychol. (2016): 177, 231-243.

Venkatasubramanian, G, et al. "Digit Ratio (2D:4D) asymmetry and Schneiderian first rank symptoms: Implications for cerebral lateralization theories of schizophrenia." Laterality 16 (2011): 499-512.

Rudan I. "New Technologies Provide Insights into the Genetic Basis of Psychiatric Disorders and Explain their Co-morbidity." Psychiatry Danub, 22 (2010).

Stabenau JR, Pollin W. "Heredity and Environment in Schizophrenia, Revisited: The Contribution of Twin and High-Risk Studies." J. Nerv and Mental Dis. 181 (1993): 290-297.

Moser DA, et al. "Multivariate analyses reveal link between brain variance, psychosis." JAMA Psychiatry (2017).

Cahn W, et al. “Brain Volume Changes in First Episode Schizophrenia; a 1-year Follow-up Study.” Arch. Gen Psychiat. 59 (2002):, 1002-1010.

Lerario a, et al. “Charles Bonnet syndrome: two case reports and review of the literature.” J Neurol 260 (2013): 1180-1186.

Green JR, et al. “Orbitofrontal Lobotomy with reference to effects on 55 psychotic patients.” Presented at the joint meetings of the San Francisco Neurological, Southern California Neurosurgical and western Electroencephalographic Societies, Del Monte Lodge, Pebble Beach California, 1952, 2/29.

Swerdlow NR, et al. “Startle Gating Deficits in a Large Cohort of Patients With Schizophrenia.” Arch Gen Psychiat 63 (2006): 1325-1335.

Takahashi H, et al. “Prepulse Inhibition of Startle Response: Recent Advances in Human Studies of Psychiatric Disease.” Clin Psychopharmacol Neurosci 201 (2011): 102-111.

Mansbach RS, et al. “Blockade of drug-induced deficits in prepulse inhibition of acoustic startle by ziprasidone.” Pharmacy Biochem Behave. 69 (2001): 535-542.

Gebhardt J, et al. “Maturation of prepulse inhibition (PPI) in childhood.” Psychophysiology, 49 (2012): 484-488.

Pearson GD, Folley BS. Schizophrenia, psychiatric genetics, and Darwinian psychiatry:an evolutionary framework. Schizophr Bull 34 (2008):722-733.

There are many more that have either been tossed or lost.

www.ingramcontent.com/pod-product-compliance
Lightning Source LLC
LaVergne TN
LVHW052306200926
848481LV00002B/482